Señorita Dhondt

Room 429

# Our

# Country's

# Founders

ALSO BY WILLIAM J. BENNETT

*The Book of Virtues for Young People*

# OUR
# COUNTRY'S
# FOUNDERS

*A Book of Advice for Young People*

*Edited with Commentary by*

# WILLIAM J. BENNETT

BROADMAN
& HOLMAN
PUBLISHERS

Nashville, Tennessee

Our Country's Founders: A Book of Advice for Young People *has been adapted from*
Our Sacred Honor: Words of Advice from the Founders in Stories, Letters, Poems, and
Speeches *by William J. Bennett, but there are also new selections in this volume.*

*Published in 1998 by Broadman & Holman Publishers, Nashville, Tennessee*

*The text for this book is set in Garamond Light.*
*Printed and bound in the United States of America*

*ISBN 0-8054-1600-5*

# CONTENTS

# INTRODUCTION

*This* is, in large part, a book of advice for how to be a good citizen and a worthy member of civil society. The advice comes not from me but from the men and women who founded this nation, our Founders. In many ways, they are our political parents, and this is part of their story. The Founders embarked on a revolution that was to change the world. At stake were several questions: Could men and women govern themselves without kings or titles? Could there be a country governed by the consent of the people rather than arbitrary rule? And could there be a country in which the rights of conscience and religious freedom, rather than religious persecution, reigned?

In 1776, the world had never witnessed anything quite as radical as this before (and there are still countries which do not honor these principles today). Yet the Founders believed that it was possible to establish a country on these principles of freedom and equality. But they also knew that they, let alone subsequent generations of Americans, would not succeed without the right virtues. Freedom, the Founders were aware, can easily turn into license unless it is guided by moral principles. This book focuses on the deeds and thoughts of some of our most celebrated Founders and draws lessons from them for how we can successfully carry on their great experiment in self-government.

Let us go back over two hundred years to Philadelphia's Independence Hall. For nearly four months, delegates to the Constitutional Convention of 1787 deliberated in secret over what form of government America would have. When it was finally over and the delegates were leaving the great hall, a citizen of Philadelphia, Mrs. Powel, "asked Dr. Franklin, 'Well, Doctor, what have we got, a republic or a monarchy?' 'A republic,' replied the Doctor, 'if you can keep it.' "

What does it mean to "keep" a republic? What was Franklin thinking? Didn't the Founders design a constitution with political institutions, such as the presidency, the congress, and the courts that would do the job? The Founders certainly constructed a brilliant constitution of government. It is the longest-lasting written political constitution and one of the most imitated political documents in the world. But the Founders knew that the Constitution alone would not be enough to keep America going. More was needed. After all, history is full of examples of the rise and the fall of great republics. Why should America be any different?

The Founders believed that America, unlike republics of the past, would survive—but only if the people possessed the virtues and habits necessary to maintain it. In other words, the U.S. Constitution and our political institutions endure not of their own accord, but because of the kind of people Americans are. Franklin's challenge of 1787 remains our challenge: Can "we the people" cultivate the right virtues to "keep" the political institutions and the country our Founders gave us over two hundred years ago?

This book takes us back to our founding principles and points us in the direction of what we must do to make America endure and live up to its great potential. The Founders were an exceptional group of men and women, among the greatest to have ever walked this land. They worked hard and aimed high. They dedicated their lives to establishing a country that would be a moral and political example to the rest of the world. They, in George Washington's words, founded this country on the "firmest props" of moral and religious teachings. But our Founders were aware that these "props" must be renewed and sustained by each generation of Americans.

The Founders left behind plenty of advice to future generations of Americans for how to make this great republic last. This
book contains much of that advice and focuses on the virtues
the Founders thought were necessary for establishing and maintaining this country. Some of the virtues are political and public
ones, such as patriotism, civility, and justice. Others are more
personal, such as love and friendship. This is a reflection of the
full lives our Founders lived. Their lives were dedicated to serving their country, enjoying their families, and working toward
self-improvement.

The Founders were thoughtful, brave, and learned men and
women who tried, though they sometimes failed, to lead lives
of virtue. Of course the Founders were not perfect. They were
not angels. They were human, just like us. They knew how
difficult, yet how important, it was to try to overcome their own
personal shortcomings and live meaningful, worthwhile lives.
Some of them had bad tempers, some were vain, some were
not good husbands, and some were spendthrifts. Most serious
of all, some owned slaves. However, though they themselves
did not abolish the evil institution of slavery, they provided
the high ideals of liberty and equality that inspired subsequent
generations of Americans to emancipate the slaves and struggle
for racial harmony.

This collection shares the great vision our Founders held for
this country in its earliest years. Although much has changed
over the last two centuries, their advice on the fundamentals,
such as how to be a good friend, a good citizen, a successful
entrepreneur, or how a nation might keep its purposes high, is
still highly relevant and worth revisiting.

# I

# PATRIOTISM AND COURAGE

❦

*Patriotism* means love of country. How do we demonstrate our love of country? At the most basic level, we do so by voting with our feet—by remaining here in this country rather than living elsewhere. But there are more active ways to be a patriot. We stand for the national anthem. We obey the laws. We vote, and hold elective offices. We celebrate our national birthday, the Fourth of July, and throughout the year, we observe other national holidays, such as Presidents Day, Memorial Day, Veterans Day, and Thanksgiving. And in times of war, Americans risk their lives to fight for their country and its ideals.

Another way for us to be patriotic is to learn about the deeds of the Founders. Without knowledge about the men and women who fought for the establishment of this country and who formed our political institutions, it would be difficult for us to carry on the American experiment in self-government.

The Founders' love of country was deep and profound. On a hot July day in 1776, the signers of the Declaration of Independence pledged to each other their "lives," "fortunes," and "sacred honor." By signing the Declaration, those men were signing their own "death warrants," as Benjamin Rush, one of the signers, put it. Many lost their fortunes, some their lives, but despite their struggles, the signers stood firm for independence. Their "sacred honor" and their patriotism sustained them throughout the struggle to become a nation.

This chapter contains the examples of the patriotic deeds of the Father of our Country, George Washington, on and off the battlefield. Washington made many sacrifices to serve his country. He served as the commander-in-chief of the Continental Army and as our first president (without pay, for he believed we should all gladly serve our country). Washington once wrote that "when my country demands the sacrifice, personal ease must always be a secondary consideration." Many of our patriots paid the ultimate price for our country, including Nathan Hale, whose story of courage and sacrifice is retold here as well.

Some of our other Founders served their country off the battlefield, and fought with the pen, not the sword. James Madison, Thomas Jefferson, and John Adams were brilliant men who thought long and hard about how to devise a government that would render justice and liberty to all. And they made their own sacrifices as well—in time, energy, and enduring long separations from their loved ones while they served their country. James Madison, who was a frail and often sickly man, worked so hard at the Constitutional Convention that he confided to a friend that his labors "nearly killed me." Abigail Adams noted that women make difficult sacrifices for the country as well and that those sacrifices are equal to those of men.

The Founders remain inspiring to us today because of what they did for their country, and for us. We have much to learn from them. For example, Thomas Jefferson advised a young boy, who had been named after him, to "Love your neighbor as yourself, and your country more than yourself." To love one's country more than oneself is not an easy thing to do. But so many heroic Americans, from the Revolutionary War to the present, have risked and even sacrificed their own lives because they did love America and her ideals that much.

# Benjamin Rush to John Adams, July 20, 1811

THE SIGNERS of the Declaration of Independence were men of courage. By affixing their names to that document, they risked death by hanging. And they knew it. But some of the signers bravely (or perhaps nervously) laughed in the face of danger: While writing his bold and now famous signature, John Hancock, the first to sign, reportedly said: "There! His Majesty can now read my name without glasses. And he can double the reward on my head!" To encourage the other signers, Hancock would later tell them that they must all hang together. To which Benjamin Franklin quipped: "We must all hang together, or we most assuredly will hang separately." In this letter, Benjamin Rush, a fellow signer of the Declaration of Independence, remembers another humorous exchange that took place at the signing. But he also recalls the "pensive and awful silence" that filled the room as these patriots of '76 prepared to make the ultimate sacrifice for their country.

DEAR OLD FRIEND,

The 4th of July has been celebrated in Philadelphia in the manner I expected. The military men, and particularly one of them, ran away with all the glory of the day. Scarcely a word was said of the solicitude and labors and fears and sorrows and sleepless nights of the men who projected, proposed, defended, and subscribed the Declaration of Independence. Do you recollect your memorable speech upon the day on which the vote was taken? Do you recollect the pensive and awful silence which pervaded the house when we were called up, one after another, to the table of the President of Congress to subscribe what was believed by many at that time to be our own death warrants? The silence and the gloom of the morning were interrupted, I well recollect, only for a moment by Colonel Harrison of Virginia, who said to Mr. Gerry at the table: "I shall have a great advantage over you, Mr. Gerry, when we are all hung for what we are now doing. From the size and weight of my body I shall die in a few minutes, but from the lightness of your body you will dance in the air an hour or two before you are dead." This speech procured a transient smile, but it was soon succeeded by the solemnity with which the whole business was conducted.

∞

## *Richard Stockton, Delegate from New Jersey, Signer of the Declaration of Independence*

MANY OF the signers of the Declaration of Independence suffered reprisals from the British. Consider the delegates from New Jersey—Francis Hopkinson, John Witherspoon, Abraham Clark, John Hart, and Richard Stockton. Hopkinson and his family fled their home shortly before British soldiers came and destroyed it. Witherspoon, who was also president of the College of New Jersey (now Princeton) and James Madison's teacher, had to flee his home with his family, as the British raided the college, occupied its buildings as well as nearby homes, and burned its library, which contained many of Witherspoon's prized books from Europe. Enemy soldiers aggressively pursued Hart, who had to leave his wife at her sickbed and go into hiding. He finally returned to his farm, now destroyed, to find his wife had died from the trauma, his children scattered. He died a despondent man a few years later. And Clark's son, who was a captain in the American army and a prisoner of war on a British prison ship, was singled out for his father's deeds and tortured and nearly starved to death.

In the following, I share a re-telling of the ordeal Richard Stockton went through—an ordeal that eventually killed him. Who could have blamed any of these men if they had renounced the cause of independence to avoid persecution to themselves and their families? But none did—their "sacred honor" was at stake, and that sustained them.

*The* families of those who had signed the instrument which severed the colonies from the parent state, were peculiarly obnoxious to the British forces; and Mr. Stockton was constrained to retire from congress to convey his own to a place of safety. After having conducted them into the county of Monmouth, about thirty miles from his residence, he resided with Mr. Covenhoven, a patriotic friend of his; and he, together with Mr. Covenhoven, was surprised, and made a prisoner, by a party of refugees, who had been informed of the place of his temporary residence, by a treacherous wretch. They were dragged from their beds at a late hour of the night; stripped and plundered of their property, and conducted to New York. They first conveyed him to Amboy, shut him in the common gaol, exposed him, thus destitute, to severe suffering by the cold weather; and in New York, he was subjected to a similar confinement, and extreme suffering. The severities he endured, during his imprisonment in Amboy and New York, laid the foundation for the disease which closed his life not long after. While in the latter place, the enemy withheld from him, not only the comforts, but even the necessaries of life; and this, notwithstanding his respectability of character and standing in life, and a very delicate state of health. At one time he was left absolutely without food more than twenty-four hours; and afterwards supplied with that which was coarse in quality, and scanty in amount.

The complicated sufferings he endured while in captivity, the burning of his papers and fine library, the plundering of his property, particularly of his stock of horses and cattle; the general depredations committed on his estate, real and personal, wherever it was exposed to the ravages of an incensed foe, and the losses he sustained by reason of the ruinous depreciation of the continental paper currency, left him only the remnants of a large fortune, exhausted so entirely that it seemed to him only a mass of ruins; and finding himself so destitute of the means for providing comfortably for his family, he was compelled to resort to friends for a temporary accommodation, to procure the absolute necessaries of life. This caused a depression of spirits, out of which he never fully rose; and aggravated a lingering disease which terminated his life. He languished for a time under this calamity which, in the latter part of his life, was much increased by a cancer in his neck, whose insidious and fatal approaches are always clearly perceived, without the least hope of remedy. He died on the twenty-eighth day of February, 1781, in the fifty-first year of his age.

A minute delineation of character, does not comport with the design or limits of this work; only a brief summary can be given. The character of Mr. Stockton as a patriot, inflexibly devoted to the liberty, rights, and independence of his country, may be easily understood by what has been already stated. He not only pledged "his life, his fortune, and his sacred honor," for the attainment of his country's independence; but he fully redeemed the pledge by becoming a martyr to her cause. His life was a sacrifice; his fortune was nearly so; and his sacred honor attended him to his grave; and remains behind him an untarnished legacy to his posterity and his country.

—From Nathaniel Dwight, *The Lives of the Signers,* 1876

∞

## "Give Me Liberty Or Give Me Death"
## Patrick Henry, Speech at St. Johns Church,
## March 23, 1775

T HIS IS one of the most famous speeches of the revolutionary era. With the growing presence of British forces in the colonies, Patrick Henry introduced a set of resolutions for organizing and arming a state militia. Henry believed it was time to prepare for war with Great Britain, which he believed to be inevitable.

The church in which Henry gave the speech was packed, and the windows were thrown open to allow more people to hear. When Henry finished, his fellow delegates, who included Thomas Jefferson and George Washington, sat in awed silence.

"*We*have petitioned—we have remonstrated—we have supplicated—we have prostrated ourselves before the throne, and have implored its interposition to arrest the tyrannical hands of the ministry and parliament. Our petitions have been slighted; our remonstrances have produced additional violence and insult; our supplications have been disregarded; and we have been spurned, with contempt, from the foot of the throne. In vain, after these things, may we indulge the fond hope of peace and reconciliation. *There is no longer any room for hope.* If we wish to be free—if we mean to preserve inviolate those inestimable privileges for which we have been so long contending—if we mean not basely to abandon the noble struggle in which we have been so long engaged, and which we have pledged ourselves never to abandon, until the glorious object of our contest shall be obtained—we must fight!—I repeat it, sir, we must fight!! An appeal to arms and to the God of hosts, is all that is left us!

"They tell us, sir," continued Mr. Henry, "that we are weak—

unable to cope with so formidable an adversary. But when shall we be stronger. Will it be the next week or the next year? Will it be when we are totally disarmed, and when a British guard shall be stationed in every house? Shall we gather strength by irresolution and inaction? Shall we acquire the means of effectual resistance by lying supinely on our backs, and hugging the delusive phantom of hope, until our enemies shall have bound us hand and foot? Sir, we are not weak, if we make a proper use of those means which the God of nature hath placed in our power. Three millions of people armed in the holy cause of liberty, and in such a country as that which we possess, are invincible by any force which our enemy can send against us. Besides, sir, we shall not fight our battles alone. There is a just God who presides over the destinies of nations, and who will raise up friends to fight our battles for us. The battle, sir, is not to the strong alone; it is to the vigilant, the active, the brave. Besides, sir, we have no election. If we were base enough to desire it, it is now too late to retire from the contest. There is no retreat but in submission and slavery! Our chains are forged. Their clanking may be heard on the plains of Boston! The war is inevitable—and let it come!! I repeat it, sir, let it come!!!

"It is vain, sir, to extenuate the matter. Gentlemen may cry, peace, peace—but there is no peace. The war is actually begun! The next gale that sweeps from the north will bring to our ears the clash of resounding arms! Our brethren are already in the field! Why stand we here idle? What is it that gentlemen wish? What would they have? Is life so dear, or peace so sweet, as to be purchased at the price of chains and slavery? Forbid it, Almighty God!—I know not what course others may take; but as for me," cried he, with both his arms extended aloft, his brows knit, every feature marked with the resolute purpose of his soul, and his voice swelled to its boldest note of exclamation—"give me liberty, or give me death!"

—From William Wirt,
  *Sketches of the Life and Character of Patrick Henry*

∞

## *Thomas Paine,* The American Crisis, *December 19, 1776*

THOMAS PAINE was a writer who was born and raised in England. He came to America in 1774 and soon became a strong advocate for the American cause. For those colonists who didn't know why American independence was so important and worth fighting for, Paine's famous pamphlet, *Common Sense,* released in January 1776, told them. The following excerpt is taken from a later work, *The American Crisis,* written at a critical juncture of the Revolution. George Washington was leading the Continental Army on a retreat through New Jersey after a disastrous defeat in New York. Paine accompanied Washington and his troops and saw firsthand the growing sense of desperation among the army. The American troops were greatly outnumbered by the British. Many were ready to give up and reconcile with Great Britain. It looked as if the rebellion was coming to an abrupt end.

Paine wrote *The American Crisis*—reportedly using a battle drum for a desk—by the light of campfire to boost morale. He left the camp for Philadelphia to have copies printed, which Washington ordered to be read aloud to his men on Christmas Eve 1776. After it was read, the American troops crossed the Delaware and launched a surprise attack on the Hessian soldiers at Trenton. The American victory at Trenton infused new life into the patriots' cause and showed the British that the American army was not ready to bow out just yet.

NUMBER I.

*These* are the times that try men's souls. The summer soldier and the sunshine patriot will, in this crisis, shrink from the service of his country; but he that stands it NOW, deserves the love and thanks of man and woman. Tyranny, like hell, is not easily conquered; yet we have this consolation with us, that the harder the conflict, the more glorious the triumph. What we obtain too cheap, we esteem too lightly: 'tis dearness only that gives every thing its value. Heaven knows how to put a proper price upon its goods; and it would be strange indeed, if so celestial an article as FREEDOM should not be highly rated. Britain, with an army to enforce her tyranny, has declared that she has a right (*not only to* TAX) but "to BIND *us in* ALL CASES WHATSOEVER," and if being *bound in that manner,* is not slavery, then is there not such a thing as slavery upon earth. Even the expression is impious, for so unlimited a power can belong only to God. . . .

I call not upon a few, but upon all: not on *this* state or *that* state, but on *every* state; up and help us; lay your shoulders to the wheel; better have too much force than too little, when so great an object is at stake. Let it be told to the future world, that in the depth of winter, when nothing but hope and virtue could survive, the city and the country, alarmed at one common danger, came forth to meet and to repulse it. Say not that thousands are gone, turn out your tens of thousands; throw not the burden of the day upon Providence, but *"show your faith by your works,"* that God may bless you. It matters not where you live, or what rank of life you hold, the evil or the blessing will reach you all. The far and the near, the home counties and the back, the rich and the poor, will suffer or rejoice alike. The heart that feels not now, is dead: the blood of his children will curse his cowardice, who shrinks back at a time when a little might have saved the whole, and made *them* happy. I love the man that can smile in trouble, that can gather strength from distress, and grow brave by reflection. 'Tis the business of little minds to shrink; but he whose heart is firm, and whose conscience approves his conduct, will pursue his principles unto death. My own line of reasoning is to myself as straight and clear as a ray of light. Not all the treasures of the world, so far as I believe, could have induced me to support an offensive war, for I think it murder; but if a thief breaks into my house, burns and destroys my property, and kills or threatens to kill me, or those that are in it, and to *"bind me in all cases whatsoever,"* to his absolute will, am I to suffer it? What signifies it to me, whether he who does it is a king or a common man; my countryman or not my countryman: whether it be done by an individual villain, or an army of them? If we reason to the root of things we shall find no difference; neither can any just cause be assigned why we should punish in the one case and pardon in the other. Let them call me rebel, and welcome, I feel no concern from it . . .

*Thomas Paine*

I thank God that I fear not. I see no real cause for fear. I know our situation well, and can see the way out of it.

∾

## Abigail Adams to John Adams, June 18, 1775, and John to Abigail, July 7, 1775

JOHN ADAMS, America's second president, and Abigail Adams were married for fifty-four years. During their courtship, Abigail Adams asked John: "Don't you think me a courageous being? Courage is laudable, a glorious virtue in your sex, why not in mine?"

Abigail's courage was to be later tested many times and in many different ways during the revolutionary war years. The following exchange between John and Abigail Adams concerns the Battle of Bunker Hill (which actually took place on Breed's Hill). John Adams was in Philadelphia serving in the Second Continental Congress; Abigail was alone, taking care of the farm and their four children in Braintree, Massachusetts. John Quincy Adams, her son, would later recall that during this time his mother along with his siblings were "liable every hour of the day and night to be butchered in cold blood, or taken and carried into Boston as hostages."

On a hill near her farm with her young son Johnny, Abigail watched the smoke rising from the sky of Charlestown from the battle of Bunker Hill. A week later, John Adam's "heroine" would reassure him that although she and others "live in continual Expectation of Hostilities" that "like good Nehemiah[,] having made our prayer with God, and set the people with their Swords, their Spears[,] and their bows[,] we will say unto them, Be not affraid of them."* And she was not afraid.

---

* Abigail to John, June 25, 1775. I've adjusted the punctuation slightly.

ABIGAIL ADAMS TO JOHN ADAMS

*Dearest* Friend

The Day; perhaps the decisive Day is come on which the fate of America depends. My bursting Heart must find vent at my pen. I have just heard that our dear Friend Dr. Warren is no more but fell gloriously fighting for his Country—saying better to die honourably in the field than ignominiously hang upon the Gallows. Great is our Loss. He has distinguished himself in every engagement, by his courage and fortitude, by animating the Soldiers and leading them on by his own example. A particular account of these dreadful, but I hope Glorious Days will be transmitted you, no doubt in the exactest manner.

The race is not to the swift, nor the battle to the strong, but the God of Israel is he that giveth strength and power unto his people. Trust in him at all times, ye people pour out your hearts before him. God is a refuge for us.—Charlstown is laid in ashes. The Battle began upon our intrenchments upon Bunkers Hill, a Saturday morning about 3 o'clock and has not ceased yet and tis now 3 o'clock Sabbeth afternoon.

Tis expected they will come out over the Neck to night, and a dreadful Battle must ensue. Almighty God cover the heads of our Country men, and be a shield to our Dear Friends. How [many ha]lve fallen we know not—the constant roar of the cannon is so [distre]ssing that we can not Eat, Drink or Sleep. May we be supported and sustaind in the dreadful conflict. I shall tarry here till tis thought unsafe by my Friends, and then I have secured myself a retreat at your Brothers who has kindly offerd me part of his house. I cannot compose myself to write any further at present. I will add more as I hear further.

JOHN ADAMS TO ABIGAIL ADAMS

*It* gives me more Pleasure than I can express to learn that you sustain with so much Fortitude, the Shocks and Terrors of the Times. You are really brave, my dear, you are an Heroine.

And you have Reason to be. For the worst that can happen, can do you no Harm. A soul, as pure, as benevolent, as virtuous and pious as yours has nothing to fear, but every Thing to hope and expect from the last of human Evils.

Am glad you have secured an Assylum, tho I hope you will not have occasion for it.

∾

## George Washington Crosses the Delaware

ONE OF the great turning points of the Revolutionary War was the American victory at the Battle of Trenton. In the summer and fall of 1776, General George Washington and his army had been defeated in New York and chased throughout New Jersey by British troops. Morale was fast sinking among the American soldiers. It looked like the American rebellion was coming to a quick end. In December of 1776, Washington decided it was time to go on the offensive and planned a surprise attack on the Hessian soldiers (German soldiers fighting on the British side). On December 25, 1776, Washington led his men on a perilous crossing over the Delaware River to reach the Hessian camp at Trenton, New Jersey. The river was swirling with frozen chunks of ice that threatened to capsize their boats, which were propelled through the water with long poles. Once the American troops reached land, a storm of frozen sleet and snow made their march extremely treacherous. Many marched barefoot and left bloody footprints in the snow. Somehow, these men, led by George Washington, persevered and went on to defeat the Hessian soldiers at Trenton.

On the 150th anniversary of the Battle of Trenton, President Calvin Coolidge celebrated the courage and leadership of the Father of our Country, George Washington.

*Intrenched* behind the Delaware with a ragged, starving army, poorly equipped, broken in morale, dwindling through the expiration of enlistments and daily desertions, while the patriotic cause was as its lowest ebb, on December 18 Washington wrote to his brother:

> You can form no idea of the perplexity of my situation. No man, I believe, ever had a greater choice of difficulties and less means to extricate himself from them. However, under a full persuasion of the justice of our cause I can not entertain an idea that it will finally sink, though it may remain for some time under a cloud.

There you have the full measure of the Father of his Country. He faced the facts. He recognized the full import of their seriousness. But he was firm in the faith that the right would prevail. To faith he proposed to add works. If ever a great cause depended for its success on one man, if ever a mighty destiny was identified with one person in these dark and despondent hours, that figure was Washington.

Such was the prelude to the historic events which, notwithstanding their discouraging beginning, were soon to culminate in the brilliant victories of the patriotic armies in the Battles of Trenton and Princeton. . . .

After a series of engagements and retreats which can only be characterized as defeats, running from April to late December, Washington now decided to take the offensive.

It was finally decided to attempt the crossing of the Delaware from Pennsylvania into New Jersey on Christmas night, 1776, for the purpose of a surprise attack on the Hessians who occupied Trenton. Orders were issued to Colonel Cadwalader, commanding three Philadelphia battalions, to cross at Trenton Ferry. Washington planned to take his army over at McKonkeys Ferry. The crossing has ever since been well-known history. The cold, the sleet, the wind, the great cakes of floating ice made the effort well-nigh impossible. But for the skill of a regiment of fishermen from Marblehead, Massachusetts, under the command of Colonel Glover, the effort would have failed. The commands of Cadwalader and Ewing were unable to reach the New Jersey shore. Tradition relates that Washington said to General Knox: "The fate of an empire depends upon this night." It was not until 4 o'clock in the morning that the little army of 2,500 men began their march on Trenton. The password was "Victory or death." The storm of sleet was freezing as it fell, the mud was deep, the night was dark. Being told the muskets were too wet to use, Washington continued the advance and ordered that where gunpowder failed the bayonets be used.

About 8 o'clock the Americans emerging through the storm surprised the Hessians at Trenton, then a village of about 800 inhabitants, killed their commander, Colonel Rall, and captured between 1,000 and 1,500 men. It is said that Washington personally directed the artillery fire. Alexander Hamilton commanded a battery. Being unsupported and outnumbered three to one, Washington recrossed the Delaware and again took up his position on the Pennsylvania shore.

It can not be said that this ranks as a great battle, but it was the turning point in the Revolutionary War at which defense and defeat became offense and victory. From that hour the spirit of the patriot cause rose. The inhabitants of this region began to remove their loyalist flags and to manifest their open adherence to the American cause. Early on New Year morning Robert Morris was busy waking people in Philadelphia making appeals for money to support the army. He secured $50,000, which went largely to pay the soldiers, encouraging them to remain after their enlistments had expired. . . .

Washington and his generals are gone. The bloody tracks which their barefoot armies often left on the frozen ground have long since been washed away. The smoke of the conflict in which they engaged has cleared. The civil strife and disorder which followed have been dissipated. But the institutions which they founded, the Government which they established, have not only remained, but have grown in strength and importance and extended their influence throughout the earth. We can never go to their assistance with supplies and reinforcements. We can never lend our counsel to their political deliberations. But we can support the Government and institutions which are their chief titles to the esteem and reverence in which they are held by the common consent of all humanity.

—From Address of President Coolidge at the
150th Anniversary of the Battles of Trenton and Princeton
Trenton, NJ, Dec. 29, 1926

∞

## *"Yankee Doodle"*

WE ARE all familiar with this tune, but perhaps we are unfamiliar with its origins. According to the Oxford English Dictionary, the tune was written by a British surgeon in 1755 out of "derision of the provincial troops" of American colonists who had fought with the British against the French in the French-Indian War. In British eyes, these American soldiers appeared to be a bunch of country bumpkins. "Yankee" was a derogatory term for a New Englander; "doodle" meant a "silly or foolish fellow;" and "macaroni" meant a "fop or dandy." During the Revolutionary War, the American colonists, however, soon claimed "Yankee Doodle" as their own song, and sang it with pride on their way to defeating the world's biggest empire.

Yankee Doodle went to town,
A-ridin' on a pony,
Stuck a feather in his cap
And called it Macaroni.

Father and I went down to camp,
Along with Captain Gooding,
And there we saw the men and boys
As thick as hasty pudding.

And there we saw a thousand men,
As rich as Squire David;
And what they wasted every day,
I wish it could be saved.

And there was Captain Washington
Upon a slapping stallion,
A-giving orders to his men;
I guess there was a million.

And there I saw a little keg,
Its head was made of leather;
They knocked upon it with two sticks
To call the men together.

And there I saw a swamping gun,
As big as a log of maple,
Upon a mighty little cart,
A load for father's cattle.

And every time they fired it off
It took a horn of powder,
And made a noise like father's gun.
Only a nation louder.

I can't tell you half I saw,
They kept up such a smother,
So I took my hat off, made a bow
And scampered home to mother.

Yankee Doodle is the tune
Americans delight in,

'Twill do to whistle, sing or play
And just the thing for fightin'.

CHORUS:
Yankee Doodle, keep it up,
Yankee Doodle Dandy,
Mind the music and the step
And with the girls be handy.

∞

## Abigail Adams to John Adams,
## June 17, 1782

IT SHOULD not be forgotten that during the Revolutionary
War, both men *and* women made sacrifices for their country. While women did not fight on the battlefield, they
contributed to the war efforts in their own indispensable
way. John Adams's service to his country took him away
from wife Abigail for a total of ten years during their marriage. Below, as John served a diplomatic mission in France,
Abigail gives voice to the form of patriotism that she and
so many other women displayed. Abigail Adams makes an
extremely powerful argument in this letter that women's
patriotic virtue, arising from profound sacrifices, "equals
the most Heroick" of men.

*Ardently* as I long for the return of my dearest Friend, I
cannot feel the least inclination to a peace but upon the most
liberal foundation. Patriotism in the female Sex is the most disinterested of all virtues. Excluded from honours and from offices, we cannot attach ourselves to the State or Government
from having held a place of Eminence. Even in the freeest coun-
trys our property is subject to the controul and disposal of our
partners, to whom the Laws have given a soverign Authority.
Deprived of a voice in Legislation, obliged to submit to those

Laws which are imposed upon us, is it not sufficient to make us indifferent to the publick Welfare? Yet all History and every age exhibit Instances of patriotick virtue in the female Sex; which considering our situation equals the most Heroick of yours. "A late writer observes that as Citizens we are calld upon to exhibit our fortitude, for when you offer your Blood to the State, it is ours. In giving it our Sons and Husbands we give more than ourselves. You can only die on the field of Battle, but we have the misfortune to survive those whom we Love most."

I will take praise to myself. I feel that it is my due, for having sacrificed so large a portion of my peace and happiness to promote the welfare of my country which I hope for many years to come will reap the benifit, tho it is more than probable unmindfull of the hand that blessed them.

∽

## Nathan Hale, Captain in the American Army

NATHAN HALE'S extraordinary example of patriotism is here retold. Hale's sense of duty is inspiring to all Americans: It shows how sacred honor has a claim on all of us.

*Perhaps* the fate of America was never suspended by a more brittle thread than previously to this memorable retreat. A spectacle is here presented of an army destined for the defence of a great continent, driven to the narrow borders of an island, with a victorious army double its number in front, with navigable waters in its rear; constantly liable to have its communication cut off by the enemy's navy, and every moment exposed to an attack.

This retreat left the British in complete possession of Long Island. What would be their future operations remained uncertain. To obtain information of their situation, their strength, and future movements, was of high importance. For this purpose,

*Nathan Hale*

General Washington applied to Colonel Knowlton, who commanded a regiment of light infantry, which formed the rear of the American army, and desired him to adopt some mode of gaining the necessary information. Colonel Knowlton communicated this request to Captain NATHAN HALE, of Connecticut, who was a captain in his regiment.

This young officer, animated by a sense of duty, and considering that an opportunity presented itself by which he might be useful to his country, at once offered himself a volunteer for this hazardous service. He passed in disguise to Long Island, and examined every part of the British army, and obtained the best possible information respecting their situation and future operations.

In his attempt to return, he was apprehended, carried before Sir William Howe, and the proof of his object was so clear, that he frankly acknowledged who he was, and what were his views. Sir William Howe at once gave an order to have him executed the next morning.

The order was accordingly executed in the most unfeeling manner, and by as great a savage as ever disgraced humanity. A clergyman, whose attendance he desired, was refused him; a Bible, for a few moments' devotion, was not procured, although he wished it. Letters which, on the morning of his execution, he wrote to his mother and other friends, were destroyed; and this very extraordinary reason given by the provost-martial, *"That the rebels should not know they had a man in their army who could die with so much firmness."*

Unknown to all around him, without a single friend to offer him the least consolation, thus fell as amiable and as worthy a young man as America could boast, with this as his dying observation, that *"he only lamented that he had but one life to lose for his country."*

> —From *Lives of the Heroes of the American Revolution*
> by John Frost, 1848

∝∞

## *"The Atlas of Independence,"*
## *John Adams to Timothy Pickering, August 6, 1822*

JOHN ADAMS performed many patriotic deeds. He served in the First and Second Continental Congress, was the leading advocate for independence at the Second Continental Congress, served abroad in Europe to help secure loans to finance the revolutionary war and establish peace alliances, served as vice-president under George Washington, and was our second president, and the father of our sixth president.

However, there were in addition two decisions of his that were to have a most monumental impact on this country: one was his nomination of George Washington as commander-in-chief of the Continental Army; the second was his selection of Thomas Jefferson to write the Declaration of Independence. Two decisions without which this nation would not have been born were both made by this astounding and underappreciated man.

Adams and Jefferson served on the subcommittee to draft the Declaration of Independence, along with Roger Sherman, Benjamin Franklin, and Robert R. Livingston. Below, Adams records the thoughts that led to his endorsement of Jefferson to write the Declaration. Adams had the dream of American independence long before most Americans. Richard Stockton, delegate from New Jersey, called Adams "the Atlas of Independence." It has been written that later on in life, Adams smarted a little every Fourth of July when all credit was given to Jefferson. It was no small sacrifice to give the pen to his friend, but Adams, always a patriot, put the cause ahead of his own fame. In recent surveys Jefferson has been regarded by many as the most influential man of the last millennium. The case can be made that he is such for no small part because Adams handed him the pen in Philadelphia.

These were men of enormous self-knowledge. Adams here candidly admits to his own shortcomings and trades on them to make Jefferson take the lead in the drafting and in history.


*August 6, 1822*

*Mr.* Jefferson came into Congress in June, 1775, and brought with him a reputation for literature, science, and a happy talent of composition. Writings of his were handed about, remarkable for the peculiar felicity of expression. Though a silent member in Congress, he was so prompt, frank, explicit and decisive upon committees and in conversation—not even Samuel Adams was more so—that he soon seized upon my heart; and upon this occasion I gave him my vote, and did all in my power to procure the votes of others. I think he had one more vote than any other, and that placed him at the head of the committee. I had the next highest number, and that placed me the second. The committee met, discussed the subject, and then appointed Mr. Jefferson and me to make the draught, I suppose because we were the two first on the list.

The sub-committee met. Jefferson proposed to me to make the draught.

I said, "I will not."

"You should do it."

"Oh! no."

"Why will you not? You ought to do it."

"I will not."

"Why?"

"Reason enough."

"What can be your reasons?"

"Reason first—You are a Virginian, and a Virginian ought to appear at the head of this business. Reason second—I am obnoxious, suspected and unpopular. You are very much otherwise. Reason third—You can write ten times better than I can."

"Well," said Jefferson, "if you are decided, I will do as well as I can."

"Very well. When you have drawn it up, we will have a meeting."

A meeting we accordingly had, and conned the paper over. I was delighted with its high tone and the flights of oratory with which it abounded, especially that concerning Negro slavery, which, though I knew his Southern brethren would never suffer to pass in Congress, I certainly never would oppose. There were other expressions which I would not have inserted, if I had drawn it up, particularly that which called the King tyrant. I thought this too personal; for I never believed George to be a tyrant in disposition and in nature; I always believed him to be deceived by his courtiers on both sides of the Atlantic, and, in his official capacity only, cruel. I thought the expression too passionate, and too much like scolding, for so grave and solemn a document; but as Franklin and Sherman were to inspect it afterwards, I thought it would not become me to strike it out. I consented to report it, and do not now remember that I made or suggested a single alteration.

We reported it to the committee of five. It was read, and I do not remember that Franklin or Sherman criticized any thing. We were all in haste. Congress was impatient, and the instrument was reported, as I believe, in Jefferson's handwriting, as he first drew it. Congress cut off about a quarter of it, as I expected they would; but they obliterated some of the best of it, and left all that was exceptionable, if any thing in it was. I have long wondered that the original draught has not been published. I suppose the reason is the vehement philippic against Negro slavery.

∞

## *Betsy Ross*

WE DON'T know for certain whether Betsy Ross actually made the first flag. But her story has become familiar to nearly all Americans and provides a wonderful example of a patriotic citizen rising to her country's call. More specifically, it shows how women then made their own sacrifices for their country. For example, in addition to sewing the flag, Ross mourned the loss of her husband, who died a soldier in the war.

*The* story of the making of the first flag with stars and stripes is as follows. Betsy Ross, or, to speak more respectfully, Mrs. Elizabeth Griscom Ross, lived on Arch Street, Philadelphia, in a tiny house of two stories and an attic. She was called the most skillful needlewoman in the city, and there is a tradition that before Washington became commander-in-chief, she embroidered ruffles for his shirts—quite an important branch of fine sewing in those days. Whether she ever embroidered the great man's ruffles or not, it is said that, whenever folk wanted any especially fine work done, they always went to "Betsy Ross." She could do more than sew, for she could draw freehand the complicated patterns that were used in quilting, the supreme proof of artistic ability in the household. One day three gentlemen entered her house through its humble doorway. One was her uncle by marriage, Colonel Ross; one is thought to have been Robert Morris; one was General Washington.

The commander-in-chief told her that they had come from Congress to ask her if she could make a flag. "I don't know," she replied, "but I can try." Then they showed her a rough sketch of a flag and asked what she thought of it. She replied that she thought it ought to be longer, that a flag looked better if the length was one third greater than the width. She ventured to make two more suggestions. One was that the stars which they had scattered irregularly over the blue canton would look better if they were arranged in some regular form, such as a circle or a star or in parallel rows. The second suggestion was that a star with five points was prettier than one with six. Some one seems to have remarked that it would be more difficult to make; and thereupon the skillful little lady folded a bit of paper and with one clip of her scissors produced a star with five points. The three gentlemen saw that her suggestions were good, and General Washington drew up his chair to a table and made another sketch according to her ideas.

Mrs. Ross could make wise suggestions about flags, but how to sew them she did not know; so it was arranged that she should call on a shipping merchant and borrow a flag from him. This she soon did. He opened a chest and took out a ship's flag to show her how the sewing was done. She carried it home to use as a guide, and when she reached the little house on Arch Street, she set to work to make the first flag bearing the stars and stripes. To try the effect, it was run up to the peak of one of the vessels in the Delaware, and the result was so pleasing that it was carried into Congress on the day that it was completed. Congress approved of the work of the little lady. Colonel Ross told her to buy all the material she could and make as many flags as possible. And for more than fifty years she continued to make flags for the Government.

This is the account that has come down to us, not by tradition merely, but by written statements of Mrs. Ross's daughters, grandchildren, and others, to whom she often told the story.

The significance of the new flag no one has expressed better than Washington. "We take the star from Heaven," he said, "red from our mother country, separating it by white stripes, thus showing that we have separated from her, and the white stripes shall go down to posterity representing liberty."

—From Eva March Tappan,
*The Little Book of the Flag*

## Israel Putnam at Bunker Hill

SHORTLY BEFORE the Battle of Bunker Hill on June 17, 1775, Abigail Adams made the following observation about the valor of her fellow patriots: "Courage I know we have in abundance, conduct I hope shall not want, but powder —where shall we get a sufficient supply?"

American troops fought valiantly at Bunker Hill and miraculously held off two charges by the British. They could have fought the redcoats off even longer had they had enough ammunition, but they ran out. Still, it was a great victory for the colonists to have stood up to the British Army. The American soldiers who fought on that day were led by Israel Putnam, who later became a major general in the Continental Army.

Legend has it that Putnam once faced down an angry

wolf in a cave. Redcoats (with more ammunition) did not frighten him either.

*At* the close of the war, in 1764, Putnam went home, hung up his sword, swung over his door a signboard with General Wolfe's picture on it, and for ten years was a quiet farmer and innkeeper. One day, he had eaten his dinner and gone out to the field with his oxen. Suddenly he heard the sound of a drum. A man was galloping furiously along the road, beating his drum and calling, "To arms! To arms! The British have fired upon us! The country is ablaze!" Then Putnam forgot his beloved farm. He forgot to say good-bye to his family. He forgot that he was an officer, and was going to war without his uniform. He forgot everything except which of his horses was the swiftest. He leaped upon its back, and while the oxen stood in the field waiting patiently for him to return, he was galloping along the road to make his second visit to Boston, one hundred miles away.

The Continental Army had gathered from all directions. The British were in possession of Boston. "We must seize those hills," declared the British General Gage, "if we are to stay in the city."

"We must seize those hills," declared the Americans, "if we are to drive the British out of the city." Colonel Prescott and General Putnam marched out by night and began to fortify Breed's Hill and Bunker Hill.

At daybreak the British discovered what was going on. "We might take Charlestown Neck," said one officer, "and starve them out."

"That's too slow," objected another. "I believe the best way will be to charge upon them."

"Not so easy to charge up that hill."

"Why not? They're only farmers. They don't know anything about fighting. The chances are that they will run long before we are at the foot of the hill."

So the British talked, and at length they decided to make a charge. The march began. The scarlet lines came nearer and nearer. Prescott and Putnam were going back and forth among their men at the top of the hill. "Remember there isn't much powder," they said. And Putnam added, "Men, you know how to aim. Don't fire till you can see the whites of their eyes."

Up the hill marched the British, stopping only to fire; but the Americans stood motionless. It seemed to them hours before the word rang out, "Fire!" That fire was like a cannonade, and the British, brave old soldiers as they were, ran pell-mell down the hill. "Hurrah! hurrah!" shouted the Americans. The British formed and rushed up the hill again; again the lines broke, and they retreated. They came a third time, but now no volleys met them; the powder had given out. The Americans had no bayonets, but they fought furiously with stones and the butt ends of their muskets, with clubs, knives, even with their fists; but no such weapons could withstand British veterans, and the Americans had to retreat.

News of the battle went through the colonies like wildfire. All their lives the Americans had looked up to the British regulars as the greatest of soldiers: and they, the untrained colonists who had never seen two regiments in battle, had twice driven them back! The hill was lost, but to repulse the British regulars was a mighty victory. Couriers galloped from one colony to another to carry the news. Everywhere there was rejoicing; but Putnam could not bear to think that after such a fight the hill had at last been given up, and he growled indignantly, "We ought to have stood. Powder or no powder, we ought to have stood."

—Adapted from Eva March Tappan, *American Hero Stories*

❧

# John Adams to Abigail Adams,
## July 3, 1776

ON JUNE 7, 1776, Richard Henry Lee of Virginia proposed a resolution in the Second Continental Congress: "That these United Colonies are and of right ought to be free and independent states." On July 2, 1776, the delegates of twelve colonies (New York abstained) voted unanimously to adopt Lee's resolution for independence, thanks to Adams's leadership. The next day in a letter to his wife, Adams shares his thoughts on how American independence would be celebrated by future generations—with pomp and parade, games and sports.

Of course, we celebrate American Independence on July 4, the date that the Declaration of Independence was approved, rather than on July 2, the date that the resolution for independence was adopted. Adams may have predicted the wrong date for future celebrations, but his thoughts are indeed prophetic. In the midst of our barbecues and fireworks, I hope Americans will take a minute or two to remember this brave warrior who made the birth of our nation possible and remember as well his words about toil, blood, treasure and trust in God.

*But* the Day is past. The Second Day of July 1776, will be the most memorable Epocha, in the History of America.—I am apt to believe that it will be celebrated, by succeeding Generations, as the great anniversary Festival. It ought to be commemorated, as the Day of Deliverance by solemn Acts of Devotion to God Almighty. It ought to be solemnized with Pomp and Parade, with Shews, Games, Sports, Guns, Bells, Bonfires and Illuminations from one End of this Continent to the other from this Time forward forever more.

You will think me transported with Enthusiasm but I am not. —I am well aware of the Toil and Blood and Treasure, that it will cost Us to maintain this Declaration, and support and defend these States.—Yet through all the Gloom I can see the Rays of ravishing Light and Glory. I can see that the End is more than worth all the Means. And that Posterity will tryumph in that Days Transaction, even altho We should rue it, which I trust in God We shall not.

∞

## Washington's Glasses

HERE'S A story of the inimitable example of George Washington. In 1783, unpaid officers from the Continental Army threatened a military coup to overthrow Congress. Washington could have been America's first dictator. Instead, he persuaded his fellow officers to live under the rule of law. On and off the field of battle, this man was a leader of the highest principles.

At the end of the Revolutionary War, the new United States came close to disaster. The government owed back pay to many officers in the army, men who had fought long and hard for the nation's freedom. But Congress had no money, and rumors abounded that it intended to disband the armed forces and send them home without pay.

As the weeks passed, the army's cry for pay grew louder. The soldiers insisted that they had performed their duty faithfully, and now the government should do the same. They sent appeals to Congress, with no effect. Patience began to wear thin. Tempers smoldered. At last some of the officers, encamped at Newburgh, New York, issued what amounted to a threat. The army would not disband until paid; if necessary, it would march on Congress. Mutiny was close at hand.

There was no doubt in anyone's mind that one man alone could persuade the army to give the government more time.

On March 15, 1783, George Washington strode into the Temple of Virtue, a large wooden hall built by the soldiers as a chapel and dance hall. A hush fell over the gathered officers as the tall figure took to the lectern at the front of the room. These men had come to love their commander-in-chief during the lean, hard years of fighting; now, for the first time, they glared at him with restless and resentful eyes. A deathlike stillness filled the room.

Washington began to speak. He talked of his own dedicated service, and reminded the group that he himself had served without pay. He spoke of his love for his soldiers. He urged them to have patience, and pointed out that Congress in the past had acted slowly, but in the end would act justly. He promised he would do everything in his power to see that the men received what they deserved.

He asked them to consider the safety and security of their new country, begging them not to "open the flood gates of civil discord, and deluge our rising empire in blood." He appealed to their honor. "Let me entreat you, gentlemen, on your part," he said, "not to take any measures which, viewed in the calm light of reason, will lessen the dignity and sully the glory you have hitherto maintained."

He paused. A restlessness pervaded the air. His audience did not seem moved. The men stared at him tensely.

Washington produced a letter from a congressman explaining the difficulties the government now faced. He would read it to them. It would help them comprehend the new government's difficulties. He unfolded the paper. He started to read, slowly. He stumbled over some of the words, then stopped. Something was wrong. The general seemed lost, slightly confused. The officers leaned forward.

Then Washington pulled from his pocket something the men had never seen their commander-in-chief use before—spectacles.

"Gentlemen, you must pardon me," he said quietly. "I have grown gray in your service, and now find myself growing blind."

It was not merely what the beloved general said, but the way he spoke the few, simple words. The humble act of this majestic man touched the soldiers in a way his arguments had failed to do. There were lumps in many throats, tears in every eye. The general quietly left the hall, and the officers voted to give the Congress more time.

George Washington had saved his new country from armed rebellion. As Thomas Jefferson later said, "The moderation and virtue of a single character probably prevented this Revolution from being closed, as most others have been, by a subversion of that liberty it was intended to establish."

∞

## Benjamin Franklin Defends the Constitution, 1787

ON SEPTEMBER 17, 1787, Franklin rose and handed the following written speech to James Wilson to read aloud. Franklin was not without his own reservations about the Constitution—for example, he believed in a one house legislature instead of two and opposed giving the president a salary. Nonetheless, Franklin showed intellectual and moral courage; he sacrificed his own ideas and endorsed the Constitution and gave a motion for a unanimous vote from the delegates from the eleven states who were present. Not all the delegates to the Constitutional Convention were in agreement—of the fifty-five delegates, only thirty-nine actually signed the Constitution.

This speech was, perhaps, Franklin's last political contribution to a nation he had been so instrumental in building. What follows is James Madison's account of the speech.

*Monday Sep. 17, 1787: In Convention*
The engrossed Constitution being read,
Doc.ᴿ Franklin rose with a speech in his hand, which he had reduced to writing for his own conveniency, and which Mr. Wilson read in the words following.

Mr. President

I confess that there are several parts of this constitution which I do not at present approve, but I am not sure I shall never approve them: For having lived long, I have experienced many instances of being obliged by better information, or fuller consideration, to change opinions even on important subjects, which I once thought right, but found to be otherwise. It is therefore that the older I grow, the more apt I am to doubt my own judgment, and to pay more respect to the judgment of others.

In these sentiments, Sir, I agree to this Constitution with all its faults, if they are such; because I think a general Government necessary for us, and there is no form of Government but what may be a blessing to the people if well administered, and believe farther that this is likely to be well administered for a course of years, and can only end in Despotism, as other forms have done before it, when the people shall become so corrupted as to need despotic Government, being incapable of any other. I doubt too whether any other Convention we can obtain, may be able to make a better Constitution. For when you assemble a number of men to have the advantage of their joint wisdom, you inevitably assemble with those men, all their prejudices, their passions, their errors of opinion, their local interests, and their selfish views. From such an assembly can a perfect production be expected? It therefore astonishes me, Sir, to find this system approaching so near to perfection as it does; and I think it will astonish our enemies, who are waiting with confidence to hear that our councils are confounded like those of the Builders of Babel; and that our States are on the point of separation, only to meet hereafter for the purpose of cutting one another's throats. Thus I consent Sir, to this Constitution because I expect no better, and because I am not sure, that it is not the best. The opinions I have had of its errors, I sacrifice to the public good. I have never whispered a syllable of them abroad. Within these walls they were born and here they shall die. If every one of us in returning to our Constituents were to report the objections he has had to it, and endeavor to gain partizans in support of them, we might prevent its being generally received, and thereby lose all the salutary effects & great advantages resulting naturally in our favor among foreign Nations as well as among ourselves, from our real or apparent unanimity. Much of the strength & efficiency of any Government in procuring and securing happiness to the people, depends, on opinion, on the general opinion of the goodness of the Government, as well as of the wisdom and integrity of its Governors. I hope therefore that for our own sakes as a part of the people, and for the sake of posterity, we shall act heartily and unanimously in recommending this Constitution (if approved by Congress & confirmed by the Conventions) wherever our influence may extend, and turn our future thoughts & endeavors to the means of having it well administred.

On the whole, Sir, I can not help expressing a wish that every member of the Convention who may still have objections to it, would with me, on this occasion doubt a little of his own infallibility, and to make manifest our unanimity, put his name to this instrument.—

He then moved that the Constitution be signed by the members and offered the following as a convenient form viz. "Done in Convention by the unanimous consent of *the States* present the 17th of Sept &c—In Witness whereof we have hereunto subscribed our names."

## *Alexander Hamilton,* Federalist No. 1, *October 27, 1787*

AFTER MONTHS of arduous work, the delegates to the Constitutional Convention submitted the Constitution before the people of each state for ratification. Adoption of the Constitution was not a foregone conclusion—there were many opponents to it, known as the "Anti-Federalists," who worried that the Constitution consolidated national power at the expense of the state governments.

Adopting the pen name "Publius," Alexander Hamilton, James Madison, and John Jay wrote a series of essays urging passage of the Constitution. These eighty-five essays appeared in newspapers mainly in New York and were later compiled in book form as *The Federalist.* They are a genuine work of political theory and still do a better job of explaining the principles of American government than any other book I know. I would encourage every American to read and reread them.

In this, one of the most famous passages from *The Federalist,* Alexander Hamilton, who later became America's first Secretary of the Treasury, explains why love of America means so much more. The fate of *our* republic is tied up with the fate of the universal principles upon which it is founded. As Hamilton points out, the spirit of patriotism *and* philanthropy support America's founding.

*To the People of the State of New York*

*After* an unequivocal experience of the inefficacy of the subsisting Federal Government, you are called upon to deliberate on a new Constitution for the United States of America. The subject speaks its own importance; comprehending in its consequences, nothing less than the existence of the Union, the safety and welfare of the parts of which it is composed, the fate of an empire, in many respects, the most interesting in the world. It has been frequently remarked, that it seems to have been reserved to the people of this country, by their conduct and example, to decide the important question, whether societies of men are really capable or not, of establishing good government from reflection and choice, or whether they are forever destined to depend, for their political constitutions, on accident and force. If there be any truth in the remark, the crisis, at which we are arrived, may with propriety be regarded as the æra in which that decision is to be made; and a wrong election of the part we shall act, may, in this view, deserve to be considered as the general misfortune of mankind.

This idea will add the inducements of philanthropy to those of patriotism to heighten the solicitude, which all considerate and good men must feel for the event.

∾

## *"One Great Respectable and Flourishing Empire"*
## *James Madison,* Federalist No. 14,
## *November 30, 1787*

JAMES MADISON has rightfully been called the "father of the Constitution." But Madison himself would not take sole credit and wrote that the Constitution "was not, like the fabled Goddess of Wisdom, the offspring of a single brain. It ought to be regarded as the work of many heads and many hands." Madison could protest as much as he wanted—as the scholar T.V. Smith once wrote, Madison had a "passion for anonymity," but he was the principal mind and force behind the Constitution. Madison arrived eleven days early in Philadelphia for the Constitutional

Convention so that he could get a running start on the proceedings.

In *Federalist No. 14,* Madison explains why the "experiment of an extended republic" is not something to dismiss simply because it has never been tried before. In the past, most republics had been small and homogenous states, rocked by factions and convulsions and decline. It was Madison's vision that American could become "one great respectable and flourishing empire."

*Is* it not the glory of the people of America, that whilst they have paid a decent regard to the opinions of former times and other nations, they have not suffered a blind veneration for antiquity, for custom, or for names, to overrule the suggestions of their own good sense, the knowledge of their own situation, and the lessons of their own experience? To this manly spirit, posterity will be indebted for the possession, and the world for the example of the numerous innovations displayed on the American theatre, in favor of private rights and public happiness. Had no important step been taken by the leaders of the revolution for which a precedent could not be discovered, no government established of which an exact model did not present itself, the people of the United States might, at this moment, have been numbered among the melancholy victims of misguided councils, must at best have been labouring under the weight of some of those forms which have crushed the liberties of the rest of mankind. Happily for America, happily we trust for the whole human race, they pursued a new and more noble course. They accomplished a revolution which has no parallel in the annals of human society: They reared the fabrics of governments which have no model on the face of the globe. They formed the design of a great confederacy, which it is incumbent on their successors to improve and perpetuate. If their works betray imperfections, we wonder at the fewness of them. If they erred most in the structure of the union; this was the work most difficult to be executed; this is the work which has been new modelled by the act of your Convention, and it is that act on which you are now to deliberate and to decide.

—Publius

❧

## George Washington, Farewell Address, September 19, 1796

HERE IS a man whose dedication to his country was as consistent as it was deep. For his leadership on the battlefield and for his willingness to serve as our first President, despite his well-known preference for private life, Washington is remembered, in the words of Henry Lee, as "first in war, first in peace, and first in the hearts of his countrymen."

Washington, the greatest American, was very clear about the "just claim" that government has on us. We have lost sight of that in the anti-government climate that so dominates public discourse.

Devoting more than half his life to the service of his country, Washington here gives a moving farewell address as he repairs to private life.

*In* looking forward to the moment, which is intended to terminate the career of my public life, my feelings do not permit me to suspend the deep acknowledgment of that debt of gratitude wch. I owe to my beloved country, for the many honors it has conferred upon me; still more for the stedfast confidence with which it has supported me; and for the opportunities I have thence enjoyed of manifesting my inviolable attachment, by services faithful and persevering, though in usefulness unequal to my zeal. If benefits have resulted to our country from these services, let it always be remembered to your praise, and as an instructive example in our annals, that, under circumstances in which the Passions agitated in every direction were liable to mislead, amidst appearances sometimes dubious, viscissitudes of fortune often discouraging, in situations in which not unfrequently want of Success has countenanced the spirit of criticism, the constancy of your support was the essential prop of the efforts, and a guarantee of the plans by which they were effected. Profoundly penetrated with this idea, I shall carry it with me to my grave, as a strong incitement to unceasing vows that Heaven may continue to you the choicest tokens of its beneficence; that your Union and brotherly affection may be perpetual; that the free constitution, which is the work of your hands, may be sacredly maintained; that its Administration in every department may be stamped with wisdom and Virtue; that, in fine, the happiness of the people of these States, under the auspices of liberty, may be made complete, by so careful a preservation and so prudent a use of this blessing as will acquire to them the glory of recommending it to the applause, the affection, and adoption of every nation which is yet a stranger to it. . . .

This government, the offspring of our own choice uninfluenced and unawed, adopted upon full investigation and mature deliberation, completely free in its principles, in the distribution of its powers, uniting security with energy, and containing within itself a provision for its own amendment, has a just claim to your confidence and your support. Respect for its authority, compliance with its Laws, acquiescence in its measures, are duties enjoined by the fundamental maxims of true Liberty. The basis of our political systems is the right of the people to make and to alter their Constitutions of Government. But the Constitution which at any time exists, 'till changed by an explicit and authentic act of the whole People, is sacredly obligatory upon all.

## James Madison, "Advice to My Country," Fall 1834

MADISON LIVED to the age of eighty-five and was the last surviving member of the Philadelphia Constitutional Convention. He died on June 28, 1836—six days before the sixtieth anniversary of America's independence. It has been reported that someone suggested to Madison that he take some medicine to delay his death until July 4, so that he could die a patriotic death on that date just as former presidents Thomas Jefferson, John Adams, and James Monroe had done. Madison thought the suggestion was ridiculous and that a man should die when he was meant to.*

Though in a state of physical debilitation, his mind remained sharp to the end, and he continued dictating letters and signing them with a trembling hand. One visitor during his last days remarked that "never have I seen so much mind in so little matter!"

His death, like his life, was full of serene dignity. Here's one account: "That morning Sukey brought him breakfast, as usual. He could not swallow. His niece, Mrs. Wilis, said: 'What is the matter, Uncle James?'

" 'Nothing more than a change of *mind*, my dear.' His head instantly dropped, and he ceased breathing as quietly as the snuff of a candle goes out." †

Madison continued to give advice from the grave. Madison's "Advice to My Country" was his final contribution to a nation that he had been so instrumental in building. As John Quincy Adams said of Madison: "Is it not in a pre-

* Cited in Rutland, *James Madison*.

† Paul Jennings, *A Colored Man's Reminiscences of James Madison,* 1865, cited in Andrienne Koch, *Madison's "Advice to My Country,"* pp. 156–57.

eminent degree by emanations from *his* mind, that we are assembled here as the representatives of the people and the states of this union? Is it not transcendentally by his exertions that we address each other here by the endearing appellations of country-men and fellow citizens?" *

As the last, and perhaps the greatest, of the Founding Fathers, no one was more entitled to give advice.

*As* this advice, if it ever see the light will not do it till I am no more, it may be considered as issuing from the tomb, where truth alone can be respected, and the happiness of man alone consulted. It will be entitled therefore to whatever weight can be derived from good intentions, and from the experience of one who has served his country in various stations through a period of forty years, who espoused in his youth and adhered through his life to the cause of its liberty, and who has borne a part in most of the great transactions which will constitute epochs of its destiny.

The advice nearest to my heart and deepest in my convictions is that the Union of the States be cherished and perpetuated. Let the open enemy to it be regarded as a Pandora with her box opened; and the disguised one, as the Serpent creeping with his deadly wiles into Paradise.

* Cited in Koch, *Madison's "Advice to My Country,"* p.158.

∞

# George Washington, Last Will and Testament, July 1799, and George Mason, Last Will and Testament, October 1792

GEORGE WASHINGTON and George Mason's love of country knew no bounds. George Mason was a Virginian planter who, in 1776, wrote the Virginia Declaration of Rights, which served as a model for the Declaration of Independence. At the Constitutional Convention of 1787, Mason said: "If I had a vein which did not beat with the love of my country, I myself would open it." * Washington, in his First Inaugural speech, said that "I was summoned by my Country, whose voice I can never hear but with veneration and love."

Here, even in death, their patriotism is passed on to their descendants.

*To* each of my Nephews, William Augustine Washington, George Lewis, George Steptoe Washington, Bushrod Washington and Samuel Washington, I give one of the Swords or Cutteaux of which I may die possessed; and they are to chuse in the order they are named. These Swords are accompanied with an injunction not to unsheath them for the purpose of shedding blood, except it be for self defence, or in defence of their Country and its rights; and in the latter case, to keep them unsheathed, and prefer falling with them in their hands, to the relinquishment thereof.

—From the last will and testament
of George Washington

---

* Catherine Drinker Bowen, *Miracle at Philadelphia*, p. 76.

I recommend it to my sons, from my own experience in life, to prefer the happiness of independence and a private station to the troubles and vexations of public business; but if either their own inclinations or the necessity of the times should engage them in public affairs, I charge them, on a father's blessing, never to let the motives of private interest or ambition to induce them to betray, nor the terrors of poverty and disgrace, or the fear of danger or of death deter them from asserting the liberty of their country, and endeavoring to transmit to their posterity those sacred rights to which themselves were born.

—From the last will and testament
of George Mason

# "Independence Forever!"
## Deaths of John Adams and Thomas Jefferson, July 4, 1826

*On* July 4, 1826—the fiftieth anniversary of the adoption of the Declaration of Independence—Thomas Jefferson, the author of that document, and John Adams, its leading advocate, died. It was surely one of the great coincidences of history—one might say, it was providential. How else could it be explained? Perhaps the two Founders sensed they could finally rest, their work now complete, and turn the American experiment over to a new generation of Americans. In life and in death, these men were patriots.

It was as if Adams and Jefferson willed themselves to live to see July 4, 1826. There was much anticipation regarding the Fiftieth Anniversary of America's Independence in Adams's hometown of Quincy, Massachusetts. Adams was too weak to attend any of the planned festivities, so a local committee approached him in late June to ask him for a toast. Adams replied,

"Independence forever!" and refused to add another word. Though bedridden, when the great anniversary arrived, Adams asked to be seated in his chair in front of the window, so that he could take in the festivities. Soon after he slipped into a state of unconsciousness, and his doctor predicted he would not live to see another day. Adams's last thought—at least the last one he uttered out loud—was of his friend and fellow laborer for independence, Thomas Jefferson. Adams woke from his coma and said, "Jefferson still survives." Those were his last words. He died that evening."*

But Adams was mistaken—Jefferson did not survive him. Jefferson's health had been on the decline. He told his grandson in the spring of 1826 that he did not expect to live to see midsummer. In mid-June, he sent for his physician to stay with him at Monticello. In the weeks that followed, Jefferson prepared for his death. He met with all his grandchildren and told them "to pursue virtue, be true and truthful."† His thoughts during his last days kept returning to the revolutionary years— as he began his final decline he said something about warning the Committee of Safety. On the morning of July 3, Jefferson's doctor reported that his "stupor" or coma was "almost permanent." However, Jefferson woke up at seven o'clock in the evening and asked the doctor, "Is it the Fourth?" The doctor assured him it soon would be. According to the testimony of his doctor, those were Jefferson's last words. He clung to life long enough to die peacefully at around one o'clock in the afternoon on July 4, 1826.

"Adams and Jefferson are no more," said Daniel Webster in his famous eulogy of both men:

> "On our fiftieth anniversary, the great day of national jubilee, in the very hour of public rejoicing, in the midst of echoing and reechoing voices of thanksgiving, while their own names were

* Charles Francis Adams, *Life and Works of John Adams,* vol. 1, pp. 634–44.
† Testimony of Thomas Jefferson Randolph, *Domestic Life of Jefferson.*

on all tongues, they took their flight together to the world of spirits . . . Poetry itself has hardly terminated illustrious lives, and finished the career of earthly renown, by such a consummation. . . . It has closed; our patriots have fallen; but so fallen, at such age, with such coincidence, on such a day, that we cannot rationally lament that that end has come, which we knew could not be long deferred. . . . Their work doth not perish with them."

Independence forever!

JEFFERSON'S EPITAPH:

> Here was buried
> Thomas Jefferson
>
> Author of the Declaration of American Independence,
> of the Statute of Virginia for religious freedom
> & Father of the University of Virginia

Jefferson explained his selection of these achievements by the following: "because by these, as testimonials that I have lived, I wish most to be remembered."

John Quincy Adams composed the following epitaph for his parents. It is located at a church which John Quincy Adams attended, in Quincy, Massachusetts.

> LIBERTATEM, AMICITIAM, FIDEM RETINEBIS
> "Freedom, Friendship, Faith Thy Soul Engage"
>
> D. O. M.
> "God the best, the greatest"
>
> Beneath these walls
> Are deposited the mortal remains of

JOHN ADAMS.

Son of John and Susanna (Boylston) Adams,
Second President of the United States;
Born $\frac{19}{30}$ October, 1735.
On the Fourth of July, 1776,
He pledged his Life, Fortune, and sacred Honor
To the INDEPENDENCE OF HIS COUNTRY.
On the third of September, 1783,
He affixed his seal to the definitive treaty with Great Britain,
Which acknowledged that independence,
And consummated the redemption of his pledge.
On the Fourth of July, 1826,
He was summoned
To the Independence of Immortality,
And to the JUDGMENT OF HIS GOD.
This House will bear witness to his piety;
This Town, his birthplace, to his munificence;
History to his patriotism;
Posterity to the depth and compass of his mind.

At his side
Sleeps, till the trump shall sound,

ABIGAIL,

His beloved and only wife,
Daughter of William and Elizabeth (Quincy) Smith;
In every relation of life a pattern
Of filial, conjugal, maternal, and social virtue.
Born November $\frac{11}{22}$, 1744,
Deceased 28 October, 1818,
Aged 74.

———

Married 25 October, 1764.
During an union of more than half a century

They survived, in harmony of sentiment, principle, and affection,
The tempests of civil commotion;
Meeting undaunted and surmounting
The terrors and trials of that Revolution,
Which secured the Freedom of their Country;
Improved the condition of their times;
And brightened the prospects of Futurity
To the race of man upon Earth.

PILGRIM.

From lives thus spent thy earthly duties learn;
From fancy's dreams to active virtue turn;
Let Freedom, Friendship, Faith, thy soul engage,
And serve, like them, thy country and thy age.

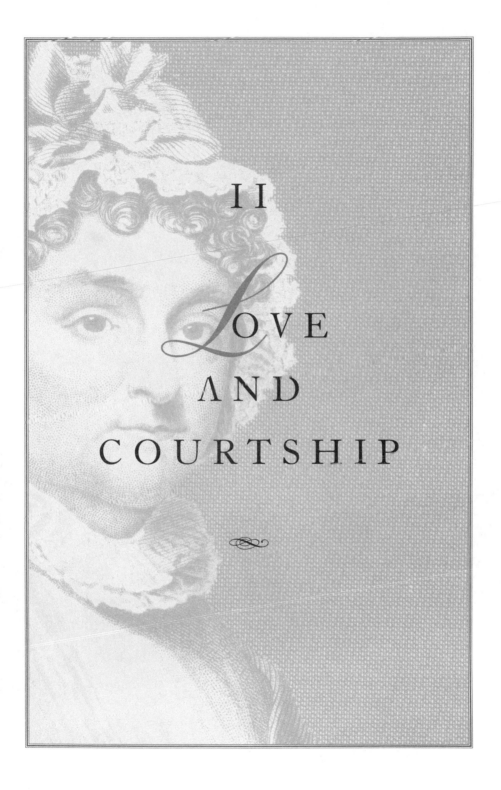

# II

# *L*OVE

# AND

# COURTSHIP

$\mathcal{The}$ Founders, who wrote extensively on political or public affairs, also had much to say on the subject of love and court-ship. And for good reason. After all, there is a connection between our private lives and our public lives. How men and women interact with each other—how they govern their "inclinations," as George Washington put it, toward each other—has long-term consequences for the well-being of both the individual and society.

The attraction between men and women is one of the first "sparks" of our natural sociability. Men and women need and are drawn toward each other—they are each parts that are meant to come together to form a whole. Left alone, each is incomplete. As Benjamin Franklin wrote: "A man without a wife is like half of a pair of scissors." The bringing together of a man and a woman forms a family, the basic building block of society. A state, as the ancient philosopher Aristotle said, is made up of many households in which a man and a woman raise a family. The French philosopher Jean Jacques Rousseau observed that the way men and women treat each other in the family sets a certain tone to society, one that will, it is hoped, create a harmonious foundation for politics. The Founders understood the importance of a happy domestic life and expected that the relations between men and women would be one of love, mutual support, and respect.

George Washington once told his adopted granddaughter that "men and women feel the same inclinations to each other *now* that they always have done, and which they will continue to do until there is a new order of things." Some things never change, it seems. Yet that does not mean that everything has been figured out. This chapter on love and courtship shows how the Founders struggled to govern the passions of the heart. Some failed, others succeeded. For example, much to his frustration, Thomas Jefferson as a young man became extremely shy and tongue-tied around young women; Benjamin Franklin admits that he had difficulties controlling "that hard-to-be-governed passion of youth;" and Alexander Hamilton had an extramarital affair that led to a political scandal. But the founding period also boasts of one of America's greatest love stories —the courtship and marriage of John and Abigail Adams. They were married for fifty-four years and provide an ideal of what love and marriage are all about. It seems safe to say that "until there is a new order of things" their story will remain inspiring to all generations.

∞

## Thomas Jefferson to John Page, October 7, 1763

THOMAS JEFFERSON was a student at William and Mary College in Virginia when he fell in love with Rebecca Burwell. Jefferson called her "Belinda" and often wrote to his good friend John Page about romantic developments. Looking back, it might be surprising to see just how shy and awkward Thomas Jefferson—the future author of the Declaration of Independence and President of the United States—was around his first love. His Belinda, perhaps from impatience at his diffidence, married somebody else.

I think most of us can relate to a time in our lives when we were just as tongue-tied as the twenty-one-year-old Jefferson at the dance he describes in the following letter.

The man whose words, perhaps more than any other, have shaped the modern political world couldn't find any to say to a young girl at a dance.

*In* the most melancholy fit that ever any poor soul was, I sit down to write to you. Last night, as merry as agreeable company and dancing with Belinda in the Apollo could make me, I never could have thought the succeeding sun would have seen me so wretched as I now am! I was prepared to say a great deal: I had dressed up in my own mind, such thoughts as occurred to me, in as moving language as I knew how, and expected to have performed in a tolerably creditable manner. But, good God! When I had an opportunity of venting them, a few broken sentences, uttered in great disorder, and interrupted with pauses of uncommon length, were the too visible marks of my strange confusion! The whole confab I will tell you, word for word, if I can, when I see you, which God send may be soon. . . . The court is now at hand, which I must attend constantly, so that unless you come to town, there is little probability of my meeting with you any where else. For God's sake come.

## *Alexander Hamilton to Catherine Livingston,*
## *April 11, 1777*

SOME HISTORIANS record that Alexander Hamilton was the most handsome of the Founding Fathers, and this letter showcases his considerable charm. Hamilton had grown up in the West Indies—his father had never married his mother and abandoned the family. Thus, Hamilton came to America without the family background that would offer entree to the highest families or social circles in America. But Hamilton, from his early days, was ambitious. With sheer brilliance, superior talents (and his charm, no doubt), Hamilton, as we all know, rose to become one of the greatest of all Americans.

This letter was written to Kitty Livingston, who was the daughter of the royal governor of New Jersey. It is not a serious attempt at courtship—Hamilton knew Kitty would not take someone with his family background seriously. But it still shows, I think, how men then went about the business of courting the woman of their dreams.

*After* knowing exactly your taste, and whether you are of a romantic, or discreet temper, as to love affairs, I will endeavour to regulate myself by it. If you would choose to be a goddess, and to be worshipped as such, I will torture my imagination for the best arguments, the nature of the case will admit, to prove you so. You shall be one of the graces, or Diana, or Venus, or something surpassing them all. And after your deification, I will cull out of every poet of my acquaintance, the choicest delicacies, they possess, as offerings at your Goddesships' shrine. But if, conformable to your usual discernment, you are content with being a mere mortal, and require no other incense, than is justly due to you, I will talk to you like one [in] his sober senses; and, though it may be straining the point a little, I will even stipulate to pay you all the rational tribute properly applicable to a fine girl.

∞

## *John Adams to Abigail Smith,*
## *October 4, 1762; 1762–1763; February 14, 1763*

IN HIS *Autobiography,* Adams described himself as possessing "an amorous disposition" and confessed that "very early, from ten or eleven years of age, he was very fond of the society of females." Instead of studying, Adams also

*Abigail Adams*

confessed that he often wasted the day "gallanting the girls" of his neighborhood. Adams was soon to court and marry one of the most exceptional women in American history, Abigail Adams. However, it was not love at first sight.

Adams met Abigail Smith, daughter of a minister, when she was but fifteen years old. Of that first encounter, Adams wrote that Abigail and her sister, Mary Smith, are "wits" but also that they are not "fond, not frank, not candid" and do not display much "tenderness."

But two years later, upon seeing Abigail again, Adams wrote in his diary, without explicitly naming her, that she is "a constant feast. Tender, feeling, sensible, friendly. A friend. Not an imprudent, not an indelicate, not a disagreeable word or action. Prudent, modest, delicate, soft, sensible, obliging, active." Soon, Adams was riding his horse the four miles to Weymouth, Massachusetts, to do legal business by day and to court Abigail by night.

As was the common practice of the day, Abigail and John adopted names from literary and classical figures in their correspondence. Abigail took the name "Diana"—the Roman goddess of purity or chastity, and later as his wife took the name "Portia"—the brave and devoted wife of the ancient Roman republican statesman Brutus; John was "Lysander"—the great Spartan admiral.

Whoever thought of the Puritans as repressed beings will be surprised by the passionate nature of young John and Abigail's courtship. Full of ardor and longing, these letters provide a wonderful example of what love can be. In the following selections, we get a delightful perspective on John Adams as the impatient and amorous pursuer—in one case, delivering a letter to "Miss Adorable" that calls for kisses upon receipt.

## JOHN ADAMS TO ABIGAIL SMITH

*Miss* Adorable

By the same Token that the Bearer hereof *satt up* with you last night I hereby order you to give him, as many Kisses, and as many Hours of your Company after 9 O'Clock as he shall please to Demand and charge them to my Account: This Order, or Requisition call it which you will is in Consideration of a similar order Upon Aurelia for the like favour, and I presume I have good Right to draw upon you for the Kisses as I have given two or three Millions at least, when one has been received, and of Consequence the Account between us is immensely in favour of yours,

John Adams

JOHN ADAMS TO ABIGAIL SMITH

*Dr:* Miss Jemima                                    *Braintree*
I have taken the best Advice, on the subject of your Billet,
and I find you cannot compell me *to pay* unless I refuse Marriage; which I never did, and never will, but on the Contrary am
ready to *have you* at any Time.
Yours,                                              Jonathan

JOHN ADAMS TO ABIGAIL SMITH

*Dear* Madam                                        *Braintree*
Accidents are often more Friendly to us, than our own Prudence.—I intended to have been at Weymouth Yesterday, but
a storm prevented.—Cruel, Yet perhaps blessed storm!—Cruel
for detaining me from so much friendly, social Company, and
perhaps blessed to you, or me or both, for keeping me at *my
Distance.* For every experimental Phylosopher knows, that the
steel and the Magnet or the Glass and feather will not fly together with more Celerity, than somebody And somebody,
when brought within the striking Distance—and, Itches, Aches,
Agues, and Repentance might be the Consequences of a Con-
tact in present Circumstances. Even the Divines pronounce ca-
suistically, I hear, "unfit to be touched these three Weeks."
    I mount this moment for that noisy, dirty Town of Boston,
where Parade, Pomp, Nonsense, Frippery, Folly, Foppery, Luxury, Polliticks, and the soul-Confounding Wrangles of the Law
will give me the Higher Relish for Spirit, Taste and Sense, at
Weymouth, next Sunday.

∞

## John Adams to Abigail Smith, August 1763, and Abigail to John, September 12, 1763

IN THESE two charming letters, John and Abigail flirta-
tiously discuss "apparitions" of each other that appeared in
their homes, no doubt a reflection of the powerful longing
they felt for each other. In today's casual style of courtship,
where obstacles to immediate gratification are like May
snowfalls—rare, brief, and easily melted—the imagination
is often left flat. We no longer believe in, or have a need
for, "apparitions." I'm not sure that love lives are the better
for it.

### JOHN ADAMS TO ABIGAIL SMITH

My dear Diana                                    *Saturday morning*

Germantown is at a great Distance from Weymouth Meeting-
House, you know; The No. of Yards indeed is not so prodi-
gious, but the Rowing and Walking that lyes between is a great
Discouragement to a weary Traveller. Could my Horse have
helped me to Weymouth, Braintree would not have held me,
last Night.—I lay, in the well known Chamber, and dreamed, I
saw a Lady, tripping it over the Hills, on Weymouth shore, and
Spreading Light and Beauty and Glory, all around her. At first I
thought it was Aurora, with her fair Complexion, her Crimson
Blushes and her million Charms and Graces. But I soon found
it was Diana, a Lady infinitely dearer to me and more charming.
—Should Diana make her Appearance every morning instead
of Aurora, I should not sleep as I do, but should be all awake
and admiring by four, at latest.—You may be sure I was morti-
fyed when I found, I had only been dreaming. The Impression
however of this dream awaked me thoroughly, and since I had

lost my Diana, I enjoy'd the Opportunity of viewing and admiring Miss Aurora. She's a sweet Girl, upon my Word. Her breath
is wholesome as the sweetly blowing Spices of Arabia, and
therefore next to her fairer sister Diana, the Properest Physician,
for your drooping

J. Adams

ABIGAIL SMITH TO JOHN ADAMS

Weymouth

*You* was pleas'd to say that the receipt of a letter from your
Diana always gave you pleasure. Whether this was designed for
a complement, (a commodity I acknowledg that you very seldom deal in) or as a real truth, you best know. Yet if I was to
judge of a certain persons Heart, by what upon the like occasion passess through a cabinet of my own, I should be apt to
suspect it as a truth. And why may I not? when I have often
been tempted to believe; that they were both cast in the same
mould, only with this difference, that yours was made, with a
harder mettle, and therefore is less liable to an impression.
Whether they have both an eaquil quantity of Steel, I have not
yet been able to discover, but do not imagine they are either of
them deficient. Supposing only this difference, I do not see,
why the same cause may not produce the same Effect in both,
tho perhaps not eaquil in degree.

Have you heard the News? that two Apparitions were seen
one evening this week hovering about this house, which very
much resembled you and a Cousin of yours. How it should ever
enter into the head of an Apparition to assume a form like
yours, I cannot devise. When I was told of it I could scarcly
believe it, yet I could not declare the contrary, for I did not see
it, and therefore had not that demonstration which generally
convinces me, that you are not a Ghost.

The original design of this letter was to tell you, that I would
next week be your fellow traveler provided I shall not be any

encumberance to you, for I have too much pride to be a clog to any body. You are to determine that point. For your—

A. Smith

∞

## Alexander Hamilton to Elizabeth Schuyler, October 27, 1780

HAMILTON COURTED and wooed Elizabeth Schuyler, daughter of General Philip and Catherine Van Rensselaer Schuyler.

In the following letter, Hamilton turns on the charm for his future wife. Unfortunately, the charm of a suitor does not always make him a good husband. Hamilton would later have an extramarital affair.

*I* had a charming dream two or three night ago. I thought I had just arrived at Albany and found you asleep on a green near the house, and beside you in an inclined posture stood a Gentleman whom I did not know. He had one of your hands in his, and seemed fixed in silent admiration. As you may imagine, I reproached him with his presumption and asserted my claim. He insisted on a prior right; and the dispute grew (heated). This I fancied (awoke) you, when yielding to a sudden impulse of joy, you flew into my arms and decided the contention with a kiss. I was so delighted that I immediately waked, and lay the rest of the night exulting in my good fortune. Tell me I pray you who is this rival of mine. Dreams you know are the messengers of Jove.

∞

## *John Adams to Abigail Smith, May 7, 1764, Abigail to John, May 9, 1764, and John to Abigail, September 30, 1764*

A BIGAIL A DAMS was clearly a woman of courage. How many of us would have the confidence to ask our love interest to provide a catalogue of our faults? But that's just what Abigail did. In April of 1764, she asked John to be her "second conscience" and to provide her with a list of her faults. She acknowledged that "although it is vastly disagreeable to be accused of faults yet no person ought to be offended when such accusations are delivered in the spirit of friendship."

It took several weeks for John Adams to answer her request, as he told Abigail that he had tried for three weeks to add more to his initial list, but found nothing more, everything else about her being "bright and luminous." John Adams finally sent the following affectionately frank assessment of his future wife.

This exchange indicates several things. It brings to light the deep bonds of trust that had developed between these young lovers. It also showcases the gallant spirit of Abigail Adams. You'll note her feisty reply to his catalogue, welcoming his criticism as most people would embrace praise. For, as she wrote, to "appear agreeable in the eyes of Lysander" is her highest ambition.

But in the end, it seemed that Adams was the one who had the most serious faults in need of reform—and he freely admitted so. In the third letter of this series, (September 30, 1764) Adams writes a letter to his fiancée one month before their wedding date, telling her that she, and only she, will form him into the man he has always wanted but struggled to be. And isn't this a large part of what marriage is all about—bringing out our beloved's finer qualities and completing each other?

JOHN ADAMS TO ABIGAIL SMITH

Boston

*I* promised you, Sometime agone, a Catalogue of your Faults, Imperfections, Defects, or whatever you please to call them. I feel at present, pretty much at Leisure, and in a very suitable Frame of Mind to perform my Promise. But I must caution you, before I proceed to recollect yourself, and instead of being vexed or fretted or thrown into a Passion, to resolve upon a Reformation—for this is my sincere Aim, in laying before you, this Picture of yourself.

In the first Place, then, give me leave to say, you have been extreamly negligent, in attending so little to Cards. You have very litle Inclination, to that noble and elegant Diversion, and whenever you have taken an Hand you have held it but aukwardly and played it, with a very uncourtly, and indifferent, Air. Now I have Confidence enough in your good sense, to rely upon it, you will for the future endeavour to make a better Figure in this elegant and necessary Accomplishment.

Another Thing, which ought to be mentioned, and by all means amended, is, the Effect of a Country Life and Education, I mean, a certain Modesty, sensibility, Bashfulness, call it by which of these Names you will, that enkindles Blushes forsooth at every Violation of Decency, in Company, and lays a most insupportable Constraint on the freedom of Behaviour. Thanks to the late Refinements of modern manners, Hypocrisy, superstition, and Formality have lost all Reputation in the World and the utmost sublimation of Politeness and Gentility lies, in Ease, and Freedom, or in other Words in a natural Air and Behaviour, and in expressing a satisfaction at whatever is suggested and prompted by Nature, which the aforesaid Violations of Decency, most certainly are.

In the Third Place, you could never yet be prevail'd on to learn to sing. This I take very soberly to be an Imperfection of the most moment of any. An Ear for Musick would be a source of much Pleasure, and a Voice and skill, would be a private solitary Amusement, of great Value when no other could be had. You must have remarked an Example of this in Mrs. Cranch, who must in all probability have been deafened to Death with the Cries of her Betcy, if she had not drowned them in Musick of her own.

In the Fourth Place you very often hang your Head like a Bulrush. You do not sit, erected as you ought, by which Means, it happens that you appear too short for a Beauty, and the Company looses the sweet smiles of that Countenance and the bright sparkles of those Eyes.—This Fault is the Effect and Consequence of another, still more inexcusable in a Lady. I mean an Habit of Reading, Writing and Thinking. But both the Cause and the Effect ought to be repented and amended as soon as possible.

Another Fault, which seems to have been obstinately persisted in, after frequent Remonstrances, Advices and Admonitions of your Frends, is that of sitting with the Leggs across. This ruins the figure and the Air, this injures the Health. And springs I fear from the former source vizt. too much Thinking.—These Things ought not to be!

A sixth Imperfection is that of Walking, with the Toes bending inward. This imperfection is commonly called Parrot-toed, I think, I know not for what Reason. But it gives an Idea, the reverse of a bold and noble Air, the Reverse of the stately strutt, and the sublime Deportment.

Thus have I given a faithful Portraiture of all the Spotts, I have hitherto discerned in this Luminary. Have not regarded Order, but have painted them as they arose in my Memory. Near Three Weeks have I conned and studied for more, but more are not to be discovered. All the rest is bright and luminous.

Having finished the Picture I finish my Letter, lest while I am recounting Faults, I should commit the greatest in a Letter, that of tedious and excessive Length. There's a prettily turned Conclusion for You! from yr.

Lysander

## ABIGAIL SMITH TO JOHN ADAMS

Weymouth

*Welcome,* Welcome thrice welcome is Lysander to Braintree, but ten times more so would he be at Weymouth, whither you are affraid to come.—Once it was not so. May not I come and see you, at least look thro a window at you? Should you not be glad to see your Diana? I flatter myself you would.

Your Brother brought your Letter, tho he did not let me see him, deliverd it the Doctor from whom received it safe. I thank you for your Catalogue, but must confess I was so hardned as to read over most of my Faults with as much pleasure, as an other person would have read their perfections. And Lysander must excuse me if I still persist in some of them, at least till I am convinced that an alteration would contribute to his happiness. Especially may I avoid that Freedom of Behaviour which according to the plan given, consists in Voilations of Decency, and which would render me unfit to Herd even with the Brutes. And permit me to tell you Sir, nor disdain to be a learner, that there is such a thing as Modesty without either Hypocricy or Formality.

As to a neglect of Singing, that I acknowledg to be a Fault which if posible shall not be complaind of a second time, nor should you have had occasion for it now, if I had not a voice harsh as the screech of a peacock.

The Capotal fault shall be rectified, tho not with any hopes of being lookd upon as a Beauty, to appear agreeable in the

Eyes of Lysander, has been for Years past, and still is the height of my ambition.

The 5th fault, will endeavour to amend of it, but you know I think that a gentleman has no business to concern himself about the Leggs of a Lady, for my part I do not apprehend any bad effects from the practise, yet since you desire it, and that you may not for the future trouble Yourself so much about it, will reform.

The sixth and last can be cured only by a Dancing School.

But I must not write more. I borrow a hint from you, therefore will not add to my faults that of a tedious Letter—a fault I never yet had reason to complain of in you, for however long, they never were otherways than agreeable to your own

A Smith

## JOHN ADAMS TO ABIGAIL SMITH

*Oh* my dear Girl, I thank Heaven that another Fortnight will restore you to me—after so long a separation. My soul and Body have both been thrown into Disorder, by your Absence, and a Month or two more would make me the most insufferable Cynick, in the World. I see nothing but Faults, Follies, Frailties and Defects in any Body, lately. People have lost all their good Properties or I my Justice, or Discernment.

But you who have always softened and warmed my Heart, shall restore my Benevolence as well as my Health and Tranquility of mind. You shall polish and refine my sentiments of Life and Manners, banish all the unsocial and ill natured Particles in my Composition, and form me to that happy Temper, that can reconcile a quick discernment with a perfect Candour.

Believe me, now & ever yr. faithful

Lysander

⌘

## *James Madison to Dolley Payne Todd,*
## *August 18, 1794*

*For* most of his young adult life, James Madison seemed to have been more interested in books than in women. Perhaps for us it's a good thing that he poured all his energies into writing the world's most imitated political document—the Constitution. Still, at the age of thirty-two, he was ready to settle down, and he became engaged to marry Kitty Floyd, who was then sixteen. Madison's friend Thomas Jefferson played a matchmaker of sorts by encouraging their union, hinting in secret code to Madison that marriage to Floyd "will render you happier than you can possibly be in a single state." Unfortunately for Madison, Floyd fell in love with someone else and broke off the engagement. Madison was devastated; Jefferson sought to comfort his friend for this "misadventure," advising him to keep busy and consoling him that "of all machines ours is the most complicated and inexplicable."

Eleven years were to pass since his failed engagement to Kitty Floyd before Madison met his future wife, the young and vivacious widow, Dorothea "Dolley" Payne Todd of Philadelphia. Madison was living in Philadelphia, serving in the Congress. This time, Aaron Burr provided matchmaking services. Dolley wrote a breathless letter to a friend: "Aaron Burr says that the great little Madison asked to be brought to see me this evening." Their meeting went well; Madison soon proposed marriage. But Dolley took some time to think it over before she finally accepted. Below, a relieved Madison responds to her acceptance:

I recd some days ago your precious favor from Fredg. I cannot express, but hope you will conceive the joy it gave me. The

delay in hearing of your leaving Hanover which I regarded as
the only satisfactory proof of your recovery, had filled me with
extreme . . . inquietude, and the consummation of that welcome
event was endeared to me by the *stile* in which it was conveyed.
I hope you will never have another *deliberation* on that subject.
If the sentiments of my heart can guarantee those of yours, they
assure me there can never be cause for it.

The great French novelist Colette distinguished between marrying "at once" and marrying "at last." Though Madison married
later than most, it is no exaggeration to say that he is remembered not only for writing the Constitution but also for his extraordinary wife. William Rives, one of Madison's biographers,
described Dolley as "the faithful and tender companion of his
bosom, the partner of his joys and sorrows . . ." James and Dolley were married for over forty years.

∞

## Abigail Adams to John Adams, March 31, 1776, and John to Abigail, April 14, 1776

THIS IS one of the more famous exchanges between Abigail and John. A few months before America had declared
independence from Great Britain, Abigail was urging her
husband, then serving in the Continental Congress, to promote independence for women. "Remember the Ladies,"
she declared. She never pressed the matter too much, and
even here, one can detect a tone of playfulness in her
request (and certainly in John's reply). Certainly, Abigail
did not count her husband as one of the tyrants. In another
letter shortly after this one, she wrote "all my desires and
all my ambition is to be esteemed and loved by my partner,

to join with him in the education and instruction of our little ones, to set under our own vines in peace, liberty and safety."

But one also detects a seed of justified discontent, one that would grow in the decades to come.

### ABIGAIL ADAMS TO JOHN ADAMS

*I* have sometimes been ready to think that the passion for Liberty cannot be Eaquelly Strong in the Breasts of those who have been accustomed to deprive their fellow Creatures of theirs. Of this I am certain that it is not founded upon that generous and christian principal of doing unto others as we would that others should do unto us.

—I long to hear that you have declared an independancy— and by the way in the new Code of Laws which I suppose it will be necessary for you to make I desire you would Remember the Ladies, and be more generous and favourable to them than your ancestors. Do not put such unlimited power into the hands of the Husbands. Remember all Men would be tyrants if they could. If perticuliar care and attention is not paid to the Laidies we are determined to foment a Rebelion, and will not hold ourselves bound by any Laws in which we have no voice, or Representation.

That your Sex are Naturally Tyrannical is a Truth so thoroughly established as to admit of no dispute, but such of you as wish to be happy willingly give up the harsh title of Master for the more tender and endearing one of Friend. Why then, not put it out of the power of the vicious and the Lawless to use us with cruelty and indignity with impunity. Men of Sense in all Ages abhor those customs which treat us only as the vassals of your Sex. Regard us then as Beings placed by providence under your protection and in immitation of the Supreem Being make use of that power only for our happiness.

JOHN ADAMS TO ABIGAIL ADAMS

*As* to your extraordinary Code of Laws, I cannot but laugh. We have been told that our Struggle has loosened the bands of Government every where. That Children and Apprentices were disobedient—that schools and Colledges were grown turbulent—that Indians slighted their Guardians and Negroes grew insolent to their Masters. But your Letter was the first Intimation that another Tribe more numerous and powerfull than all the rest were grown discontented.—This is rather too coarse a Compliment but you are so saucy, I won't blot it out.

∞

## Benjamin Franklin to Jane Franklin, January 6, 1726

**BENJAMIN FRANKLIN** sends a practical wedding gift to his favorite sister and gives her a little advice as well.

TO JANE FRANKLIN

*Dear* Sister,                    *Philadelphia, January 6, 1726–7.*
I am highly pleased with the account captain Freeman gives me of you. I always judged by your behaviour when a child that you would make a good, agreeable woman, and you know you were ever my peculiar favourite. I have been thinking what would be a suitable present for me to make, and for you to receive, as I hear you are grown a celebrated beauty. I had almost determined on a tea table, but when I considered that the character of a good housewife was far preferable to that of being only a pretty gentlewoman, I concluded to send you a *spinning wheel,* which I hope you will accept as a small token of my sincere love and affection.
Sister, farewell, and remember that modesty, as it makes the

most homely virgin amiable and charming, so the want of it infallibly renders the most perfect beauty disagreeable and odious. But when that brightest of female virtues shines among other perfections of body and mind in the same person, it makes the woman more lovely than an angel. Excuse this freedom, and use the same with me. I am, dear Jenny, your loving brother,

∞

## George Washington to Eleanor (Nelly) Parke Custis, January 16, 1795

GEORGE AND **Martha Washington adopted two of their grandchildren and raised them as their own children. One of these grandchildren was Eleanor (Nelly) Custis.**

**This letter, which is full of both levity and seriousness, gives good advice about the "inclinations" and "passions" men and women have felt toward each other since time immemorial. Nobody, President Washington tells his spirited daughter, is immune to the stirrings of the heart, but we can still direct these feelings toward people worthy of our affections.**

*Let* me touch a little now on your Georgetown ball, and happy, thrice happy, for the fair who were assembled on the occasion, that there was a man to spare; for had there been 79 ladies and only 78 gentlemen, there might, in the course of the evening, have been some disorder among the caps; notwithstanding the apathy which *one* of the company entertains for the *"youth"* of the present day, and her determination "never to give herself a moment's uneasiness on account of any of them." A hint here; men and women feel the same inclinations to each other *now* that they always have done, and which they will continue to do until there is a new order of things, and *you,* as others have done, may find, perhaps, that the passions of your sex are easier raised than allayed. Do not therefore boast too soon or too strongly of your insensibility to, or resistance of, its powers. In the composition of the human frame there is a good deal of inflammable matter, however dormant it may lie for a time, and like an intimate acquaintance of yours, when the torch is put to it, *that* which is *within you* may burst into a blaze; for which reason and especially too, as I have entered upon the chapter of advices, I will read you a lecture drawn from this text.

Love is said to be an involuntary passion, and it is, therefore, contended that it cannot be resisted. This is true in part only, for like all things else, when nourished and supplied plentifully with aliment, it is rapid in its progress; but let these be withdrawn and it may be stifled in its birth or much stinted in its growth. For example, a woman (the same may be said of the other sex) all beautiful and accomplished, will, while her hand and heart are undisposed of, turn the heads and set the circle in which she moves on fire. Let her marry, and what is the consequence? The madness *ceases* and all is quiet again. Why? not because there is any diminution in the charms of the lady, but because there is an end of hope. Hence it follows, that love may and therefore ought to be under the guidance of reason, for although we cannot avoid first impressions, we may assuredly place them under guard; and my motives for treating on this subject are to show you, while you remain Eleanor Parke Custis, spinster, and retain the resolution to love with moderation, the propriety of adhering to the latter resolution, at least until you have secured your game, and the way by which it may be accomplished.

When the fire is beginning to kindle, and your heart growing warm, propound these questions to it. Who is this invader? Have I a competent knowledge of him? Is he a man of good character; a man of sense? For, be assured, a sensible woman can never be happy with a fool. What has been his walk in life? Is he a gambler, a spendthrift, or drunkard? Is his fortune sufficient to maintain me in the manner I have been accustomed to live, and my sisters do live, and is he one to whom my friends can have no reasonable objection? If these interrogatories can be satisfactorily answered, there will remain but one more to be asked, that, however, is an important one. Have I sufficient ground to conclude that his affections are engaged by me? Without this the heart of sensibility will struggle against a passion that is not reciprocated; delicacy, custom, or call it by what epithet you will, having precluded all advances on your part. The declaration, without the *most indirect* invitation of yours, must proceed from the man, to render it permanent and valuable, and nothing short of good sense and an easy unaffected conduct can draw the line between prudery and coquetry. It would be no great departure from truth to say, that it rarely happens otherwise than that a thorough-paced coquette dies in celibacy, as a punishment for her attempts to mislead others, by encouraging looks, words, or actions, given for no other purpose than to draw men on to make overtures that they may be rejected.

∽

## Benjamin Franklin: Reply to a Piece of Advice, Pennsylvania Gazette, 1734

BENJAMIN FRANKLIN here responds to a published poem warning men against the cares and bondage of marriage. Franklin defended the institution of marriage against such naysayers and here shows the advantages of the marital state. While Franklin chose to emphasize the practical side of married life, he also believed that husbands and wives could be "like a faithful Pair of Doves" relieving "one another by turns."

*Nor* is it true that *as soon as a Man weds, his expected Bliss dissolves into slavish Cares and Bondage.* Every Man that is really a Man is Master of his own Family; and it cannot be *Bondage* to have another submit to one's Government. If there be any Bondage in the Case, 'tis the Woman enters into it, and not the Man. And as to the *Cares,* they are chiefly what attend the bringing up of Children; and I would ask any Man who has experienced it, if they are not the most delightful Cares in the World; and if from that Particular alone, he does not find the *Bliss* of a double State much greater, instead of being less than he expected. In short this *Bondage* and these *Cares* are like the Bondage of having a beautiful and fertile Garden, which a Man takes great Delight in; and the Cares are the Pleasure he finds in cultivating it, and raising as many beautiful and useful Plants from it as he can. And if common Planting and Gardening be an Honourable Employment, (as 'tis generally allow'd, since the greatest Heroes have practic'd it without any Diminution to their Glory) I think *Human Planting* must be more Honourable, as the Plants to be raised are more excellent in their Nature, and to bring them to Perfection requires the greater Skill and Wisdom.

In the next Place he insinuates, that *a Man by marrying, acts contrary to his Interest, loses his Liberty and his Friends, and soon finds himself undone.* In which he is as much mistaken as in any of the rest. A Man does not act contrary to his Interest by Marrying; for I and Thousands more know very well that we could never thrive till we were married; and have done well ever since; What we get, the Women save; a Man being fixt in Life minds his Business better and more steadily; and he that cannot thrive married, could never have throve better single; for the Idleness and Negligence of Men is more frequently fatal to Families, than the Extravagance of Women. Nor does a Man *lose his Liberty* but encrease it; for when he has no Wife to take Care of his Affairs at Home, if he carries on any Business there, he cannot go Abroad without a Detriment to that; but having a Wife, that he can confide in, he may with much more Freedom be abroad, and for a longer Time; thus the Business goes on comfortably, and the good Couple relieve one another by turns, like a faithful Pair of Doves. Nor does he *lose Friends* but gain them, by prudently marrying; for there are all the Woman's Relations added to his own, ready to assist and encourage the new-married Couple; and a Man that has a Wife and Children, is sooner trusted in Business, and can have Credit longer and for larger Sums than if he was single, inasmuch as he is look'd upon to be more firmly settled, and under greater Obligations to behave honestly, for his Family's Sake.

∞

## *Abigail Adams to John Adams, October 25, 1782*

ABIGAIL SPENT ten years of their fifty-four years of marriage apart from John. John left Abigail in 1774 for Philadelphia where he spent more than three years as a delegate to the First and Second Continental Congresses, visiting Abigail between sessions. Next, in 1777, Adams sailed for France with their son John Quincy to serve as an American commissioner, joining Benjamin Franklin and Arthur Lee. He returned to America briefly in 1779 and then sailed back to France. Abigail was finally able to join him in 1784.

Abigail had not seen John for three years when this letter, noting the passage of their eighteenth wedding anniversary, was written. Their love sustained them throughout these long separations. In fact, Abigail's devotion to John was so complete that she once told a friend that "when he is wounded, I bleed."

ABIGAIL TO JOHN ADAMS

*My* Dearest Friend                              *October 25, 1782*
The family are all retired to rest, the Busy scenes of the day are over, a day which I wished to have devoted in a particular

manner to my dearest Friend, but company falling in prevented
nor could I claim a moment untill this silent watch of the Night.

Look—(is there a dearer Name than Friend; think of it for
me;) Look to the date of this Letter—and tell me, what are the
thoughts which arise in your mind? Do you not recollect that
Eighteen years have run their annual Circuit, since we pledged
our mutual Faith to each other, and the Hymeneal torch was
Lighted at the Alter of Love. Yet, yet it Burns with unabating
fervour, old ocean has not Quenched it, nor old Time smooth-
erd it, in the Bosom of Portia. It cheers her in the Lonely Hour,
it comforts her even in the gloom which sometimes possesses
her mind.

It is my Friend from the Remembrance of the joys I have lost
that the arrow of affliction is pointed. I recollect the untitled
Man to whom I gave my Heart, and in the agony of recollection
when time and distance present themse[l]ves together, wish
he had never been any other. Who shall give me back Time?
Who shall compensate to me those *years* I cannot recall? How
dearly have I paid for a titled Husband; should I wish you less
wise, that I might enjoy more happiness? I cannot find that in
my Heart. Yet providence has wisely placed the real Blessings
of Life within the reach of moderate abilities, and he who is
wiser than his Neighbour sees so much more to pitty and Lament, that I doubt whether the balance of happiness is in his
Scale.

I feel a disposition to Quarrel with a race of Beings who have
cut me of, in the midst of my days from the only Society I
delighted in. Yet No Man liveth for himself, says an authority I
will not dispute. Let me draw satisfaction from this Source and
instead of murmuring and repineing at my Lot consider it in a
more pleasing view. Let me suppose that the same Gracious
Being who first smiled upon our union and Blessed us in each
other, endowed *(him)* my Friend with powers and talents for
the Benifit of Mankind and gave him a willing mind, to improve
them for the service of his Country.

You have obtaind honour and Reputation at Home and abroad. O may not an inglorious Peace wither the Laurels you have won.

## *Benjamin Rush to Mrs. Julia Rush, June 11, 1812: Poem*

BENJAMIN RUSH, **the physician, wrote this lovely tribute to his wife.**

> To M^rs Julia Rush
> from her husband
> Benjamin Rush
> 36 years after their marriage.

### 1

> When tossed upon the bed of pain,
> And every healing art was vain,
> Whose prayers brought back my life again?
>                          my Julia's.

### 2

> When shafts of scandal round me flew,
> And ancient friends no longer knew,
> My humble name, whose heart was true?
>                          my Julia's.

### 3

> When falsehood aimed its poisoned dart,
> And treachery pierced by bleeding heart,
> Whose friendship did a cure impart?
>                          my Julia's

4

When hope was weak, and faith was dead,
And every earthly joy was fled,
Whose hand sustained my drooping head?
                         my Julia's


5


When worn by age, and sunk in years,
My shadow at full length appears,
Who shall participate my cares?
                         my Julia.


6


When life's low wick shall feebly blaze,
And weeping children on me gaze,
Who shall assist my prayers & praise,
                         my Julia.


7


And when my mortal part shall lay,
Waiting in hope, the final day,
Who shall mourn o're my sleeping clay,
                         my Julia.


8


And when the stream of time shall end,
And the last trump, my grave shall rend,
Who shall with me to Heaven ascend?
                         my Julia.

*Benjamin Rush*

⚭

## *Death of Martha Jefferson, September 6, 1792,*

*We* began this chapter with an example of Jefferson's awkwardness around women; we end it with an example of the inexpressible love he shared with his wife.

Jefferson enjoyed ten years of married life before his wife, Martha, died. For much of their marriage, Martha was in frail health. According to their daughter, while his wife was dying Jefferson "was never out of calling" and nursed her tenderly.

On Martha's deathbed, Jefferson supposedly made a promise to her that he would never remarry; and he never did.

Below is a copy of a poem by Laurence Sterne that Martha and Thomas Jefferson had read together.* Martha began writing the first part; Jefferson finished the rest. After his death, a worn envelope containing the poem, which had been frequently opened and closed over the years, was found in his private drawer.

The first part of the poem is in Martha's handwriting:

> Time wastes too fast: every letter
> I trace tells me with what rapidity
> life follows my pen. The days and hours
> are flying over our heads like
> clouds of windy day never to return—
> more.
> Everything presses on—

Jefferson here finishes the rest:

> and every time I kiss thy hand to bid adieu, every absence
> which follows it, are preludes to that eternal separation
> which we are shortly to make!

On her gravestone, Jefferson had the following epitaph engraved, in Greek to preserve some privacy, on his wife's grave. It is taken from Homer's *Iliad:*

> If in the melancholy shades below,
> The flames of friends and lovers cease to glow,
> Yet mine shall sacred last; mine undecayed
> Burn on through death and animate my shade.

---

* Cited in Andrew Burstein, *The Inner Jefferson: Portrait of a Grieving Optimist,* pp. 61–62.

# III

## CIVILITY AND FRIENDSHIP

*The* word "civility" comes from the Latin root "civitas," meaning city, and "civis," meaning citizen. Civility is behavior worthy of people living in a city, or, more generally, in common with others. As none of us lives alone, the art of civility is important if we are to get along with others—even with those with whom we disagree. The English philosopher John Locke defined civility as: ". . . that general good will and regard for all people, which makes any one have a care not to show, in his carriage, any contempt, disrespect, or neglect of them."

Many social and political observers have written about the lack of civility or this "general good will and regard for people" in our public and private lives today. Rudeness, impatience, and self-aggrandizement have increasingly come to characterize much of our common culture and social interactions.

The Founders worked hard at practicing the art of civility for they believed it contributed not only to their own individual success but also to the well-being and harmony of the community. Thomas Jefferson told his young grandson that civility, or what he called "good humor," is "one of the preservatives of our peace and tranquillity" and ranked it "of first rate value." George Washington, as a young boy, copied down 110 "Rules of Civility" to guide him through life and help him control his temper. It must have worked—Washington is remembered as one of our most courteous and considerate presidents.

Friendship is different from civility. We should be civil or courteous to all, as Benjamin Franklin recommended, but it would be impossible to be friends with everyone. We can only have a few true friends in a lifetime. Thus, we should be very careful, George Washington warns, when it comes to choosing our friends, because that relationship is very special. The friends we "hang out" with tell the world much about ourselves —who we are and what kind of person we want to become.

So what exactly is friendship? Aristotle, the Greek philosopher, believed that friends ideally bring out "good things" in each other's characters. As Proverbs 27:17 says: "Iron sharpeneth iron; so a man sharpeneth the countenance of his friend." The Founders could not have acted so nobly had it not been for the support of their friends. In this chapter, you will read some of the correspondence from some of the more famous friendships among the Founders: the Marquis de Lafayette and George Washington; James Madison and Thomas Jefferson; and Jefferson and John Adams. Loyalty, sacrifice, and mutual interests held these special friendships together. A good life is one surrounded and sweetened by friends, "[l]aboring always at the same oar" and making "a happy port," as Jefferson put it to Adams.

∽

## Benjamin Franklin, "Rules for Making Oneself a Disagreeable Companion," Pennsylvania Gazette, *November 15, 1750*

BENJAMIN FRANKLIN freely admitted that there was a time in his life when he himself followed these rules for making oneself disagreeable in company. In his *Autobiography,* Franklin noted that a friend once told him that he could be quite rude and argumentative when he was trying to make a point. This friend got to him, and Franklin changed. Here, Franklin with his usual sharp wit, offers some advice to those who still don't get it. "Self-esteem," as Franklin describes it, is certainly not a virtue, for it ends up esteeming only itself.

*Rules,* by the Observation of which, a Man of Wit and Learning may nevertheless make himself a disagreeable Companion.

Your Business is to *shine;* therefore you must by all means prevent the shining of others, for their Brightness may make yours the less distinguish'd. To this End,

1. If possible engross the whole Discourse; and when other Matter fails, talk much of your-self, your Education, your Knowledge, your Circumstances, your Successes in Business, your Victories in Disputes, your own wise Sayings and Observations on particular Occasions, &c. &c. &c.

2. If when you are out of Breath, one of the Company should seize the Opportunity of saying something; watch his Words, and, if possible, find somewhat either in his Sentiment or Expression, immediately to contradict and raise a Dispute upon. Rather than fail, criticise even his Grammar.

3. If another should be saying an indisputably good Thing; either give no Attention to it, or interrupt him; or draw away the Attention of others; or, if you can guess what he would be at, be quick and say it before him; or, if he gets it said, and you perceive the Company pleas'd with it, own it to be a good Thing, and withal remark that it had been said by *Bacon, Locke, Bayle,* or some other eminent Writer; thus you deprive him of the Reputation he might have gain'd by it, and gain some yourself, as you hereby show your great Reading and Memory.

4. When modest Men have been thus treated by you a few times, they will chuse ever after to be silent in your Company; then you may shine on without Fear of a Rival; rallying them at the same time for their Dullness, which will be to you a new Fund of Wit.

Thus you will be sure to please *yourself.* The polite Man aims at pleasing *others,* but you shall go beyond him even in that. A

Man can be present only in one Company, but may at the same time be absent in twenty. He can please only where he *is,* you where-ever you are *not.*

∞

# Thomas Jefferson to Thomas Jefferson Randolph, November 20, 1808

IN THIS letter, Jefferson explains to his grandson and namesake why "good humor" is so essential. Jefferson believes that good humor or civility elevates social and political interactions that might otherwise be too raw or too coarse or even violent. It also can't hurt one's reputation to have a conciliatory disposition. According to Jefferson, it's the secret that will get you ahead in life. People will like you and take you more seriously if you are good-humored and polite. For example, good humor and civility certainly helped the quiet and agreeable young Jefferson, who spoke no more than three sentences in the Continental Congress in 1776. Fellow delegates, almost all of them older, chose him to write the Declaration of Independence. And yes, the world listened and is still listening to this gentleman from Virginia.

## TO THOMAS JEFFERSON RANDOLPH

*I* have mentioned good humor as one of the preservatives of our peace and tranquillity. It is among the most effectual, and it's effect is so well imitated and aided artificially by politeness, that this also becomes an acquisition of first rate value. In truth, politeness is artificial good humor, it covers the natural want of it, and ends by rendering habitual a substitute nearly equivalent to the real virtue. It is the practice of sacrificing to those whom we meet in society all the little conveniences and preferences which will gratify them, and deprive us of nothing worth a moment's consideration; it is the giving a pleasing and flattering turn to our expressions which will conciliate others, and make them pleased with us as well as themselves. How cheap a price for the good will of another! When this is in return for a rude thing said by another, it brings him to his senses, it mortifies and corrects him in the most salutary way, and places him at the feet of your good nature in the eyes of the company.

∞

## George Washington's "Rules of Civility"

GEORGE WASHINGTON was not born good— only practice and habit made him so. He was, for instance, known to have had a bad temper. Gouverneur Morris, Washington's friend and fellow delegate at the Constitutional Convention, said that Washington had those "tumultuous passions that accompany greatness" and that his "wrath" could be "terrible." But Morris also noted that these strong passions were "controlled by his stronger mind."

In large measure, Washington began the process of controlling his temper and other passions by copying, at a very young age, a translated version of a French book of etiquette, dating back to the sixteenth century. This book contained 110 rules of civility. By regularly reminding himself of these rules and practicing them when the occasion presented itself, Washington learned to master his worst inclinations.

Here's an excerpt of some of the rules. I believe that the general spirit of the rules still applies. We tend to think that liberation means breaking the rules. But it is only by respecting time-honored rules of decency, as Washington

**himself did, that we truly become masters of ourselves and worthy members of civil society.**

1.  Every action in company ought to be with some sign of respect to those present.

2.  In the presence of others sing not to yourself with a humming voice, nor drum with your fingers or feet.

3.  Speak not when others speak, sit not when others stand, and walk not when others stop.

4.  Turn not your back to others, especially in speaking; jog not the table or desk on which another reads or writes; lean not on anyone.

5.  Let your countenance be pleasant, but in serious matters somewhat grave.

6.  Show not yourself glad at the misfortune of another, though he were your enemy.

7.  Strive not with your superiors in argument, but always submit your judgment to others with modesty.

8.  Undertake not to teach your equal in the art he himself professes; it savors of arrogancy.

9.  When a man does all he can, though it succeeds not well, blame not him that did it.

10.  Being to advise or reprehend anyone, consider whether it ought to be in public or in private, presently or at some other time, also in what terms to do it; and in reproving show no signs of choler, but do it with sweetness and mildness.

11.  Mock not nor jest at anything of importance; break no jests that are sharp or biting; and if you deliver anything witty or pleasant, abstain from laughing thereat yourself.

12.  Use no reproachful language against anyone, neither curses nor revilings.

13.  Be not hasty to believe flying reports to the disparagement of anyone.

14.  In your apparel be modest, and endeavor to accommodate nature rather than procure admiration. Keep to the fashion

of your equals, such as are civil and orderly with respect to time and place.

15. Play not the peacock, looking everywhere about you to see if you be well decked, if your shoes fit well, if your stockings set neatly and clothes handsomely.

16. Associate yourself with men of good quality if you esteem your own reputation, for it is better to be alone than in bad company.

17. Let your conversation be without malice or envy, for it is a sign of tractable and commendable nature; and in all causes of passion admit reason to govern.

18. Utter not base and frivolous things amongst grown and learned men, nor very difficult questions or subjects amongst the ignorant, nor things hard to be believed.

19. Speak not of doleful things in time of mirth nor at the table; speak not of melancholy things, as death and wounds; and if others mention them, change, if you can, the discourse. Tell not your dreams but to your intimate friends.

20. Speak not injurious words, neither in jest or earnest. Scoff at none, although they give occasion.

21. Be not forward, but friendly and courteous, the first to salute, hear and answer, and be not pensive when it is time to converse.

22. Detract not from others, but neither be excessive in commending.

23. Go not thither where you know not whether you shall be welcome or not. Give not advice without being asked; and when desired, do it briefly.

24. Reprehend not the imperfection of others, for that belongs to parents, masters, and superiors.

25. Gaze not on the marks or blemishes of others, and ask not how they came. What you may speak in secret to your friend deliver not before others.

26. Think before you speak; pronounce not imperfectly, nor bring out your words too hastily, but orderly and distinctly.

27. When another speaks, be attentive yourself, and disturb not the audience. If any hesitate in his words, help him not, nor prompt him without being desired; interrupt him not, nor answer him till his speech be ended.

28. Treat with men at fit times about business, and whisper not in the company of others.

29. Be not apt to relate news if you know not the truth thereof. In discoursing of things you have heard, name not your author always. A secret discover not.

30. Be not curious to know the affairs of others, neither approach to those that speak in private.

31. Undertake not what you cannot perform; but be careful to keep your promise.

32. When your superiors talk to anybody, hear them; neither speak nor laugh.

33. Be not tedious in discourse, make not many digressions, nor repeat often the same matter of discourse.

34. Speak no evil of the absent, for it is injust.

35. Be not angry at table, whatever happens; and if you have reason to be so show it not; put on a cheerful countenance, especially if there be strangers, for good humor makes one dish a feast.

36. When you speak of God or his attributes, let it be seriously, in reverence and honor, and obey your natural parents.

37. Let your recreations be manful, not sinful.

38. Labor to keep alive in your breast that little spark of celestial fire called conscience.

∽

## *Benjamin Franklin,* Autobiography, *On His Newspapers*

THE FIRST patron saint of printers was St. Augustine of Hippo. But in America, the title goes to Benjamin Franklin. The oldest of America's Founders began his career in insurgency and in printing simultaneously when, at the age of twelve, he rebelled against his father's desire that he become a tallow candle maker and instead became a printer's apprentice for his brother in Boston. Franklin later fled his apprenticeship, found work for a printer in Philadelphia, mastered his craft in England, and returned home, where he produced some of the most famous editorial broadsides in American history and published both the *Pennsylvania Gazette* and *Poor Richard's Almanack.*

At the end of a long life accumulating honors as a scientist, diplomat, businessman, philosopher, and statesman, he chose to begin his Last Will and Testament with the words, "I, Benjamin Franklin, printer . . ." His self-composed epitaph reads:

> The body of
> B. Franklin, Printer
> (Like the Cover of an Old book
> Its Contents torn Out
> And Stript of its Lettering and Gilding)
> Lies Here, Food for Worms.
> But the Work shall not be Lost;
> For it will (as he Believ'd) Appear Once More
> In a New and More Elegant Edition
> Revised and Corrected
> By the Author.

Please note that his actual tombstone reads, rather more modestly:

Benjamin and Deborah Franklin: 1790

**In this age of tabloid journalism, Franklin's standards for what is fit to print and his worry about a polluted press are highly instructive.**

*In* the Conduct of my Newspaper I carefully excluded all Libelling and Personal Abuse, which is of late Years become so disgraceful to our Country. Whenever I was solicited to insert any thing of that kind, and the Writers pleaded as they generally did, the Liberty of the Press, and that a Newspaper was like a Stage Coach in which any one who would pay had a Right to a Place, my Answer was, that I would print the Piece separately if desired, and the Author might have as many Copies as he pleased to distribute himself, but that I would not take upon me to spread his Detraction, and that having contracted with my Subscribers to furnish them with what might be either useful or entertaining, I could not fill their Papers with private Altercation in which they had no Concern without doing them manifest Injustice. Now many of our Printers make no scruple of gratifying the Malice of Individuals by false Accusations of the fairest Characters among ourselves, augmenting Animosity even to the producing of Duels, and are moreover so indiscreet as to print scurrilous Reflections on the Government of neighbouring States, and even on the Conduct of our best national Allies, which may be attended with the most pernicious Consequences.—These Things I mention as a Caution to young Printers, & that they may be encouraged not to pollute their Presses and disgrace their Profession by such infamous Practices, but refuse steadily; as they may see by my Example; that such a Course of Conduct will not on the whole be injurious to their Interests.—

❧

## *Abigail Adams to Mary Cranch,*
## *January 5, 1790*

JOHN ADAMS served as America's first vice-president under George Washington. This meant for Abigail Adams many official duties and parties to attend. During these official receptions, the wife of the vice-president was to stand to the right of Mrs. Washington. Abigail Adams, who had never been particularly comfortable with the formalities of court life when she served as a diplomat's wife in Europe, was sometimes confused as to what she should do and where she should stand. Sometimes, other women would step in her place next to Mrs. Washington. But Washington was always mindful of making others comfortable and often came to Abigail's rescue by restoring her to her rightful place. The following description of Washington, by a grateful Abigail, captures the gentility and gracious bearing of Washington that won him the respect not only of Abigail but of a whole nation as well.

Here is the wife of the second president of the United States expressing her hope that the tenure of the first president will last "for many, many years."

*In* the Evening I attended the drawing Room, it being Mrs. W[ashington']s publick day. It was as much crowded as a Birth Night at St. James, and with company as Briliantly drest, diamonds & great hoops excepted. My station is always at the right hand of Mrs. W.; through want of knowing what is right I find it sometimes occupied, but on such an occasion the President never fails of seeing that it is relinquished for me, and having removed Ladies several times, they have now learnt to rise & give it me, but this between our selves, as *all distinction* you know is unpopular. Yet this same P[resident] has so happy a faculty of appearing to accommodate & yet carrying his point, that if he was not really one of the best intentiond men in the world he might be a very dangerous one. He is polite with dignity, affable without familiarity, distant without Haughtyness, Grave without Austerity, Modest, wise & Good. These are traits in his Character which peculiarly fit him for the exalted station he holds, and God Grant that he may Hold it with the same applause & universal satisfaction for many many years, as it is my firm opinion that no other man could rule over this great people & consolidate them into one mighty Empire but He who is set over us.

∾

## *Benjamin Franklin,* Autobiography

BENJAMIN FRANKLIN called pride the strongest of all our natural passions. Franklin tried to conquer his ample portion of pride, but like most of us, he admits he never overcame it. That didn't seem to bother him, however, for he notes, with wit and some jocularity, that if he conquered his pride he would probably be proud of his humility. Franklin settled for *appearing* to be humble. He marveled at how "soon" he "found the advantage of this change in his manners." Franklin's point is not that we be hypocrites but that where moral purity is impossible the practice of good manners is not. And who knows, the more we practice, the better we may actually become.

*My* list of virtues contain'd at first but twelve; but a Quaker friend having kindly informed me that I was generally thought proud; that my pride show'd itself frequently in conversation; that I was not content with being in the right when discussing any point, but was overbearing, and rather insolent, of which he convinc'd me by mentioning several instances; I determined endeavouring to cure myself, if I could, of this vice or folly among the rest, and I added *Humility* to my list, giving an extensive meaning to the word.

I cannot boast of much success in acquiring the *reality* of this virtue, but I had a good deal with regard to the *appearance* of it. I made it a rule to forbear all direct contradiction to the sentiments of others, and all positive assertion of my own. I even forbid myself, agreeably to the old laws of our Junto, the use of every word or expression in the language that imported a fix'd opinion, such as *certainly, undoubtedly,* etc., and I adopted, instead of them, *I conceive, I apprehend,* or *I imagine* a thing to be so or so; or it *so appears to me at present.* When another asserted something that I thought an error, I deny'd myself the pleasure of contradicting him abruptly, and of showing immediately some absurdity in his proposition; and in answering I began by observing that in certain cases or circumstances his opinion would be right, but in the present case there *appear'd* or *seem'd* to me some difference, etc. I soon found the advantage of this change in my manner; the conversations I engag'd in went on more pleasantly. The modest way in which I propos'd my opinions procur'd them a readier reception and less contradiction; I had less mortification when I was found to be in the wrong, and I more easily prevail'd with others to give up their mistakes and join with me when I happened to be in the right.

And this mode, which I at first put on with some violence to natural inclination, became at length so easy, and so habitual to me, that perhaps for these fifty years past no one has ever heard a dogmatical expression escape me. And to this habit (after my character of integrity) I think it principally owing that I had early so much weight with my fellow-citizens when I proposed new institutions, or alterations in the old, and so much influence in public councils when I became a member; for I was but a bad speaker, never eloquent, subject to much hesitation in my choice of words, hardly correct in language, and yet I generally carried my points.

In reality, there is, perhaps, no one of our natural passions so hard to subdue as *pride*. Disguise it, struggle with it, beat it down, stifle it, mortify it as much as one pleases, it is still alive, and will every now and then peep out and show itself; you will see it, perhaps, often in this history; for, even if I could conceive that I had compleatly overcome it, I should probably be proud of my humility.

∞

## Thomas Jefferson and Benjamin Franklin at the Second Continental Congress

PART OF being a true friend is knowing just the right words to give comfort to and cheer up a friend. Here's a great example.

*After* this had been adopted Congress went into Committee of the Whole to consider Jefferson's statement of the reasons which had led to this act; but the hour being late, it was agreed to postpone discussion to another day. On the 3d of July further reasons for delay presented themselves, but on the 4th the way was clear, and the Declaration as Jefferson wrote it had to stand the criticism of one surveyor, one planter, one clergyman, one shoemaker, one sailor, one general, one printer, one soldier, eight merchants, two statesmen, six farmers, six doctors and twenty-four lawyers, who made up the Continental Congress. Some suggested verbal changes. Others wanted to strike out whole paragraphs. Objection was made to calling King George a tyrant. Somebody took exception to Jefferson's observations on the wickedness of slavery. Between them all they discarded about a quarter of what he had written—"as I expected," said John Adams, who felt that some of the best passages had been sacrificed. Timothy Pickering, on the other hand, thought the document distinctly improved. To Jefferson the well-meant changes seemed little short of butchery. He sat quiet, however, leaving the task of defense to Mr. Adams, and glad that Mr. Adams was a good fighter. . . .

On the day when his work was running the gauntlet of discussion, Benjamin Franklin, seated near Jefferson, noted with sympathy, not untinged by amusement, that his young friend "writhed a little," and to divert him told under his breath an incident of his own youth, which had taught him, he said, never to write anything to be offered for public criticism. An acquaintance of his, a hatter's apprentice, about to set up in business for himself, devised a fine new sign and exhibited it with pride to his friends. It read: "John Thompson Hatter makes and sells hats for ready money," this information being followed by an impressive picture of a hat. Asked what they thought of it, one man said the word "hatter" might be dispensed with, since it was followed by "makes hats." Another thought "makes" quite superfluous, the public not caring who made the hats; and so it went on until nothing was left except John Thompson's name and the portrait of a hat. If Jefferson failed to see any humor in this while his masterpiece was being hacked to pieces, he savored it to the full later on, and the story, with Franklin's kindly intent in telling it, strongly emphasized, became one of his favorite anecdotes.

—From Helen Nicolay, *Boys Life of Thomas Jefferson*

## *George Washington to Bushrod Washington, January 15, 1783*

BUSHROD WASHINGTON was George Washington's favorite nephew. Bushrod was studying law in Philadelphia when Washington, "as a friend," gave him some moral guidance. Washington couldn't resist giving out a little advice every now and then to his extended family members. To give more incentive to Bushrod to behave properly, he told him, at the end of this letter, that it makes him happy "to find those, to whom I am so nearly connected, pursuing the right walk of life." Bushrod grew up to become an associate justice of the U.S. Supreme Court.

*That* the Company in which you will improve most, will be least expensive to you; and yet I am not such a Stoic as to suppose you will, or to think it right that you ought, always to be in Company with Senators and Philosophers; but, of the young and juvenile kind let me advise you to be choice. It is easy to make acquaintances, but very difficult to shake them off, however irksome and unprofitable they are found after we have once committed ourselves to them; the indiscretions, and scrapes which very often they involuntarily lead one into, proves equally distressing and disgraceful.

Be courteous to all, but intimate with few, and let those few be well tried before you give them your confidence; true friendship is a plant of slow growth, and must undergo and withstand the shocks of adversity before it is entitled to the appellation.

∞

## *George Washington to George Washington Custis, November 28, 1796*

GEORGE WASHINGTON CUSTIS was Washington's adopted grandson, whom he raised, along with Custis's sister, Eleanor, at Mount Vernon. George Washington Custis was a student at Princeton University when George wrote the letter of advice. Custis needed a lot of guidance. He was a handful—not very disciplined and prone to idleness.

He dropped out of Princeton University and returned to Mount Vernon.

*'Tis* well to be on good terms with all your fellow students, and I am pleased to hear you are so, but while a courteous behavior is due to all, select the most deserving only for your friendships, and before this becomes intimate, weigh their dispositions and character *well*. True friendship is a plant of slow growth; to be sincere, there must be a congeniality of temper and pursuits. Virtue and vice can not be allied; nor can idleness and industry; of course, if you resolve to adhere to the two former of these extremes, an intimacy with those who incline to the latter of them, would be extremely embarrassing to you; it would be a stumbling-block in your way, and act like a mill-stone hung to your neck, for it is the nature of idleness and vice to obtain as many votaries as they can.

∞

## *Thomas Jefferson to Martha Jefferson Randolph, July 17, 1790*

MARTHA'S FATHER-IN-LAW was about to remarry a woman half his age. This had agitated Martha and her husband. Jefferson wrote the following note stressing the importance of comity between those we must live with.

*If* the lady has any thing difficult in her dispositions, avoid what is rough, and attach her good qualities to you. Consider what are otherwise as a bad stop in your harpsichord. Do not touch on it, but make yourself happy with the good ones. Every human being, my dear, must thus be viewed according to what it is good for, for none of us, no not one, is perfect; and were we to love none who had imperfections, this world would be a desart for our love. All we can do is to make the best of our friends: love and cherish what is good in them, and keep out of the way of what is bad: but no more think of rejecting them for it than of throwing away a piece of music for a flat passage or two. Your situation will require peculiar attentions and respects to both parties. Let no proof be too much for either your patience or acquiescence. Be you my dear, the link of love, union, and peace for the whole family. The world will give you the more credit for it, in proportion to the difficulty of the task. And your own happiness will be the greater as you percieve that you promote that of others.

∞

## Alexander Hamilton, Private Papers, 1804

SHAKESPEARE WROTE of Henry V: "If it be a sin to covet honor, he was the most offending soul alive." The same may be said of Alexander Hamilton. Hamilton entered a gun duel with Aaron Burr to defend his honor. In it, he lost his life.

The animosity between Burr and Hamilton escalated during the presidential election of 1800. The vote in the electoral college ended in a tie between the two Republican candidates Jefferson and Burr. As provided in article 2, section 2 of the still-new Constitution, the election was thrown to the House of Representatives, where the results were far from certain. Though Hamilton had strong and long-established political differences with Jefferson, he threw his support (reluctantly) behind Jefferson for the good of the country. Hamilton wrote to a friend that Burr was "the most unfit man in the U.S. for the office of President," a man "without probity" or for that matter, any "principle[,] public or private." Believing that Burr's ambitions would not be satisfied with the office of the presidency and that he would be a serious threat to the stability of the young republic, Hamilton urged fellow Federalists to "save our country from so great a calamity." With the help of Hamilton, Jefferson won.

Their paths crossed again a few years later when Burr was nominated for governor in New York. Hamilton again spoke out against him and played a prominent role in Burr's defeat. Burr heard of some derogatory remarks Hamilton had made about him. He demanded an apology. Hamilton and Burr exchanged several letters; Burr, however, was not satisfied with Hamilton's responses and thus challenged him to a duel.

Hamilton, who had lost a son to a duel, did not believe in the practice of dueling and worried that his example might encourage others. Many wonder why he couldn't have resolved his differences with Burr peaceably. But Hamilton had an aristocratic idea of honor and believed that, given his out-of-wedlock birth, he had much to prove, as his honor was often held in question. Thus he acquiesced.

Some reports indicate that Hamilton never intended to shoot at Burr and fired his gun into the air. Burr had no such qualms and with his first shot delivered a fatal wound to Hamilton's chest. After much suffering, Hamilton died the next day. As for Burr, he was indicted but fled. He later engaged in secessionist plans to break up the Union for which he was tried but not convicted for lack of evidence.

Gouverneur Morris said that Hamilton "was ambitious of glory only" and told mourners at his funeral to "protect his fame. It is all that he has left. . . ." There is no denying that this out-of-wedlock son of a Scotsman certainly achieved that.

*On* my expected interview with Col. Burr, I think it proper to make some remarks explanatory of my conduct, motives, and views. I was certainly desirous of avoiding this interview for the most cogent reasons:

(1) My religious and moral principles are strongly opposed to the practice of dueling, and it would ever give me pain to be obliged to shed the blood of a fellow-creature in a private combat forbidden by the laws.

(2) My wife and children are extremely dear to me, and my life is of the utmost importance to them in various views.

(3) I feel a sense of obligation towards my creditors; who, in case of accident to me by the forced sale of my property, may be in some degree sufferers. I did not think myself

*Alexander Hamilton*

at liberty as a man of probity lightly to expose them to this hazard.

(4) I am conscious of no ill-will to Col. Burr, distinct from political opposition, which, as I trust, has proceeded from pure and upright motives.

Lastly, I shall hazard much and can possibly gain nothing by the issue of the interview.

But it was, as I conceive, impossible for me to avoid it. There were intrinsic difficulties in the thing and artificial embarrassments, from the manner of proceeding on the part of Col. Burr.

Intrinsic, because it is not to be denied that my animadversions on the political principles, character, and views of Col. Burr have been extremely severe; and on different occasions I, in common with many others, have made very unfavorable criticisms on particular instances of the private conduct of this gentleman. In proportion as these impressions were entertained with sincerity and uttered with motives and for purposes which might appear to me commendable, would be the difficulty (until they could be removed by evidence of their being erroneous) of explanation or apology.

The disavowal required of me by Col. Burr in a general and indefinite form was out of my power, if it had really been proper for me to submit to be questioned, but I was sincerely of opinion that this could not be, and in this opinion I was confirmed by that of a very moderate and judicious friend whom I consulted. Besides that, Col. Burr appeared to me to assume, in the first instance, a tone unnecessarily peremptory and menacing, and, in the second, positively offensive.

Yet I wished, as far as might be practicable, to leave a door open to accommodation. This, I think, will be inferred from the written communication made by me and by my directions, and would be confirmed by the conversations between Mr. Van Ness and myself which arose out of the subject. I am not sure whether, under all the circumstances, I did not go further in the attempt to accommodate than a punctilious delicacy will justify. If so, I hope the motives I have stated will excuse me.

It is not my design, by what I have said, to affix any odium on the conduct of Col. Burr in this case. He doubtless has heard of animadversions of mine which bore very hard upon him, and it is probable that as usual they were accompanied with some falsehoods. He may have supposed himself under a necessity of acting as he has done. I hope the grounds of his proceeding have been such as ought to satisfy his own conscience.

I trust, at the same time, that the world will do me the justice to believe that I have not censured him on light grounds nor from unworthy inducements. I certainly have had strong reasons for what I have said, though it is possible that in some particulars I may have been influenced by misconstruction or misinformation. It is also my ardent wish that I may have been more mistaken than I think I have been; and that he, by his future conduct, may show himself worthy of all confidence and esteem and prove an ornament and a blessing to the country. As well, because it is possible that I may have injured Col. Burr, however convinced myself that my opinions and declarations have been well-founded, as from my general principles and temper in relation to similar affairs, I have resolved, if our interview is conducted in the usual manner and if pleases God to give me the opportunity to reserve and throw away my first fire, and I have thoughts even of reserving my second fire, and thus giving a double opportunity to Col. Burr to pause and reflect.

It is not, however, my intention to enter into any explanations on the ground. Apology from principle, I hope, rather than pride, is out of the question. To those who, with me, abhorring the practice of duelling, may think that I ought on no account to have added to the number of bad examples, I answer that my relative situation, as well in public as private, enforcing all the considerations which constitute what men of the world denominate honor, imposed on me (as I thought) a peculiar necessity not to decline the call. The ability to be in future useful, whether in resisting mischief or in effecting good, in those crises of our public affairs which seem likely to happen, would probably be inseparable from a conformity with public prejudice in this particular.

∾

## Comity at Valley Forge

GEORGE WASHINGTON described the plight of the continental army at Valley Forge in the following: "To see Men without Cloathes to cover their nakedness, without Blankets to lay on, without Shoes, by which their Marches might be traced by the blood from their feet, and almost as often without Provisions as with; Marching through frost and Snow, and at Christmas taking up their Winter Quarters within a day's March of the enemy, without a House or Hutt to cover them till they could be built and submitting to it without a murmur, is a mark of patience and obedience which in my opinion can scarce be parallel'd."

Despite the suffering and death, the brutal conditions of Valley Forge could not suppress a spirit of comity that arose among the officers and their men. Below is a narrative describing the fellow feeling that characterized the relationships among Washington's men.

*Howe's* troops lay through the cold weather in comfort in the city, while the privations in Washington's gloomy camp were the most severe that the Americans were called upon to endure. But during the terrible winter at Valley Forge, Washington's ragged host was welded into an army of which any general might be proud. He was proud of them. "Naked and starving as they are," he wrote, "we cannot sufficiently admire the incomparable patience and fidelity of the soldiers." The weather was intensely cold. There was not enough food or shelter or clothing. The barefooted soldiers left bloody footprints in the snow, and men actually died of starvation. Conspiracy tried to undermine faith in Washington, even to bribe to its side the gallant young Lafayette who had come to America in time to receive his wound at Brandywine. Lafayette was as loyal as his heart was big, and his presence was not the least among the small bits of comfort that Washington was able to extract from the situation.

Before he knew Lafayette, Washington's personal dealings with Frenchmen had been limited to those he met in the French and Indian War, and his experience of officers who had served abroad to such unfortunate examples as Charles Lee and General Horatio Gates, a little man with a plausible tongue and a cuckoo's gift for slipping into places to which he had no right. Washington had been distinctly uncordial in thought toward the foreign officers who came over during the summer of 1777 to join his army and, fearing that Lafayette would put on airs, was annoyed at having to welcome him. But their meeting proved a case of friendship at first sight, which speedily deepened into real affection. Far from putting on airs the young Frenchman was willing and eager to bear his share of hardship. One of his small acts of kindness that only came to light half a century after it happened was done during this cold winter at Valley Forge. The last time Lafayette was in America an aged man came up to shake his hand. He was dressed in a faded Continental uniform, and across his shoulders he wore a piece of old and dingy blanket. He asked the general if he remembered a stormy night when he took the musket from the hands of a shivering sentry and sent him to his own tent with orders to bring back stockings and a blanket, promising to do duty for him till he returned. The soldier found that even a general at Valley Forge owned only one covering for his bed, but when he brought the desired articles, Lafayette bade him put on the stockings and, taking out his sword, fraternally divided the blanket in half.

The story not only portrays the want in that winter camp, but the spirit in which it was borne. John Marshall, who was in after years to become America's great chief justice, joked about his discomforts. Young Alexander Hamilton, whom Washington loved like a son, was there to ease his chief's burden where he could, giving long and laborious days to clerical duty, using that wonderful brain of his on a thousand perplexing problems, and seasoning the fare at the frugal mess-table with his brilliant talk. Scores of officers proved their mettle that winter; thousands of soldiers, their heroism. In December, Baron von Steuben brought his great knowledge and skill to the camp and gave officers and men alike what would now be called "intensive training." They came out from the trial welded in a spirit of comradeship and devotion that was destined to be the seed of the spirit of a great nation.

—From Helen Nicolay, *The Book of American Wars*

※

## Washington's Farewell to Military Officers

GEORGE WASHINGTON, AS a leader, worked to preserve some distance from those he led. Thus, his conduct was often marked by formality. Yet, underneath this exterior was a warm heart that formed the firmest and deepest attachments to his fellow military officers. Below is a moving testament to Washington's capacity for friendship and love.

*In* the course of a few days Washington prepared to depart for Annapolis, where Congress was assembling, with the intention of asking leave to resign his command. A barge was in waiting about noon on the 4th of December [1783] at Whitehall Ferry to convey him across the Hudson to Paulus Hook. The principal officers of the army assembled at Fraunces's Tavern in the neighborhood of the ferry to take a final leave of him.

On entering the room and finding himself surrounded by his old companions in arms, who had shared with him so many scenes of hardship, difficulty and danger, his agitated feelings overcame his usual self-command. Filling a glass of wine and turning upon them his benignant but saddened countenance, "With a heart full of love and gratitude," said he, "I now take leave of you, most devoutly wishing that your latter days may be as prosperous and happy as your former ones have been glorious and honorable."

Having drunk this farewell benediction, he added with emotion, "I cannot come to each of you to take my leave, but shall be obliged if each of you will come and take me by the hand."

General Knox, who was nearest, was the first to advance. Washington, affected even to tears, grasped his hand and gave him a brother's embrace. In the same affectionate manner he took leave severally of the rest. Not a word was spoken. The deep feeling and manly tenderness of these veterans in the parting moment could find no utterance in words. Silent and solemn they followed their loved commander as he left the room, passed through a corps of light infantry and proceeded on foot to Whitehall Ferry. Having entered the barge, he turned to them, took off his hat and waved a silent adieu. They replied in the same manner, and having watched the barge until the intervening point of the battery shut it from sight, returned, still solemn and silent, to the place where they had assembled.

—From Washington Irving's *Life of Washington*

∽

## Marquis de Lafayette and George Washington Correspondence, 1779–1784

WHEN GENERAL John J. "Black Jack" Pershing arrived in France in World War I with allied American troops, he reportedly said: "Lafayette, we are here."

Lafayette was certainly here for us during the critical years of the Revolutionary War. Born an aristocrat, Lafayette came to America from France at the age of nineteen to volunteer in the struggling continental army. Washington invited Lafayette to become a member of his military "family." Lafayette had lost his father in battle when he was just two years old. Washington became like a father to Lafayette; Lafayette a loyal son to the childless Washington.

Lafayette endured the hardships of Valley Forge and stood loyally by Washington. Lafayette named one of his sons George Washington (and a daughter Virginia). Lafayette, as it turns out, was not only one of Washington's best friends, but America's as well. Below is some of their correspondence. It is readily apparent that Lafayette brings out the most affectionate side of George Washington.

GEORGE WASHINGTON TO LAFAYETTE, SEPTEMBER 30, 1779

*Your* forward zeal in the cause of liberty; Your singular attachment to this infant World; Your ardent and persevering efforts, not only in America but since your return to France to serve the United States; Your polite attention to Americans, and your strict and uniform friendship for *me,* has ripened the first impressions of esteem and attachment which I imbibed for you into such perfect love and gratitude that neither time nor ab-

sence can impair which will warrant my assuring you, that
whether in the character of an Officer at the head of a Corps of
gallant French (if circumstances should require this) whether as
a Major Genl. commanding a division of the American Army;
Or whether, after our Swords and Spears have given place to
the plough share and pruning hook, I see you as a private
Gentleman, a friend and Companion, I shall welcome you in all
the warmth of friendship to Columbia's shore; and in the latter
case, to my rural Cottage, where homely fare and a cordial
reception shall be substituted for delicacies and costly living.
this from past experience I know *you* can submit to; and if the
lovely partner of your happiness will consent to participate with
*us* in such rural entertainment and amusemts. I can undertake
in behalf of Mrs. Washington that she will do everything in
her power to make Virginia agreeable to the Marchioness. My
inclination and endeavours to do this cannot be doubted when
I assure you that I love everybody that is dear to you.

### LAFAYETTE TO WASHINGTON, JUNE 29, 1782

*Adieu,* my dear General, I hope you will approuve my conduct and in every thing I do I first consider what your opinion
would be had I an opportunity to consult it. I anticipate the
happiness to be again with you, my dear General, and I hope I
need not assuring you that nothing can exceed the sentiments
of respect and tenderness I have the honor to be with
Your most h^ble serv and for
ever your most devoted affectionate
friend
Lafayette

### WASHINGTON TO LAFAYETTE, DECEMBER 8, 1784

*In* the moment of our separation upon the road as I trav-
elled, and every hour since, I felt all that love, respect and

attachment for you, with which length of years, close connexion and your merits have inspired me. I often asked myself, as
our carriages distended, whether that was the last sight, I ever
should have of you? And tho' I wished to say no, my fears
answered yes. I called to mind the days of my youth, and found
they had long since fled to return no more; that I was now
descending the hill, I had been 52 years climbing, and that tho'
I was blessed with a good constitution, I was of a short lived
family, and might soon expect to be entombed in the dreary
mansions of my father's. These things darkened the shades and
gave a gloom to the picture, consequently to my prospects of
seeing you again: but I will not repine, I have had my day.

It is unnecessary, I persuade myself to repeat to you my Dr.
Marqs. the sincerity of my regards and friendship, nor have I
words which could express my affection for you, were I to
attempt it.


LAFAYETTE TO WASHINGTON

> *On board the Nimph Newyork Harbour*
> *December the 21st 1 /84*

*My* dear General

I have received your affectionate letter of the 8th inst, and
from the known sentiments of my heart to you, you will easely
guess what my feelings have been in perusing the tender expressions of your friendship —No, my beloved General, our
late parting was not by any means a last interwiew. My whole
soul revolts at the idea—and could I harbour it an instant,
indeed my dear General, it would make miserable. I well see
you never will go to France—The unexpressible pleasure of
embracing you in my own house, of well coming you in a
family where your name is adored, I do not much expect to
experience—But to you, I shall return, and in the walls of
Mount Vernon we shall yet often speack of old times. My firm
plan is to visit now and then my friends on this side of the

Atlantick, and the most beloved of all friends I ever had, or ever will have any where, is too strong an inducement for me to return to him, not to think that, when ever it is possible, I will renew my so pleasing visits to Mount Vernon. . . .

Adieu, adieu, my dear General, it is with unexpressible pain that I feel I am going to be severed from you by the Atlantick— every thing that admiration, respect, gratitude, friendship, and filial love can inspire, is combined in my affectionate heart to devote me most tenderly to you—In your friendship I find a delight which words cannot express—Adieu, my dear General, it is not without emotion that I write this word—Altho' I know I shall soon visit you again—Be attentive to your health—Let me hear from you every month—Adieu, adieu.

L.f.

∞

## Marquis de Lafayette and Thomas Jefferson in 1824

AT THE invitation of Congress, Lafayette returned to America for a tour in 1824. The reception for America's adopted son—the "knight of liberty"—was overwhelming. Jefferson told Lafayette that he was afraid Lafayette would "be killed with kindness." Throngs of Americans turned out in all towns and cities across the nation to welcome Lafayette. He spent some time alone at the tomb of Washington and tried to visit as many surviving heroes of the Revolutionary War years as he could. That included Jefferson, who Lafayette had known both in America and in France.

Thomas Jefferson Randolph, Jefferson's grandson, recounts the emotional reunion of these aging heroes of the Revolutionary War.

The lawn on the eastern side of the house at Monticello contains not quite an acre. On this spot was the meeting of

Jefferson and Lafayette, on the latter's visit to the United States. The barouche containing Lafayette stopped at the edge of this lawn. His escort—one hundred and twenty mounted men—formed on one side in a semicircle extending from the carriage to the house. A crowd of about two hundred men, who were drawn together by curiosity to witness the meeting of these two venerable men, formed themselves in a semicircle on the opposite side. As Lafayette descended from the carriage, Jefferson descended the steps of the portico. The scene which followed was touching. Jefferson was feeble and tottering with age—Lafayette permanently lamed and broken in health by his long confinement in the dungeon of Olmutz. As they approached each other, their uncertain gait quickened itself into a shuffling run, and exclaiming, "Ah, Jefferson!" "Ah, Lafayette," they burst into tears as they fell into each other's arms. Among the four hundred men witnessing the scene there was not a dry eye—no sound save an occasional suppressed sob. The two old men entered the house as the crowd dispersed in profound silence.

## *Thomas Jefferson to James Madison,*
## *February 20, 1784*

JEFFERSON AND Madison met in 1776 as fellow delegates to the Virginia Assembly. Their friendship was to continue "uninterrupted" for fifty years.

It is impossible to understand either of them without understanding both of them. They often collaborated in political projects, and on the few occasions where disagreement made such cooperation impossible, it did not harm their friendship or their intellectual kinship. Their friendship was an education for both of them and fostered

and secured some of the most important political developments and institutions of our nation, from the Virginia statute for religious liberty to the Bill of Rights.

In this letter, Jefferson was attempting to lure Madison,
James Monroe, and William Short to set up their homes
near his Monticello. For as Jefferson put it in another letter,
"Agreeable society is the first essential in constituting the
happiness and of course the value of our existence."

There is something wondrous in Jefferson's ideal of
friendship as a rational society in which the minds of each
friend would be refined and sharpened by the others. No
one can ascend intellectual or moral virtue alone—it must
be done with the help of like-minded friends. One can
imagine Albermarle County, Virginia, becoming the Athens
of America under Jefferson's plan. Madison never relocated
to Jefferson's neighborhood, but he always remained Jefferson's most constant intellectual partner and friend.

*I* hope you have found access to my library. I beg you to
make free use of it. Key, the steward is living there now and of
course will be always in the way. Monroe is buying land almost
adjoining me. Short will do the same. What would I not give
you could fall into the circle. With such a society I could once
more venture home and lay myself up for the residue of life,
quitting all it's contentions which grow daily more and more
insupportable. Think of it. To render it practicable only requires
you to think it so. Life is of no value but as it brings us gratifica-
tions. Among the most valuable of these is rational society. It
informs the mind, sweetens the temper, chears our spirits, and
promotes health. There is a little farm of 140 as. adjoining me,
and within two miles, all of good land, tho' old, with a small
indifferent house on it, the whole worth not more than £250.
Such a one might be a farm of experiment and support a little
table and houshold. It is on the road to Orange and so much
nearer than I am. It is convenient enough for supplementary
supplies from thence. Once more think of it, and Adieu.

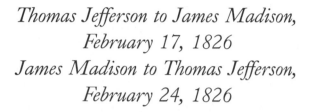

## Thomas Jefferson to James Madison, February 17, 1826
## James Madison to Thomas Jefferson, February 24, 1826

NEARING DEATH, Jefferson worried about how he would be remembered. He also worried about the future state of his beloved University of Virginia. Jefferson wrote to his friend, James Madison, for support. He asked him "to take care of me when dead."

Madison devoted himself to taking care of Jefferson and his university. Madison became the rector of the University of Virginia, donated money to the university, and gave books to the library. Madison also responded to many requests from biographers and historians about Jefferson's political views and legacy. He even corrected one biographer's unflattering description of Jefferson's nose. (Madison told him that Jefferson's nose was "rather under, certainly not above, common size.")

Below is a moving exchange between lifelong friends.

### JEFFERSON TO MADISON

*But* why afflict you with these details? Indeed, I cannot tell, unless pains are lessened by communication with a friend. The friendship which has subsisted between us, now half a century, and the harmony of our political principles and pursuits, have been sources of constant happiness to me through that long period. And if I remove beyond the reach of attentions to the University, or beyond the bourne of life itself, as I soon must, it is a comfort to leave that institution under your care, and an assurance that it will not be wanting. It has also been a great solace to me, to believe that you are engaged in vindicating to posterity the course we have pursued for preserving to them, in all their purity, the blessings of self-government, which we had assisted too in acquiring for them. If ever the earth has beheld a system of administration conducted with a single and steadfast eye to the general interest and happiness of those committed to it, one which, protected by truth, can never know reproach, it is that to which our lives have been devoted. To myself you have been a pillar of support through life. Take care of me when dead, and be assured that I shall leave with you my last affections.

*James Madison*

MADISON TO JEFFERSON

*You* cannot look back to the long period of our private friendship and political harmony, with more affecting recollections than I do. If they are a source of pleasure to you, what ought they not to be to me? We cannot be deprived of the happy consciousness of the pure devotion to the public good with which we discharged the trusts committed to us. And I indulge a confidence that sufficient evidence will find its way to another generation, to ensure, after we are gone, whatever of justice may be withheld whilst we are here. The political horizon is already yielding in your case at least, the surest auguries of it. Wishing and hoping that you may yet live to increase the debt which our Country owes you, and to witness the increasing gratitude, which alone can pay it, I offer you the fullest return of affectionate assurances.

∽

## *John Adams–Thomas Jefferson Reconciliation 1809–1812* *

JOHN ADAMS and Thomas Jefferson became friends in 1775, when they were both serving in the Continental Congress. They made an unlikely pair. Adams was a short and paunchy Northerner; Jefferson was a tall and lean Southerner. Adams, as he himself put it, was "obnoxious, suspected, and unpopular"; Jefferson was "very much otherwise." But they owned in common a fierce devotion to the cause of independence. Their dedication to this cause cemented a deep friendship that was to last for over fifty years.

However, political differences soon surfaced that almost

---

* Details of the Adams–Jefferson reconciliation taken from L.H. Butterfield, "The Dream of Benjamin Rush: The Reconciliation of John Adams and Thomas Jefferson," *Yale Review,* vol. 40, 1950–1951.

destroyed their friendship. Jefferson thought that Adams was betraying the spirit of the revolution by embracing monarchical sentiments. Some of Jefferson's concerns were inadvertently published. Adams viewed Jefferson's remarks as an "open personal attack." Adams himself thought that Jefferson's radical republicanism and unqualified support for the French Revolution would itself subvert the experiment in self-government. Thus, shortly before leaving office, President Adams made "midnight appointments" of judges before Jefferson's inauguration, putting on the bench Federalist judges who would oppose the new president's initiatives. This time it was Jefferson who was infuriated.

They didn't speak to each other or exchange any correspondence for eleven years. Benjamin Rush, a fellow signer of the Declaration of Independence and mutual friend of both, wanted these two men to reconcile with each other. He spent several years corresponding with both of them in order to persuade them to bury the hatchet. He believed that posterity would be made better off from a renewed correspondence between these eminent founders. But how could Rush get these two proud old men, both feeling hurt by the other, back together? Who would make the first move?

As it turned out, John Adams, prompted by Rush's urging, made the first move. In the following letter, Adams found the excuse of sending to Jefferson "two pieces of Homespun" which turned out to be John Quincy Adams's treastise of rhetoric and oratory. As the second letter shows, Jefferson eagerly responded, and the two exchanged a rich correspondence for many years. In the third letter of this series, Benjamin Rush rejoiced in their happy reunion.

⚭

# John Adams to Thomas Jefferson, January 1, 1812, and Jefferson to Adams, January 21, 1812

## ADAMS TO JEFFERSON

*Dear* Sir

As you are a Friend to American Manufactures under proper restrictions, especially Manufactures of the domestic kind, I take the Liberty of sending you by the Post a Packett containing two Pieces of Homespun lately produced in this quarter by One who was honoured in his youth with some of your Attention and much of your kindness.

All of my Family whom you formerly knew are well. My Daughter Smith is here and has successfully gone through a perilous and painful Operation, which detains her here this Winter, from her Husband and her Family at Chenango: where one of the most gallant and skilful Officers of our Revolution is probably destined to spend the rest of his days, not in the Field of Glory, but in the hard Labours of Husbandry.

I wish you Sir many happy New Years and that you may enter the next and many succeeding Years with as animating Prospects for the Public as those at present before Us. I am Sir with a long and sincere Esteem your Friend and Servant

JOHN ADAMS

## JEFFERSON TO ADAMS

*Dear* Sir

. . . A letter from you calls up recollections very dear to my mind. It carries me back to the times when, beset with difficulties and dangers, we were fellow laborers in the same cause, struggling for what is most valuable to man, his right of self-government. Laboring always at the same oar, with some wave ever ahead threatening to overwhelm us and yet passing harmless under our bark, we knew not how, we rode through the storm with heart and hand, and made a happy port. Still we did not expect to be without rubs and difficulties; and we have had them.

Sometimes indeed I look back to former occurrences, in remembrance of our old friends and fellow laborers, who have fallen before us. Of the signers of the Declaration of Independance I see now living not more than half a dozen on your side of the Potomak, and, on this side, myself alone. You and I have been wonderfully spared, and myself with remarkable health, and a considerable activity of body and mind. I am on horseback 3. or 4. hours of every day; visit 3. or 4. times a year a possession I have 90 miles distant, performing the winter journey on horseback. I walk little however; a single mile being too much for me; and I live in the midst of my grandchildren, one of whom has lately promoted me to be a great grandfather. I have heard with pleasure that you also retain good health, and a greater power of exercise in walking than I do. But I would rather have heard this from yourself, and that, writing a letter, like mine, full of egotisms, and of details of your health, your habits, occupations and enjoyments, I should have the pleasure of knowing that, in the race of life, you do not keep, in it's physical decline, the same distance ahead of me which you have done in political honors and atchievements. No circumstances have lessened the interest I feel in these particulars respecting yourself; none have suspended for one moment my sincere esteem for you; and I now salute you with unchanged affections and respect.

TH: JEFFERSON

∽

## Benjamin Rush to John Adams, February 17, 1812

RUSH REJOICED in the reunion of these two friends and fellow patriots and wrote a wonderful tribute to them both.

*I* rejoice in the correspondence which has taken place between you and your old friend Mr. Jefferson. I consider you and him as the North and South Poles of the American Revolution. Some talked, some wrote, and some fought to promote and establish it, but you and Mr. Jefferson *thought* for us all. I never take a retrospect of the years 1775 and 1776 without associating your opinions and speeches and conversations with all the great political, moral, and intellectual achievements of the Congresses of those memorable years.

∽

## John Adams to Thomas Jefferson, December 8, 1818

JOHN ADAMS responds to Thomas Jefferson's condolence letter on the death of his wife Abigail and expresses his hope to meet Jefferson in the next world.

*Dear* Sir                                    December 8, 18.
     Your Letter of Nov. 13 gave me great delight not only by the divine Consolation it Afforded me under my great Affliction: but as it gave me full Proof of your restoration to Health.
     While you live, I seem to have a Bank at Montecello on which I can draw for a Letter of Friendship and entertainment when I please.

I know not how to prove physically that We shall meet and know each other in a future State; Nor does Revelation, as I can find give Us any possitive Assurance of such a felicity. My reasons for believing, it, as I do, most undoubtingly, are all moral and divine.

I believe in God and in his Wisdom and Benevolence: and I cannot conceive that such a Being could make such a Species as the human merely to live and die on this Earth. If I did not believe a future State I should believe in no God. This Un[i]verse, this all; this . . . ["totality"]; would appear with all its swelling Pomp, a boyish Fire Work.

And if there be a future State Why should the Almighty dissolve forever all the tender Ties which Unite Us so delightfully in this World and forbid Us to see each other in the next?

Sick or Well the frien[d]ship is the same of your old Acquaintance

JOHN ADAMS

∞

## Thomas Jefferson to John Adams, March 25, 1826

THIS WAS to be the last letter Jefferson wrote to his friend. They both were soon to be reunited in death, "in an ecstatic meeting with the friends [they] have loved and lost," as Jefferson had once put it.

*Dear* Sir

My grandson Th: Jefferson Randolph, being on a visit to Boston, would think he had seen nothing were he to leave it without having seen you. Altho' I truly sympathise with you in the trouble these interruptions give, yet I must ask for him permission to pay to you his personal respects. Like other young people, he wishes to be able, in the winter nights of old age, to recount to those around him what he has heard and learnt of the Heroic age preceding his birth, and which of the Argonauts particularly he was in time to have seen. It was the lot of our early years to witness nothing but the dull monotony of colonial subservience, and of our riper ones to breast the labors and perils of working out of it. Theirs are the Halcyon calms succeeding the storm which our Argosy had so stoutly weathered. Gratify his ambition then by recieving his best bow, and my solicitude for your health by enabling him to bring me a favorable account of it. Mine is but indifferent, but not so my friendship and respect for you.

# IV

## EDUCATION OF THE HEAD AND HEART

◈

*The* Founders believed in the fundamental importance of individual rights and liberty. But they also believed that citizens needed a solid education in order to exercise those rights without abusing them. Receiving an education is important if we are to be informed citizens, ones who read the newspaper, keep up with the day's events, and are capable of making sound decisions about who and what to vote for. For the Founders thought that without an educated populace, the American experiment would fail. As Thomas Jefferson wrote to James Madison: "Above all things I hope the education of the common people will be attended to; convinced that on their good sense we may rely with the most security for the preservation of a due degree of liberty."

Jefferson, as well as the rest of our Founders, believed that in America, unlike any other country of that time, every citizen, no matter how poor, should be entitled to an education. Jefferson hoped for what he called a "general diffusion of knowledge" to keep citizens aware of their basic rights and to help them guard against any abuses of those rights by crafty or corrupt politicians.

Our first teachers are our parents. This chapter contains the Founders' letters filled with advice and precepts aimed at shaping the moral sense and character of their own children and the other young charges. For no matter how smart one might become, the Founders believed that knowledge without virtue would be incomplete. Abigail Adams told her young son, John Quincy Adams: "Great Learning and superior abilities, should you ever possess them, will be of little value and small Estimation, unless Virtue, Honour, Truth and integrety are added to them."

In our country, it should be in the schools and homes where we are taught to respect our nation's laws and the rights of our fellow citizens and, in short, where we first learn our basic civic duties. The Founders hoped students would study America's founding political documents, such as the Declaration of Independence and the Constitution, so that future generations would continue to cherish liberty and the political institutions which safeguard that liberty. Part of a civic education also includes learning about the great men and women who risked their lives for the cause of freedom and equality. As Noah Webster suggested, as soon as a child "opens his lips . . . he should lisp the praise of liberty and of those illustrious heroes" of our Founding. In other words, American students should learn to love their country and to take pride in and contribute to the American experience.

∞

## "I Can't Tell a Lie"
## Mason Weems, The Life of George Washington

"I CAN'T tell a lie" is perhaps the most famous quotation ever attributed to George Washington. As it happens, we don't know that he ever said it, but his biographer Parson Weems, who inserted it into the fifth edition of *The Life and Memorable Actions of George Washington,* has made it part of the Washington story.

While Weems took considerable artistic license in depicting the life of George Washington—which doubtless made for enjoyable reading—the integrity of his subject did not require any such embellishment. Washington himself said, "I hope I shall always possess firmness and virtue enough to maintain what I consider the most enviable of all titles, the character of an 'Honest Man.' " And Washington, by all accounts, always acted with that title more than anything else in mind, maintaining it throughout his life. However, it is in part thanks to Weems that we do remember Washington as an honest man, and for that reason, I have included Weems's famous account of Washington and the cherry tree in this chapter. But I do so not on my judgment alone. I can think of no higher recommendation for including it here than the fact that another famous president avidly read Weems's biography of Washington—Abraham Lincoln, whose moniker was "Honest Abe." Truth or fiction, myth or not, it certainly had an impact on this boy, who would later hail Washington as the "mightiest name" in "moral reformation."

*"When* George," said she, "was about six years old, he was made the wealthy master of a *hatchet!* of which, like most little boys, he was immoderately fond, and was constantly going about chopping every thing that came in his way. One day, in the garden, where he often amused himself hacking his mother's pea-sticks, he unluckily tried the edge of his hatchet on the body of a beautiful young English cherry-tree, which he barked so terribly, that I don't believe the tree ever got the better of it. The next morning the old gentleman finding out what had befallen his tree, which, by the by, was a great favourite, came into the house, and with much warmth asked for the mischievous author, declaring at the same time, that he would not have taken five guineas for his tree. Nobody could tell him any thing about it. Presently George and his hatchet made their appearance. *George,* said his father, *do you know who killed that beautiful little cherry-tree yonder in the garden?* This was a *tough question;* and George staggered under it for a moment; but quickly recovered himself: and looking at his father, with the

sweet face of youth brightened with the inexpressible charm of all-conquering truth, he bravely cried out, *"I can't tell a lie, Pa; you know I can't tell a lie. I did cut it with my hatchet."—Run to my arms, you dearest boy,* cried his father in transports, *run to my arms; glad am I, George, that you killed my tree; for you have paid me for it a thousand fold. Such an act of heroism in my son, is more worth than a thousand trees, though blossomed with silver, and their fruits of purest gold."*

It was in this way, by interesting at once both his *heart* and *head,* that Mr. Washington conducted George with great ease and pleasure along the happy paths of virtue.

∞

## Thomas Jefferson's Decalogue, February 25, 1825

A FRIEND asked Thomas Jefferson to pass on some advice to his young son, whom he had named after Jefferson. Jefferson wrote a letter of advice, attached a poem, and wrote a set of ten commandments for practical life.

Jefferson's wisdom is timeless—it's a good list of rules to remember.

*The Portrait of a Good Man by the most sublime of Poets, for your Imitation.*

Lord, who's the happy man that may to thy blest courts repair;
Not stranger-like to visit them, but to inhabit there?

'Tis he whose every thought and deed by rules of virtue moves;
Whose generous tongue disdains to speak the thing his heart
    disproves.

Who never did a slander forge, his neighbor's fame to wound;
Nor hearken to a false report by malice whispered round.

Who vice in all its pomp and power, can treat with just neglect;
And piety, though clothed in rags, religiously respect.

Who to his plighted vows and trust has ever firmly stood;
And though he promise to his loss, he makes his promise good.

Whose souls in usury disdains his treasure to employ;
Whom no rewards can ever bribe the guiltless to destroy.

The man who, by this steady course, has happiness insured,
When earth's foundations shake, shall stand by Providence
    secured.

*A Decalogue of Canons for Observation in Practical Life.*

1.  Never put off till to-morrow what you can do to-day.
2.  Never trouble another for what you can do yourself.
3.  Never spend your money before you have it.
4.  Never buy what you do not want because it is cheap; it will be dear to you.
5.  Pride costs us more than hunger, thirst, and cold.
6.  We never repent of having eaten too little.
7.  Nothing is troublesome that we do willingly.
8.  How much pain have cost us the evils which have never happened.
9.  Take things always by their smooth handle.
10. When angry, count ten before you speak; if very angry, an hundred.

∞

# Abigail Adams to John Quincy Adams,
# January 21, 1781

JOHN QUINCY ADAMS was thirteen years old and in Europe when he received this letter from his mother. Though separated by an ocean (John Quincy was with his father), Abigail continued to raise and shape her son through letters like this one. She urged John Quincy to take advantage of his time abroad, to study the varied scenes carefully so that he might arrive at a better understanding of himself and human nature.

*You* must not be a superficial observer, but study Men and Manners that you may be Skilfull in both. Tis said of Socrates, that the oracle pronounced him the wisest of all Men living because he judiciously made choice of Humane Nature for the object of his Thoughts. Youth is the proper season for observation and attention—a mind unincumberd with cares may seek instruction and draw improvement from all the objects which surround it. The earlier in life you accustome yourself to consider objects with attention, the easier will your progress be, and more sure and successfull your enterprizes. What a Harvest of true knowledge and learning may you gather from the numberless varied Scenes through which you pass if you are not wanting in your own assiduity and endeavours. Let your ambition be engaged to become eminent, but above all things support a virtuous character, and remember that "an Honest Man is the Noblest work of God."

❧

## *Teach Her to Be Good,*
## *Thomas Jefferson to Martha Jefferson,*
## *April 7, 1787*

THOMAS JEFFERSON'S surviving daughters, Martha ("Patsy") and Mary ("Polly") Jefferson were only ten and four years old respectively when their mother died. Jefferson, who had acted as both mother and father to his young daughters, had been in Paris for three years with Patsy when he sent for eight-year-old Polly to join them. (Jefferson's sister had been taking care of her in Virginia, as Jefferson thought it would be too dangerous for such a young girl to cross the ocean with him and Patsy.) Jefferson tells Patsy of her duties to her younger sister. Patsy is to teach her sister to be good, "because without that," Jefferson writes, "we can neither be valued by others, nor set any value on ourselves."

*I* have received letters which inform me that our dear Polly will certainly come to us this summer. By the time I return it will be time to expect her. When she arrives, she will become a precious charge on your hands. The difference of your age, and your common loss of a mother, will put that office on you. Teach her above all things to be good: because without that we can neither be valued by others, nor set any value on ourselves. Teach her to be always true. No vice is so mean as the want of truth, and at the same time so useless. Teach her never to be angry. Anger only serves to torment ourselves, to divert others, and alienate their esteem. And teach her industry and application to useful pursuits. I will venture to assure you that if you inculcate this in her mind you will make her a happy being in herself, a most inestimable friend to you, and precious to all the world. In teaching her these dispositions of mind, you will be more fixed in them yourself, and render yourself dear to all your acquaintance. Practice them then, my dear, without ceasing. If ever you find yourself in difficulty and doubt how to extricate yourself, do what is right, and you will find it the easiest way of getting out of the difficulty. Do it for the additional incitement of increasing the happiness of him who loves you infinitely, and who is my dear Patsy your's affectionately.

∾

## *George Washington to George Washington Custis*

WASHINGTON WROTE the following letters to his adopted grandson, George Washington Custis, who was studying at Princeton. Custis was not a very serious student and often lacked self-discipline. Washington's advice to students about to enter upon "the grand theatre of life" (a.k.a. the real world) is as good today as it was then; Custis did not heed it and eventually dropped out of the College of New Jersey.

*December 19, 1796*

*The* same consequences would follow from inconstancy and want of steadiness—for 'tis to close application and constant perseverance, men of letters and science are indebted for their knowledge and usefulness; and you are now at that period of life (as I have observed to you in a former letter) when these are to be acquired, or lost for ever. But as you are well acquainted with my sentiments on this subject, and know how anxious all your friends are to see you enter upon the grand theatre of life, with the advantages of a finished education, a highly culivated mind, and a proper sense of your duties to God and man, I shall only add one sentiment more before I close this letter (which, as I have others to write, will hardly be in time for the mail), and that is, to pay due respect and obedience to your tutors, and affectionate reverence to the president of the college, whose character merits your highest regards. Let no bad example, for such is to be met in all seminaries, have an improper influence upon your conduct. Let this be such, and let it be your pride, to demean yourself in such a manner as to obtain the good will of your superiors, and the love of your fellow-students.

Adieu—I sincerely wish you well, being your attached and affectionate friend,

*January 11, 1797*

Another thing I would recommend to you—not because *I* want to know how *you* spend your money—and that is, to keep an account-book, and enter therein every farthing of your receipts and expenditures. The doing of which would initiate you into a habit, from which considerable advantages would result. Where no account of this sort is kept, there can be no investigation; no correction of errors; no discovery from a recurrence thereto, wherein too much, or too little, has been appropriated to particular uses. From an early attention to these matters, important and lasting benefits may follow.

We are all well, and all unite in best wishes for you; and with sincere affection I am always yours,

∾

## *George Washington to George Steptoe Washington, December 5, 1790*

GEORGE STEPTOE WASHINGTON was the son of George Washington's brother, Sam. When Sam died, Washington took on the responsibility of educating Sam's son. George Steptoe Washington was heading to college in Philadelphia when Washington wrote him the following letter. Knowledge without virtue would be incomplete, Washington tells his nephew. As John Locke put it: "Virtue is harder to be got than knowledge; and, if lost in a young man, is seldom recovered." We have lost sight of the fact that the proper end of any education is moral education. As Martin Buber wrote: "All education is the education of character."

*Should* you enter upon the course of studies here marked out you must consider it as the finishing of your education, and, therefore, as the time is limited, that every hour misspent is lost for ever, and that future *years* cannot compensate for lost *days* at this period of your life. This reflection must shew the necessity of an unremitting application to your studies. To point out the importance of circumspection in your conduct, it may be proper to observe that a good moral character is the first essential in a man, and that the habits contracted at your age are generally indelible, and your conduct here may stamp your character through life. It is therefore highly important that you should endeavor not only to be learned but virtuous. Much more might be said to shew the necessity of application and regularity, but when you must know that without them you can never be qualified to render service to your country, assistance to your friends, or consolation to your retired moments, nothing further need be said to prove their utility.

∞

## *James Madison to William Bradford, Jr., November 9, 1772*

MADISON WROTE this letter when he was twenty-one years old. He had recently returned from Princeton where he had stayed an extra six months after graduation to study Hebrew and theology with his teacher John Witherspoon. Studying Hebrew and theology, not politics, Madison thought, would serve him well in the pursuit of public policy. He was right.

Back home, this young college graduate began educating his younger brothers and sisters. His health was never very good, and he had exhausted himself by his intellectual exertions at Princeton. But during this time, he suffered from

what some historians say was a "nervous disorder" or depression. He was unsure of what he wanted to do in life—
he didn't want to go into the ministry, but he found the
study of law to be tedious. A good friend of his from
Princeton, who had graduated early with him, had recently
died. Madison thought that his life would be cut short as
well, given his weak and frail constitution (some claim that
he was barely five feet six inches and weighed ninety-eight
pounds).

Like many young people today, he was having an "iden-
tity crisis" and thought very little of himself. Despite the
low expectations expressed here, he was, of course, to
become one of the greatest men in our history. Every soul
has valleys of despair and self-doubt, even the souls of the
greatest human beings.

This letter is to William Bradford, a good friend of his
from the College of New Jersey (Princeton).

*However* nice and cautious we may be in detecting the follies of mankind, and framing our economy according to the
precepts of Wisdom and Religion, I fancy there will commonly
remain with us some latent expectation of obtaining more than
ordinary happiness and prosperity till we feel the convincing
argument of actual disappointment. Though I will not determine whether we shall be much the worse for it if we do not
allow it to intercept our views towards a future state, because
strong desires and great hopes instigate us to arduous enter-
prises, fortitude, and perseverance. Nevertheless, a watchful
eye must be kept on ourselves, lest while we are building ideal
monuments of renown and bliss here, we neglect to have our
names enrolled in the annals of Heaven.

These thoughts come into my mind because I am writing to
you, and thinking of you. As to myself, I am too dull and infirm
now to look out for any extraordinary things in this world, for I
think my sensations for many months past have intimated to

me not to expect a long or healthy life; though it may be better with me after some time, [but] I hardly dare expect it, and therefore have little spirit and alacrity to set about anything that is difficult in acquiring and useless in possessing after one has exchanged time for eternity. But you have health, youth, fire, and genius, to bear you along through the high track of public life, and so may be more interested and delighted in improving on hints that respect the temporal though momentous concerns of man.

∞

## John Quincy Adams to John Adams, March 16, 1780, and John Adams to John Quincy Adams, March 17, 1780

TWELVE-YEAR-OLD John Quincy Adams was enrolled in school in Passy, a suburb of Paris. Here Adams carefully goes over his curriculum and even nags his son for his bad penmanship. It would be hard to have John Adams for a father. Then again the hard road can pay off. John Quincy Adams did become president of the United States, which John Adams lived to see. It is interesting that for Adams, one of the most brilliant and politically astute men of his time, it is Greek and Latin that he recommends above all to a future president. The same priorities are certainly not found in many schools or universities today.

JOHN QUINCY ADAMS TO JOHN ADAMS

*My Work for a day.*
  Make Latin,
  Explain Cicero
        Erasmus
        Appendix
  Peirce Phædrus
  Learn greek Racines
      greek Grammar
  Geography
  geometry
  fractions
  Writing
  Drawing

As a young boy can not apply himself to all those Things and keep a remembrance of them all I should desire that you would let me know what of those I must begin upon at first. I am your Dutiful Son,

John Quincy Adams

JOHN ADAMS TO JOHN QUINCY ADAMS

*My* dear Son

I have received your Letter giving an Account of your Studies for a day. You should have dated your Letter.

Making Latin, construing Cicero, Erasmus, the Appendix de Diis et Heroibus ethnicis, and Phædrus, are all Exercises proper for the Acquisition of the Latin Tongue; you are constantly employed in learning the Meaning of Latin Words, and the Grammar, the Rhetorick and Criticism of the Roman Authors: These Studies have therefore such a Relation to each other, that I think you would do well to pursue them all, under the Direction of your Master.

The Greek Grammar and the Racines I would not have you omit, upon any Consideration, and I hope your Master will soon put you into the Greek Testament, because the most perfect Models of fine Writing in history, Oratory and Poetry are to be found in the Greek Language.

Writing and Drawing are but Amusements and may serve as Relaxations from your studies.

As to Geography, Geometry and Fractions I hope your Master will not insist upon your spending much Time upon them at present; because altho they are Useful sciences, and altho all Branches of the Mathematicks, will I hope, sometime or other engage your Attention, as the most profitable and the most satisfactory of all human Knowledge, yet my Wish at present is that your principal Attention should be directed to the Latin and Greek Tongues, leaving the other studies to be hereafter attained, in your own Country.

I hope soon to hear that you are in Virgil and Tully's orations, or Ovid or Horace or all of them.

I am, my dear Child, your affectionate Father, John Adams
P.S. The next Time you write me, I hope you will take more care to write well. Cant you keep a steadier Hand?

∽

## *Thomas Jefferson to Martha Jefferson, December 11, 1783*

PATSY JEFFERSON was only eleven years old when her father made her confront something that many adults avoid: that death "puts an end" to us all. To prepare for this is to find one's conscience—one's "internal monitor"—and to strive never to do wrong. Learning we are to die teaches us how to live right. It is a lesson that the young should learn—that in this coil life is not forever.

*My* Dear Patsy

. . . I hope you will have good sense enough to disregard those foolish predictions that the world is to be at an end soon. The almighty has never made known to any body at what time he created it, nor will he tell any body when he means to put an end to it, if ever he means to do it. As to preparations for that event, the best way is for you to be always prepared for it. The only way to be so is never to do or say a bad thing. If ever you are about to say any thing amiss or to do any thing wrong, consider before hand. You will feel something within you which will tell you it is wrong and ought not to be said or done: this is your conscience, and be sure to obey it. Our maker has given us all this faithful internal Monitor, and if you always obey it, you will always be prepared for the end of the world: or for a much more certain event which is death. This must happen to all: it puts an end to the world as to us, and the way to be ready for it is never to do a wrong act.

∞

## Abigail Adams to Mercy Warren, July 6, 1773, and Mercy to Abigail, July 25, 1773

ABIGAIL ADAMS and Mercy Otis Warren were good friends who maintained a lifelong correspondence. As a young mother with four children under the age of five, Abigail was eager for advice on how to raise "the tender twigs alloted to my care." Warren recommends instilling in children, first and foremost, a "sacred regard for Veracity." It makes everything else come easier.

### ABIGAIL ADAMS TO MERCY WARREN

*I* am sensible I have an important trust committed to me; and tho I feel my-self very uneaquel to it, tis still incumbent upon me to discharge it in the best manner I am capable of. I was really so well pleased with your little offspring, that I must beg the favour of you to communicate to me the happy Art of "rearing the tender thought, teaching the young Idea how to shoot, and pouring fresh instruction o'er the Mind." May the Natural Benevolence of your Heart, prompt you to assist a young and almost inexperienced Mother in this Arduous Business, that the tender twigs alloted to my care, may be so cultivated as to do honour to their parents and prove blessing[s] to the riseing generation. When I saw the happy fruits of your attention in your well ordered family, I felt a Sort of Emulation glowing in my bosom, to imitate the

> "Parent who vast pleasure find's
> In forming of her childrens minds
> In midst of whom with vast delight
> She passes many a winters Night
> Mingles in every play to find
> What Bias Nature gave the mind
> Resolving thence to take her aim
> To guide them to the realms of fame
> And wisely make those realms the way
> To those of everlasting day.
>
> Each Boisterous passion to controul
> And early Humanize the Soul
> In simple tales beside the fire,
> The noblest Notions to inspire.
> Her offspring conscious of her care
> Transported hang around her chair."

MERCY WARREN TO ABIGAIL ADAMS

*You* ask if the sentiments of this Lady coincide with the Rules perscribed myself in the Regulation of my Little flock and to answer you ingeneously I must acknowledge I fall so far short of the Methods I heretofore Laid down as the Rule of my Conduct that I dispaire of Reaching those more perfect plans

Exhibited by superior Hands. Much less shall I presume to dictate to those who have had Equal advantages with myself and who I think Likly to make a much better improvement thereof. I shall Esteem it a happiness indeed if I can acquit myself of the important Charge (by providence devovled on Every Mother), to the approbation of the judicious Observer of Life, but a much more noble pleasure is the conscious satisfaction of having Exerted our utmost Efforts to rear the tender plant and Early impress the youthful mind, with such sentiments that if properly Cultivated when they go out of our hands they may become useful in their several departments on the present theatre of action, and happy forever when the immortal mind shall be introduced into more Enlarged and Glorious scenes.

But before I quit this subject I would ask if you do not think Generosity of sentiment as it is mention'd in the ninth Letter of the above treatise too Comprehensive a term to be given as the first principle to be impress'd on the infant mind. This temper doubtless includes many other Virtues but does it argue an

*Mercy Warren*

invariable Attachment to truth. I have ever thought a careful Attention to fix a sacred regard to Veracity in the Bosom of Youth the surest Gaurd to Virtue, and the most powerful Barrier against the sallies of Vice through Every future period of Life. I cannot but think it is of much the most importance of any single principle in the Early Culture, for when it has taken deep root it usually produces not only Generosity of mind but a train of other Exelent qualities. And when I find a heart that will on no terms deviate from the Law of truth I do not much fear its Course will Ever Run very Eccentrick from the path of Rectitude, provided we can obtain any degree of that Childs Confidence: A point at which I think Every mother should aim.

∞

## Thomas Jefferson to Peter Carr, August 19, 1785

"HOW WOULD you act were all the world looking at you?" Jefferson asked his fifteen-year-old nephew, Peter Carr. "Act accordingly," he advised. Jefferson here offers some good advice that stands the test of time and scrutiny.

*When* your mind shall be well improved with science, nothing will be necessary to place you in the highest points of view but to pursue the interests of your country, the interests of your friends, and your own interests also with the purest integrity, the most chaste honour. The defect of these virtues can never be made up by all the other acquirements of body and mind. Make these then your first object. Give up money, give up fame, give up science, give [up] the earth itself and all it contains rather than do an immoral act. And never suppose that in any possible situation or under any circumstances that it is best for you to do a dishonourable thing however slightly so it may appear to you. Whenever you are to do a thing tho' it can never be known but to yourself, ask yourself how you would act were all the world looking at you, and act accordingly. Encourage all your virtuous dispositions, and exercise them whenever an opportunity arises, being assured that they will gain strength by exercise as a limb of the body does, and that exercise will make them habitual. From the practice of the purest virtue you may be assured you will derive the most sublime comforts in every moment of life and in the moment of death. If ever you find yourself environed with difficulties and perplexing circumstances, out of which you are at a loss how to extricate yourself, do what is right, and be assured that that will extricate you the best out of the worst situations. Tho' you cannot see when you fetch one step, what will be the next, yet follow truth, justice, and plain-dealing, and never fear their leading you out of the labyrinth in the easiest manner possible. The knot which you thought a Gordian one will untie itself before you. Nothing is so mistaken as the supposition that a person is to extricate himself from a difficulty, by intrigue, by chicanery, by dissimulation, by trimming, by an untruth, by an injustice. This increases the difficulties tenfold, and those who pursue these methods, get themselves so involved at length that they can turn no way but their infamy becomes more exposed. It is of great importance to set a resolution, not to be shaken, never to tell an untruth. There is no vice so mean, so pitiful, so contemptible and he who permits himself to tell a lie once, finds it much easier to do it a second and third time, till at length it becomes habitual, he tells lies without attending to it, and truths without the world's beleiving him. This falshood of the tongue leads to that of the heart, and in time depraves all it's good dispositions.

∾

## Abigail Adams to John Quincy Adams, June 1778

ABIGAIL ADAMS shows what "tough love" is all about in this letter to her eleven-year-old son, John Quincy Adams, who was in Europe with his father. Her letter may seem overly stern, but she is well aware that "the welfare and prosperity of all countries, communities and I may add individuals depend upon their morals." Abigail Adams took to heart the fundamental task of the education of the young, knowing that self-government rests on the piety and moral seriousness of each new generation of citizens.

Her sentiment that she would prefer John Quincy dead to being immoral or "a Graceless child" may not be literally true, but it probably caught his attention.

*My* Dear Son

. . . The most amiable and most usefull disposition in a young mind is diffidence of itself, and this should lead you to seek advise and instruction from him who is your natural Guardian, and will always counsel and direct you in the best manner both for your present and future happiness. You are in possession of a natural good understanding and of spirits unbroken by adversity, and untamed with care. Improve your understanding for acquiring usefull knowledge and virtue, such as will render you an ornament to society, an Honour to your Country, and a Blessing to your parents. Great Learning and superior abilities, should you ever possess them, will be of little value and small Estimation, unless Virtue, Honour, Truth and integrety are added to them. Adhere to those religious Sentiments and principals which were early instilled into your mind and remember that you are accountable to your Maker for all your words and actions. Let me injoin it upon you to attend constantly and steadfastly to the precepts and instructions of your Father as you value the happiness of your Mother and your own welfare. His care and attention to you render many things unnecessary for me to write which I might otherways do, but the inadvertency and Heedlessness of youth, requires line upon line and precept upon precept, and when inforced by the joint efforts of both parents will I hope have a due influence upon your Conduct, for dear as you are to me, I had much rather you should have found your Grave in the ocean you have crossd, or any untimely death crop you in your Infant years, rather than see you an immoral profligate or a Graceless child.

You have enterd early in life upon the great Theater of the world which is full of temptations and vice of every kind. You are not wholly unacquainted with History, in which you have read of crimes which your unexperienced mind could scarcly believe credible. You have been taught to think of them with Horrour and to view vice as

> a Monster of so frightfull Mein
> That to be hated, needs but to be seen

Yet you must keep a strict guard upon yourself, or the odious monster will soon loose its terror, by becomeing familiar to you. The Modern History of our own times furnishes as Black a list of crimes as can be paralleld in ancient time, even if we go back to Nero, Caligula or Caesar Borgia. Young as you are, the cruel war into which we have been compelld by the Haughty Tyrant of Britain and the Bloody Emissarys of his vengance may stamp upon your mind this certain Truth, that the welfare and prosperity of all countries, communities and I may add individuals depend upon their Morals. That Nation to which we were once united as it has departed from justice, eluded and subverted the wise Laws which formerly governd it, suffer'd the worst of crimes to go unpunished, has lost its valour, wisdom and Humanity, and from being the dread and terror of Europe, has sunk into derision and infamy.

∞

## Thomas Jefferson to Mary Jefferson, April 11, 1790

GEORGE WASHINGTON appointed Thomas Jefferson to be America's first secretary of state. In March of 1790, he began his official duties as secretary of state in New York, which was then the nation's capital. This meant that he was separated from his eleven-year-old daughter Mary, whom he often called "Maria" or "Polly." He referred to himself in this letter as a "vagrant" father. Yet although public service often took him away from his children, he remained attentive to the moral upbringing and education of his daughter, as this letter demonstrates.

TO MARY JEFFERSON

*New York Apr. 11. 1790.*

*Where* are you, my dear Maria? How do you do? How are you occupied? Write me a letter by the first post and answer me all these questions. Tell me whether you see the sun rise every day? How many pages a day you read in Don Quixot? How far you are advanced in him? Whether you repeat a Grammar lesson every day? What else you read? How many hours a day you sew? Whether you have an opportunity of continuing your music? Whether you know how to make a pudding yet, to cut out a beef stake, to sow spinach or to set a hen? Be good my dear, as I have always found you, never be angry with any body, nor speak harm of them, try to let every body's faults be forgotten, as you would wish yours to be; take more pleasure in giving what is best in another than in having it yourself, and then all the world will love you, and I more than all the world. If your sister is with you kiss her and tell her how much I love her also, and present my affections to Mr. Randolph. Love your Aunt and Uncle and be dutiful and obliging to them for all their kindness to you. What would you do without them, and with such a vagrant for a father? Say to both of them a thousand affectionate things for me: and Adieu my dear Maria.

TH: JEFFERSON

∽

## Benjamin Franklin, "On Constancy," Pennsylvania Gazette, *April 4, 1734*

**CONSTANCY — OR steadiness and perseverance — Franklin considered a great enabler to the other virtues. Indeed, he considered it a virtue in its own right. Having a high IQ or good intentions does not make one a good citizen or good friend or guarantee success in life. It is the virtue of perseverance that is a more likely ally.**

*When* I have sometimes observ'd Men of Wit and Learning, in Spite of their excellent natural and acquir'd Qualifications, fail of obtaining that Regard and Esteem with Mankind, which their Inferiors in point of Understanding frequently arrive at, I have, upon a slight Reflection, been apt to think, that it was owing to the ill Judgment, Malice, or Envy of their Acquaintance: But of late two or three flagrant Instances of this kind have put me upon thinking and deliberating more maturely, and I find within the Compass of my Observation the greatest part of those fine Men have been ruined for want of *CONSTANCY,* a Virtue never too highly priz'd, and whose true Worth is by few rightly understood.

A Man remarkably wavering and inconstant, who goes through with no Enterprize, adheres to no Purpose that he has resolv'd on, whose Courage is surmounted by the most trifling Obstacles, whose Judgment is at any time byass'd by his Fears, whose trembling and disturb'd Imagination will at every Turn suggest to him Difficulties and Dangers that actually have no Existence, and enlarge those that have; A Man, I say, of this Stamp, whatever natural and aquir'd Qualities he may have, can never be a truly useful Member of a Common-wealth, a sincere or amiable Friend, or a formidable Enemy; and when he is once incapable of bearing either of these Characters, 'tis no Wonder he is contemn'd and disregarded by Men of all Ranks and Conditions.

Without Steadiness or Perseverance no Virtue can long subsist; and however honest and well-meaning a Man's Principles may be, the Want of this is sufficient to render them ineffectual, and useless to himself or others. Nor can a Man pretend to enjoy or impart the lasting Sweets of a strict and glorious Friendship, who has not Solidity enough to despise the malicious Misrepresentations frequently made use of to disturb it, and which never fail of Success where a mutual Esteem is not founded upon the solid Basis of Constancy and Virtue. An Intimacy of this sort, contracted by chance, or the Caprice of an unstable Man, is liable to the most violent Shocks, and even an intire Ruin, from very trifling Causes. Such a Man's Incapacity for Friendship, makes all that know his Character absolutely indifferent to him: His known Fickleness of Temper renders him too inconsiderable to be fear'd as a Foe, or caress'd as a Friend.

I may venture to say there never was a Man eminently famous but what was distinguish'd by this very Qualification; and few if any can live comfortably even in a private Life without it; for a Man who has no End in View, no Design to pursue, is like an irresolute Master of a Ship at Sea, that can fix upon no one Port to steer her to, and consequently can call not one Wind favourable to his Wishes. . . .

∽

## Benjamin Franklin to Joseph Priestley, *September 19, 1772*

JOSEPH PRIESTLEY was an English philosopher, scientist (the discoverer of oxygen), and clergyman, with whom Franklin often discussed his scientific experiments. Priestley asked Franklin for some advice on what we might today call a "career move." Franklin shares his method of moral or "prudential algebra" with his friend. We all face choices in our lives—here's a way of avoiding rash decisions. Many people use such a method like this today. I do.

*Dear* Sir,

In the Affair of so much Importance to you, wherein you ask my Advice, I cannot for want of sufficient Premises, advise you *what* to determine, but if you please I will tell you *how.* When these difficult Cases occur, they are difficult chiefly because while we have them under Consideration all the Reasons *pro* and *con* are not present to the Mind at the same time; but sometimes one Set present themselves, and at other times another, the first being out of Sight. Hence the various Purposes or Inclinations that alternately prevail, and the Uncertainty that perplexes us. To get over this, my Way is, to divide half a Sheet of Paper by a Line into two Columns, writing over the one *Pro,* and over the other *Con.* Then during three or four Days Consideration I put down under the different Heads short Hints of the different Motives that at different Times occur to me for or against the Measure. When I have thus got them all together in one View, I endeavour to estimate their respective Weights; and where I find two, one on each side, that seem equal, I strike them both out: If I find a Reason *pro* equal to some two Reasons *con,* I strike out the three. If I judge some two Reasons *con* equal to some three Reasons *pro,* I strike out the five; and thus proceeding I find at length where the Balance lies; and if after a Day or two of farther Consideration nothing new that is of Importance occurs on either side, I come to a Determination accordingly. And tho' the Weight of Reasons cannot be taken with the Precision of Algebraic Quantities, yet when each is thus considered separately and comparatively, and the whole lies before me, I think I can judge better, and am less likely to make a rash Step; and in fact I have found great Advantage from this kind of Equation, in what may be called *Moral* or *Prudential Algebra*. Wishing sincerely that you may determine for the best, I am ever, my dear Friend, Yours most affectionately.

*Benjamin Franklin*

≈

## Thomas Jefferson to Benjamin Banneker, August 30, 1791

JEFFERSON, IN his *Notes on Virginia,* tentatively questioned the intellectual equality of blacks. In that work, he observed that blacks seemed inferior in their mental capacities. Later in life, however, he became more persuaded that the intellectual inferiority of blacks was due not to any intrinsic or natural difference but to their lack of education. They were, after all, slaves, who received no schooling whatsoever. He expresses this change of heart to Benjamin Banneker, who was a prominent black mathematician.

*Sir,*

I thank you sincerely for your letter of the 19th instant and for the Almanac it contained. No body wishes more than I do to see such proofs as you exhibit, that nature has given to our black brethren, talents equal to those of the other colors of men, and that the appearance of a want of them is owing merely to the degraded condition of their existence, both in Africa & America. I can add with truth, that no body wishes more ardently to see a good system commenced for raising the condition both of their body & mind to what it ought to be, as fast as the imbecility of their present existence, and other circumstances which cannot be neglected, will admit. I have taken the liberty of sending your Almanac to Monsieur de Condorcet, Secretary of the Academy of Sciences at Paris, and member of the Philanthropic society, because I considered it as a document to which your whole colour had a right for their justification against the doubts which have been entertained of them. I am with great esteem, Sir Your most obed t humble serv t.

∞

## Samuel Adams to Joseph Warren, November 4, 1775, and Samuel Adams to the Legislature, January 27, 1797

SAM ADAMS has been called the "last Puritan." Thomas Jefferson called him the "patriarch of liberty." Adams believed that morality and liberty go hand in hand. Here, the most rebellious of our patriots shares his thoughts on the central role of education in inculcating morality.

### SAMUEL ADAMS TO JAMES WARREN

*Let* me talk with you a little about the Affairs of our own Colony. I perswade my self, my dear Friend, that the greatest Care and Circumspection will be used to conduct its internal Police with Wisdom and Integrity. The Eyes of Mankind will be upon you to see whether the Government, which is now more popular than it has been for many years past, will be productive of more Virtue moral and political. We may look up to Armies for our Defence, but Virtue is our best Security. It is not possible that any State shd long remain free, where Virtue is not supremely honord.

. . . Since private and publick Vices, are in Reality, though not always apparently, so nearly connected, of how much Importance, how necessary is it, that the utmost Pains be taken by the Publick, to have the Principles of Virtue early inculcated on the Minds even of children, and the moral Sense kept alive, and that the wise institutions of our Ancestors for these great Purposes be encouraged by the Government. For no people will tamely surrender their Liberties, nor can any be easily subdued, when knowledge is diffusd and Virtue is preservd. On the Contrary, when People are universally ignorant, and debauchd in their Manners, they will sink under their own weight without the Aid of foreign Invaders.

SAMUEL ADAMS TO THE
LEGISLATURE OF MASSACHUSETTS

*As* Piety, Religion and Morality have a happy influence on the minds of men, in their public as well as private transactions, you will not think it unseasonable, although I have frequently done it, to bring to your remembrance the great importance of encouraging our University, town schools, and other seminaries of education, that our children and youth while they are engaged in the pursuit of useful science, may have their minds impressed with a strong sense of the duties they owe to their God, their instructors, and each other, so that when they arrive to a state of manhood, and take a part in any public transactions, their hearts having been deeply impressed in the course of their education with the moral feelings—such feelings may continue and have their due weight through the whole of their future lives.

∞

## *Thomas Jefferson, Aim and Curricula, University of Virginia, August 4, 1818*

THIS WAS Thomas Jefferson's vision of an academic community. His University of Virginia was to be modeled after a family; professor and student were to take their cue from "the affectionate deportment between father and son." Unfortunately, this vision did not bear up to reality—a student riot involving one of Jefferson's great-nephews erupted a few years after the university was founded, and stricter disciplinary provisions were instituted. Still, it is a noble vision, one that Jefferson believed should be "woven into the American character."

*The* best mode of government for youth, in large collections, is certainly a desideratum not yet attained with us. It may be well questioned whether *fear* after a certain age, is a motive to which we should have ordinary recourse. The human character is susceptible of other incitements to correct conduct, more worthy of employ, and of better effect. Pride of character, laudable ambition, and moral dispositions are innate correctives of the indiscretions of that lively age; and when strengthened by habitual appeal and exercise, have a happier effect on future character than the degrading motive of fear. Hardening them to disgrace, to corporal punishments, and servile humiliations cannot be the best process for producing erect character. The affectionate deportment between father and son, offers in truth the best example for that of tutor and pupil; and the experience and practice of other* countries, in this respect, may be worthy of enquiry and consideration with us. It will then be for the wisdom and discretion of the Visitors to devise and perfect a proper system of government, which, if it be founded in reason and comity, will be more likely to nourish in the minds of our youth the combined spirit of order and self-respect, so congenial with our political institutions, and so important to be woven into the American character.

* A police exercised by the students themselves, under proper discretion, has been tried with success in some countries, and the father as forming them for initiation into the duties and practices of civil life.—T.J.

∽

## Benjamin Rush, "Of the Mode of Education Proper in a Republic," 1798

TOCQUEVILLE ONCE observed that "everything which has a bearing on the status of women, their habits, and their thoughts is, in my view, of great political importance." Benjamin Rush believed that girls, like boys, "should be taught the principles of liberty and government" as they will have a decisive part in the perpetuation of America's institutions.

*I* beg pardon for having delayed so long to say any thing of the separate and peculiar mode of educaton proper for women in a republic. I am sensible that they must concur in all our plans of education for young men, or no laws will ever render them effectual. To qualify our women for this purpose, they should not only be instructed in the usual branches of female education, but they should be taught the principles of liberty and government; and the obligations of patriotism should be inculcated upon them. The opinions and conduct of men are often regulated by the women in the most arduous enterprizes of life; and their approbation is frequently the principal reward of the hero's dangers, and the patriot's toils. Besides, the first impressions upon the minds of children are generally derived from the women. Of how much consequence, therefore, is it in a republic, that they should think justly upon the great subject of liberty and government!

The complaints that have been made against religion, liberty and learning, have been, against each of them in a separate state. Perhaps like certain liquors, they should only be used in a state of mixture. They mutually assist in correcting the abuses, and in improving the good effects of each other. From the combined and reciprocal influence of religion, liberty and learning upon the morals, manners and knowledge of individuals, of these, upon government, and of government, upon individuals, it is impossible to measure the degrees of happiness and perfection to which mankind may be raised. For my part, I can form no ideas of the golden age, so much celebrated by the poets, more delightful, than the contemplation of that happiness which it is now in the power of the legislature of Pennsylvania to confer upon her citizens, by establishing proper modes and places of education in every part of the state.

∞

## Noah Webster, "On the Education of Youth in America," 1788

NOAH WEBSTER, whose "blue back spellers" educated and unified generations of Americans, was a constant advocate of what we today would call civic education. During Webster's time, the case for a civic education was made to promote unity and create a sense of national spirit for a nation quite young. The case for it in the twentieth century seems to me as strong as ever.

. . . *But* every child in America should be acquainted with his own country. He should read books that furnish him with ideas that will be useful to him in life and practice. As soon as he opens his lips, he should rehearse the history of his own country; he should lisp the praise of liberty, and of those illustrious heroes and statesmen who have wrought a revolution in her favor.

A selection of essays, respecting the settlement and geography of America; the history of the late revoluton and of the most remarkable characters and events that distinguished it, and a compendium of the principles of the federal and provincial governments, should be the principal school book in the United States. These are interesting objects to every man; they call home the minds of youth and fix them upon the interests of their own country, and they assist in forming attachments to it, as well as in enlarging the understanding.

"It is observed by the great Montesquieu, that the laws of education ought to be relative to the principles of the government."

In despotic governments, the people should have little or no education, except what tends to inspire them with a servile fear. Information is fatal to despotism.

In monarchies, education should be partial, and adapted to the rank of each class of citizens. But "in a republican government," says the same writer, "the whole power of education is required." Here every class of people should *know* and *love* the laws. This knowledge should be diffused by means of schools and newspapers; and an attachment to the laws may be formed by early impressions upon the mind.

When I speak of a diffusion of knowledge, I do not mean merely a knowledge of spelling books, and the New Testament. An acquaintance with ethics, and with the general principles of law, commerce, money and government, is necessary for the yeomanry of a republican state. This acquaintance they might obtain by means of books calculated for schools, and read by the children, during the winter months, and by the circulation of public papers.

. . . Every small district should be furnished with a school, at least four months in a year, when boys are not otherwise employed. This school should be kept by the most reputable and well informed man in the district. Here children should be taught the usual branches of learning; submission to superiors and to laws; the moral or social duties; the history and transactions of their own country; the principles of liberty and government. Here the rough manners of the wilderness should be softened, and the principles of virtue and good behaviours inculcated. The *virtues* of men are of more consequence to society than their *abilities;* and for this reason, the *heart* should be cultivated with more assiduity than the *head*.

Such a general system of education is neither impracticable nor difficult; and excepting the formation of a federal government that shall be efficient and permanent, it demands the first attention of American patriots. Until such a system shall be adopted and pursued; until the Statesman and Divine shall unite their efforts in *forming* the human mind, rather than in loping its excrescences, after it has been neglected; until Legislators discover that the only way to make good citizens and subjects is to nourish them from infancy; and until parents shall be convinced that the *worst* of men are not the proper teachers to make the *best;* mankind cannot know to what a degree of perfection society and government may be carried. America affords the fairest opportunities for making the experiment, and opens the most encouraging prospect of success.

# V

# INDUSTRY AND FRUGALITY

❦

*Benjamin* Franklin's *Poor Richard's Almanack,* which was written over two hundred years ago, is filled with advice that we are all familiar with today, such as: "No pains, no gains;" or "Early to bed, and early to rise, makes a man healthy, wealthy, and wise." Whatever we do, we know that if we want to be successful in life we must work hard. This is the lesson of Benjamin Franklin's life. We are fortunate to live in a country that rewards industry and frugality—or in today's terms, hard work and saving. Franklin knew about this firsthand and lived an inspiring rags-to-riches story. Franklin rose to become a world-renowned scientist, inventor, statesman, and philanthropist. In his *Autobiography* he recalled of how he "emerged from the poverty and obscurity" of his origins to "attain a degree of reputation in the world." Franklin wrote that the way to wealth and success for him and all Americans depended on "two Words, INDUSTRY and FRUGALITY."

Industry is an important virtue to cultivate, not only for financial success, but to live a good and worthwhile life. One of James Madison's teachers and a signer of the Declaration of Independence, John Witherspoon, told his students: "Do not live useless, and die contemptible." In other words, life is short. Why waste precious time?

Thomas Jefferson told his young daughter: "It is wonderful how much may be done if we are constantly doing." The Founders were "constantly doing"—rising early, keeping physically fit, studying, writing, and working. Does this mean that they did not value leisure or what we today call free time? Not at all. They worked hard so that they could have free time, which they filled with friends, family, and worthwhile pursuits. For example, Franklin worked so hard as a young man that he was able to retire from his printing business in his forties, and spent the next forty years of his life serving his country, devising useful inventions, and starting public-spirited projects, such as the first subscription library and the first volunteer fire department in Philadelphia.

The Founders knew how tempting it would be to spend all our time working so that we could buy material things—fine clothes, nice houses, and jewelry. And it is certainly tempting for us to want to make a statement about ourselves through our possessions. That is why the virtue of industry must be accompanied by the virtue of frugality. While there is nothing wrong with the desire to have nice things and lead a comfortable life, the Founders, such as Sam Adams, believed it was important not to lose sight of the more important things, such as what is on the inside of a person. As George Washington told his nephew: "Do not conceive that fine clothes make fine men . . . A plain genteel dress is more admired and obtains more credit than lace and embroidery in the eyes of the judicious and sensible." The virtue of frugality not only controls wasteful spending, but helps to remind us that our inner lives are more important than outward appearances or material things.

Together, industry and frugality have helped to make this nation a prosperous and moral one.

∞

## Benjamin Franklin, Autobiography

UNHAPPY WORKING for his older brother in his printing business, Benjamin Franklin ran away from his home in Boston at the age of seventeen. He went briefly to New York, but could not find work there, so he set sail for

Philadelphia. First, he landed in Perth Amboy, New Jersey, sick with a fever; from Perth Amboy, Franklin walked fifty miles over two days to reach Burlington, where he boarded a rowboat to cross the river to Philadelphia.

Below is Franklin's famous account of his entry into Philadelphia. Franklin shared this story with the hope that his very humble and "unlikely Beginning" would give hope to other Americans struggling to get ahead in life.

*I* have been the more particular in this Description of my Journey, & shall be so of my first Entry into that City, that you may in your Mind compare such unlikely Beginning with the Figure I have since made there. I was in my working Dress, my best Cloaths being to come round by Sea. I was dirty from my Journey; my Pockets were stuff'd out with Shirts & Stockings; I knew no Soul, nor where to look for Lodging. I was fatigu'd with Travelling, Rowing & Want of Rest. I was very hungry, and my whole Stock of Cash consisted of a Dutch Dollar and about a shilling in Copper. The latter I gave the People of the boat for my Passage, who at first refus'd it on Acc' of my Rowing; but I insisted on their taking it, a Man being sometimes more generous when he has but a little Money than when he has plenty, perhaps thro' Fear of being thought to have but little.

Then I walk'd up the Street, gazing about, till near the Market House I met a Boy with Bread. I had made many a Meal on Bread, & inquiring where he got it, I went immediately to the Baker's he directed me to in second Street; and ask'd for Bisket, intending such as we had in Boston, but they it seems were not made in Philadelphia, then I ask'd for a threepenny Loaf, and was told they had none such: so not considering or knowing the Difference of Money & the greater Cheapness nor the Names of his Bread, I bad him give me three pennyworth of any sort. He gave me accordingly three great Puffy Rolls. I was surpriz'd at the Quantity, but took it, and having no Room in my Pockets, walk'd off, with a Roll under each Arm, & eating the other. Thus I went up Market Street as far as fourth Street, passing by the Door of Mr Read, my future Wife's Father, when she standing at the Door saw me, & thought I made as I certainly did a most awkward ridiculous Appearance. Then I turn'd and went down Chestnut Street and part of Walnut Street, eating my Roll all the Way, and coming round found my self again at Market street Wharff, near the Boat I came in, to which I went for a Draught of the River Water, and being fill'd with one of my Rolls, gave the other two to a Woman & her Child that came down the River in the Boat with us and were waiting to go farther.

Thus refresh'd I walk'd again up the Street, which by this time had many clean dress'd People in it who were all walking the same Way; I join'd them, and thereby was led into the great Meeting House of the Quakers near the Market. I sat down among them, and after looking round a while & hearing nothing said, being very drowzy thro' Labour & want of Rest the preceding Night, I fell fast asleep, and continu'd so till the Meeting broke up, when one was kind enough to rouse me. This was therefore the first House I was in or slept in, in Philadelphia.

∞

## *Benjamin Franklin*, Autobiography, *Plan for Moral Perfection*

WHILE STILL in his twenties, Benjamin Franklin realized he had many faults and decided to embark on a "bold and arduous project of arriving at moral perfection." In fact, he wrote his famous *Autobiography* largely to share with the world this project and to show how it might work for anybody willing to go through with it. At first glance, Franklin's plan may appear to be a ridiculous attempt to take all the fun out of life. But this is not so. Instead, Franklin's plan shows how morality and virtue can work in one's self-interest: "Deny self for self's sake," Franklin suggested in *Poor Richard.* Virtue is an end in itself, but Franklin emphasizes how it can also be a means to making one happier and more successful in life. Morality, happiness, and success were considered by Franklin to be inseparable.

Below is Franklin's list of the thirteen virtues. These virtues have helped to make America an orderly and prosperous nation. And isn't there something especially American about Franklin's list? His list and his "plan" in many ways represent to beginning of a long American tradition of self-improvement. The list, the virtues, and their corresponding vices are still familiar. Most of us have fallen short on most of them. But that is why we put them before us. For in this country, as Franklin observes, "one man of tolerable Abilities may work great Changes, and accomplish great Affairs among Mankind, if he first forms a good Plan, and . . . makes the Execution of that same Plan his sole Study and Business." There are so many self-help books these days—Franklin's *Autobiography* is one of the best.

*It* was about this time I conceiv'd the bold and arduous project of arriving at moral perfection. I wish'd to live without committing any fault at any time; I would conquer all that either natural inclination, custom, or company might lead me into. As I knew, or thought I knew, what was right and wrong, I did not see why I might not always do the one and avoid the other. But I soon found I had undertaken a task of more difficulty than I had imagined. While my care was employ'd in guarding against one fault, I was often surprised by another; habit took the advantage of inattention; inclination was sometimes too strong for reason. I concluded, at length, that the mere speculative conviction that it was our interest to be completely virtuous, was not sufficient to prevent our slipping; and that the contrary habits must be broken, and good ones acquired and established, before we can have any dependence on a steady, uniform rectitude of conduct. For this purpose I therefore contrived the following method.

In the various enumerations of the moral virtues I had met with in my reading, I found the catalogue more or less numerous, as different writers included more or fewer ideas under the same name. Temperance, for example, was by some confined to eating and drinking, while by others it was extended to mean the moderating every other pleasure, appetite, inclination, or passion, bodily or mental, even to our avarice and ambition. I propos'd to myself, for the sake of clearness, to use rather more names, with fewer ideas annex'd to each, than a few names with more ideas; and I included under thirteen names of virtues all that at that time occurr'd to me as necessary or desirable, and annexed to each a short precept, which fully express'd the extent I gave to its meaning.

These names of virtues, with their precepts, were:

### 1. TEMPERANCE.

Eat not to dullness; drink not to elevation.

### 2. SILENCE.

Speak not but what may benefit others or yourself; avoid trifling conversation.

### 3. ORDER.

Let all your things have their places; let each part of your business have its time.

### 4. RESOLUTION.

Resolve to perform what you ought; perform without fail what you resolve.

### 5. FRUGALITY.

Make no expense but to do good to others or yourself; *i.e.,* waste nothing.

### 6. INDUSTRY.

Lose no time; be always employ'd in something useful; cut off all unnecessary actions.

### 7. SINCERITY.

Use no hurtful deceit; think innocently and justly, and, if you speak, speak accordingly.

### 8. JUSTICE.

Wrong none by doing injuries, or omitting the benefits that are your duty.

### 9. MODERATION.

Avoid extreams; forbear resenting injuries so much as you think they deserve.

### 10. CLEANLINESS.

Tolerate no uncleanliness in body, cloaths, or habitation.

### 11. TRANQUILLITY.

Be not disturbed at trifles, or at accidents common or un-avoidable.

### 12. CHASTITY.

Rarely use venery but for health or offspring, never to dullness, weakness, or the injury of your own or another's peace or reputation.

## 13. HUMILITY.

Imitate Jesus and Socrates.

FRANKLIN DIDN'T leave anything to chance in his attempt to master the thirteen virtues. He devised a "method" to expunge each bad habit, one week at a time, and recorded his progress in a "little book." When public business and travels made him too busy to repeat the course, he still carried the little book with him always.

While this might seem extreme, even odd, the larger lesson here is, I think, that nobody is born good—it takes constant application to rid ourselves of bad habits. Today we see many analogues to Franklin's book—for cardiovascular health, nutritional health, even healthy relationships —then why not for moral health? The Founding Fathers, on good precedent, thought that kind of health more important. If it takes Franklin's method, then so be it.

*My* intention being to acquire the *habitude* of all these virtues, I judg'd it would be well not to distract my attention by attempting the whole at once, but to fix it on one of them at a time; and, when I should be master of that, then to proceed to another, and so on, till I should have gone thro' the thirteen; and, as the previous acquisition of some might facilitate the acquisition of certain others, I arrang'd them with that view, . . .

I made a little book, in which I allotted a page for each of the virtues. I rul'd each page with red ink, so as to have seven columns, one for each day of the week, marking each column with a letter for the day. I cross'd these columns with thirteen red lines, marking the beginning of each line with the first letter of one of the virtues, on which line, and in its proper column, I might mark, by a little black spot, every fault I found upon examination to have been committed respecting that virtue upon that day.

I determined to give a week's strict attention to each of the virtues successfully. Thus, in the first week, my great guard was to avoid every the least offence against *Temperance,* leaving the other virtues to their ordinary chance, only marking every evening the faults of the day. Thus, if in the first week I could keep my first line, marked T, clear of spots, I suppos'd the habit of that virtue so much strengthen'd, and its opposite weaken'd, that I might venture extending my attention to include the next, and for the following week keep both lines clear of spots. Proceeding thus to the last, I could go thro' a course compleat in thirteen weeks, and four courses in a year. And like him who, having a garden to weed, does not attempt to eradicate all the bad herbs at once, which would exceed his reach and strength, but works on one of the beds at a time, and, having accomplish'd the first, proceeds to a second, so I should have, I hoped, the encouraging pleasure of seeing on my pages the progress I made in virtue, by clearing successively my lines of their spots, till in the end, by a number of courses, I should be happy in viewing a clean book, after a thirteen weeks' daily examination.

*Form of the pages.*

| TEMPERANCE | | | | | | |
|---|---|---|---|---|---|---|
| *Eat not to dulness. Drink not to elevation.* | | | | | | |
| | S. | M. | T. | W. | T. | F. | S. |
| T. | | | | | | | |
| S. | * | * | | * | | * | |
| O. | ** | * | * | | * | * | * |
| R. | | | * | | | * | |
| F. | | * | | | * | | |
| I. | | | * | | | | |
| S. | | | | | | | |
| J. | | | | | | | |
| M. | | | | | | | |
| C. | | | | | | | |
| T. | | | | | | | |
| C. | | | | | | | |
| H. | | | | | | | |

WHILE FRANKLIN certainly worked hard at his "method" for attaining moral perfection, he admits he was not successful. He says here that he had the most trouble with the virtue of "order." But he didn't worry too much about it— he still affirms that the whole "endeavor" made him "a better and happier man." Below, he corrects those who aim for complete moral purity with his story of "speckled" versus "bright" axes. Franklin is at his most charming here and shows that a little tolerance for human frailties and lapses is definitely in order.

*My* scheme of ORDER gave me the most trouble; and I found that, tho' it might be practicable where a man's business was such as to leave him the disposition of his time, that of a journeyman printer, for instance, it was not possible to be exactly observed by a master, who must mix with the world, and often receive people of business at their own hours. *Order,* too, with regard to places for things, papers, etc., I found extreamly difficult to acquire. I had not been early accustomed to it, and, having an exceeding good memory, I was not so sensible of the inconvenience attending want of method. This article, therefore, cost me so much painful attention, and my faults in it vexed me so much, and I made so little progress in amendment, and had such frequent relapses, that I was almost ready to give up the attempt, and content myself with a faulty character in that respect, like the man who, in buying an ax of a smith, my neighbour, desired to have the whole of its surface as bright as the edge. The smith consented to grind it bright for him if he would turn the wheel; he turn'd, while the smith press'd the broad face of the ax hard and heavily on the stone, which made the turning of it very fatiguing. The man came every now and then from the wheel to see how the work went on, and at length would take his ax as it was, without farther grinding. "No," said the smith, "turn on, turn on; we shall have it bright by-and-by; as yet, it is only speckled." "Yes," says the man, *"but I think I like a speckled ax best."* And I believe this may have been the case with many, who, having, for want of some such means as I employ'd, found the difficulty of obtaining good and breaking bad habits in other points of vice and virtue, have given up the struggle, and concluded that *"a speckled ax was best";* for something, that pretended to be reason, was every now and then suggesting to me that such extream nicety as I exacted of myself might be a kind of foppery in morals, which, if it were known, would make me ridiculous; that a perfect character might be attended with the inconvenience of being envied and hated; and that a benevolent man should allow a few faults in himself, to keep his friends in countenance.

In truth, I found myself incorrigible with respect to Order; and now I am grown old, and my memory bad, I feel very sensibly the want of it. But, on the whole, tho' I never arrived at the perfection I had been so ambitious of obtaining, but fell far short of it, yet I was, by the endeavour, a better and a happier man than I otherwise should have been if I had not attempted it; as those who aim at perfect writing by imitating the engraved copies, tho' they never reach the wish'd for excellence of those copies, their hand is mended by the endeavour, and is tolerable while it continues fair and legible.

It may be well my posterity should be informed that to this little artifice, with the blessing of God, their ancestor ow'd the constant felicity of his life, down to his 79th year in which this is written.

&#8734;

## Thomas Jefferson to Martha Jefferson, November 28, 1783

TO GET a sense of what Thomas Jefferson expected of his ten-year-old daughter, Martha "Patsy" Jefferson, I have included the following letter in which he put her on a schedule. This is his idea of "industry" for a ten-year-old girl.

As you can see, Jefferson set high standards for his young daughter—standards that are perhaps a little too high for us today. But we can still learn from them. Research and common sense agree that young people "learn up" to whatever is expected of them.

Dear Patsy,

After four days' journey, I arrived here without any accident, and in as good health as when I left Philadelphia. The conviction that you would be more improved in the situation I have placed you than if still with me, has solaced me on my parting with you, which my love for you has rendered a difficult thing. The acquirements which I hope you will make under the tutors I have provided for you will render you more worthy of my love; and if they cannot increase it, they will prevent its diminution. Consider the good lady who has taken you under her roof, who has undertaken to see that you perform all your exercises, and to admonish you in all those wanderings from what is right or what is clever, to which your inexperience would expose you; consider her, I say, as your mother, as the only person to whom, since the loss with which Heaven has pleased to afflict you, you can now look up; and that her displeasure or disapprobation, on any occasion, will be an immense misfortune, which should you be so unhappy as to incur by any unguarded act, think no concession too much to regain her good will. With respect to the distribution of your time, the following is what I should approve:

From 8 to 10, practice music.

From 10 to 1, dance one day and draw another.

From 1 to 2, draw on the day you dance, and write a letter next day.

From 3 to 4, read French.

From 4 to 5, exercise yourself in music.

From 5 till bed-time, read English, write, etc.

Communicate this plan to Mrs. Hopkinson, and if she approves of it, pursue it. As long as Mrs. Trist remains in Philadelphia, cultivate her affection. She has been a valuable friend to you, and her good sense and good heart make her valued by all who know her, and by nobody on earth more than me. I expect you will write me by every post. Inform me what books you read, what tunes you learn, and enclose me your best copy of every lesson in drawing. Write also one letter a week either to your Aunt Eppes, your Aunt Skipwith, your Aunt Carr, or the little lady from whom I now enclose a letter, and always put the letter you so write under cover to me. Take care that you never spell a word wrong. Always before you write a word, consider how it is spelt, and, if you do not remember it, turn to a dictionary. It produces great praise to a lady to spell well. I have placed my happiness on seeing you good and accomplished; and no distress this world can now bring on me would equal that of your disappointing my hopes. If you love me, then strive to be good under every situation and to all living creatures, and to acquire those accomplishments which I have put in your power, and which will go far towards ensuring you the warmest love of your affectionate father.

P.S. Keep my letters and read them at times, that you may always have present in your mind those things which will endear you to me.

∽

## Benjamin Franklin, *"Advice to a Young Tradesman, Written by an Old One,"* 1748, and Autobiography

HERE'S SOME more good advice from Franklin on how to succeed in business. The ever shrewd Franklin advises here that it is essential to be not only industrious and frugal in reality but also to make sure one presents oneself in that way. His observation about creditors states a timeless truth. Franklin followed his own advice quite faithfully and ran his nearest competitor, Samuel Keimer, out of town, as the next entry from his *Autobiography* recounts.

Franklin, who was nearly penniless when he ran away from home as a young teenager and rose to become one of the most successful Americans, believed that in this country, the same path to success was open to other enterprising people. In his *Autobiography,* he ascribed "[t]o Industry and Frugality the early Easiness of his circumstances, and the Acquisition of His Fortune, with all that Knowledge which enabled him to be an Useful citizen, and obtained for him some Degree of Reputation among the Learned."

ADVICE TO A YOUNG TRADESMAN,
WRITTEN BY AN OLD ONE

*To* my Friend A. B.
*As you have desired it of me, I write the following Hints, which have been of Service to me, and may, if observed, be so to you.*

Remember that TIME is Money. He that can earn Ten Shillings a Day by his Labour, and goes abroad, or sits idle one half of that Day, tho' he spends but Sixpence during his Diversion or Idleness, ought not to reckon That the only Expence; he has really spent or rather thrown away Five Shillings besides.

Remember that CREDIT is Money. If a Man lets his Money lie in my Hands after it is due, he gives me the Interest, or so much as I can make of it during that Time. This amounts to a considerable Sum where a Man has good and large Credit, and makes good Use of it.

Remember that Money is of a prolific generating Nature. Money can beget Money, and its Offspring can beget more, and so on. Five Shillings turn'd, is *Six:* Turn'd again, 'tis Seven and Three Pence; and so on 'til it becomes an Hundred Pound. The more there is of it, the more it produces every Turning, so that the Profits rise quicker and quicker. He that kills a breeding Sow, destroys all her Offspring to the thousandth Generation. He that murders a Crown, destroys all it might have produc'd, even Scores of Pounds. . . .

The most trifling Actions that affect a Man's Credit, are to be regarded. The Sound of your Hammer at Five in the Morning or Nine at Night, heard by a Creditor, makes him easy Six Months longer. But if he sees you at a Billiard Table, or hears your Voice in a Tavern, when you should be at Work, he sends for his Money the next Day. Finer Cloaths than he or his Wife wears, or greater Expence in any particular than he affords himself, shocks his Pride, and he duns you to humble you. Creditors are a kind of People, that have the sharpest Eyes and Ears, as well as the best Memories of any in the World. . . .

In short, the Way to Wealth, if you desire it, is as plain as the Way to Market. It depends chiefly on two Words, INDUSTRY and FRUGALITY; *i. e.* Waste neither Time nor Money, but make the best Use of both. He that gets all he can honestly, and saves all he gets (necessary Expences excepted) will certainly become RICH; If that Being who governs the World, to whom all should look for a Blessing on their Honest Endeavours, doth not in his wise Providence otherwise determine.

### AUTOBIOGRAPHY

I began now gradually to pay off the debt I was under for the printing-house. In order to secure my credit and character as a tradesman, I took care not only to be in *reality* industrious and frugal, but to avoid all appearances to the contrary. I drest plainly; I was seen at no places of idle diversion. I never went out a fishing or shooting; a book, indeed, sometimes debauch'd me from my work, but that was seldom, snug, and gave no scandal; and, to show that I was not above my business, I sometimes brought home the paper I purchas'd at the stores thro' the streets on a wheelbarrow. Thus being esteem'd an industrious, thriving young man, and paying duly for what I bought, the merchants who imported stationery solicited my custom; others proposed supplying me with books, and I went on swimmingly. In the mean time, Keimer's credit and business declining daily, he was at last forc'd to sell his printing-house to satisfy his creditors. He went to Barbadoes, and there lived some years in very poor circumstances.

≈

# Benjamin Franklin, Poor Richard Improved *or* "The Way to Wealth," 1758

BENJAMIN FRANKLIN was twenty-six years old when he wrote his first *Poor Richard's Almanack*. In his *Autobiography*, Franklin recounts that he filled his almanacks with "proverbial sentences, chiefly such as inculcating Industry and Frugality, as the means of procuring wealth and thereby securing virtue." His almanacks were extremely popular, and he sold more than ten thousand copies annually.

The following selection was the last *Poor Richard's Almanack*. By this time, Franklin was a very wealthy and successful man, and had already retired from his printing business. In this last almanack, Franklin culled together some of his best aphorisms on industry and frugality from past editions and put them in a speech by one of his created characters "Father Abraham." This essay was known as "The Way to Wealth."

*It* would be thought a hard Government that should tax its People one-tenth Part of their *Time,* to be employed in its Service. But *Idleness* taxes many of us much more, if we reckon all that is spent in absolute *Sloth,* or doing of nothing, with that which is spent in idle Employments or Amusements, that amount to nothing. *Sloth,* by bringing on Diseases, absolutely shortens life. *Sloth, like Rust, consumes faster than Labour wears; while the used Key is always bright,* as *Poor Richard* says. *But dost thou love Life, then do not squander Time, for that's the stuff Life is made of,* as *Poor Richard* says. How much more than is necessary do we spend in sleep, forgetting that *The sleeping Fox catches no Poultry,* and that *There will be sleeping enough in the Grave,* as *Poor Richard* says.

*If Time be of all Things the most precious, wasting Time must be,* as *Poor Richard* says, *the greatest Prodigality;* since, as he elsewhere tells us, *Lost Time is never found again;* and *what we call Time enough, always proves little enough:* Let us then up and be doing, and doing to the Purpose; so by Diligence shall we do more with less Perplexity. *Sloth makes all Things difficult, but Industry all easy,* as *Poor Richard* says; and *He that riseth late must trot all Day, and shall scarce overtake his Business at Night;* while *Laziness travels so slowly, that Poverty soon overtakes him,* as we read in *Poor Richard,* who adds, *Drive thy Business, let not that drive thee;* and *Early to Bed, and early to rise, makes a Man healthy, wealthy, and wise.*

So what signifies *wishing* and *hoping* for better Times. We may make these Times better, if we bestir ourselves. *Industry need not wish,* as *Poor Richard* says, *and he that lives upon Hope will die fasting. There are no Gains without Pains; then Help Hands, for I have no Lands,* or if I have, they are smartly taxed. Work while it is called To-day, for you know not how much you may be hindered To-morrow, which makes *Poor Richard* say, *One to-day is worth two To-morrows,* and farther, *Have you somewhat to do To-morrow, do it To-day.* If you were a Servant, would you not be ashamed that a good Master should catch you idle? Are you then your own Master, *be ashamed to catch yourself idle,* as *Poor Dick* says. When there is so much to be done for yourself, your family, your Country, and your gracious King, be up by Peep of Day; *Let not the Sun look down and say, Inglorious here he lies. . . .*

Methinks I hear some of you say, *Must a Man afford himself no Leisure?* I will tell thee, my friend, what *Poor Richard* says, *Employ thy Time well, if thou meanest to gain Leisure; and, since thou art not sure of a Minute, throw not away an Hour.* Leisure, is Time for doing something useful; this Leisure the diligent Man will obtain, but the lazy Man never; so that, as *Poor Richard* says *A Life of Leisure and a Life of Laziness are two Things.*

**THE SECOND part of "The Way to Wealth" focuses on the benefits of Frugality.**

*So* much for Industry, my Friends, and Attention to one's own Business; but to these we must add *Frugality,* if we would make our *Industry* more certainly successful. A Man may, if he knows not how to save as he gets, *keep his Nose all his Life to the Grindstone,* and die not worth a *Groat* at last. *A fat Kitchen makes a lean Will,* as *Poor Richard* says; and

> *Many Estates are spent in the Getting,*
> *Since Women for Tea forsook Spinning and Knitting,*
> *And Men for Punch forsook Hewing and Splitting.*

*If you would be wealthy,* says he, in another Almanack, *think of Saving as well as of Getting: The Indies have not made Spain rich, because her Outgoes are greater than her Incomes.*

Away then with your expensive Follies, and you will not then have so much Cause to complain of Hard Times, heavy Taxes, and chargeable Families; for, as *Poor Dick* says,

> *Women and Wine, Game and Deceit,*
> *Make the Wealth small and the Wants great.*

And farther, *What maintains one Vice, would bring up two Children.* You may think perhaps, that a *little* Tea, or a *little* Punch now and then, Diet a *little* more costly, Clothes a *little* finer, and a *little* Entertainment now and then, can be no *great* Matter; but remember what *Poor Richard* says, *Many a Little makes a Mickle;* and farther, Beware of little *Expences; A small Leak will sink a great Ship;* and again, *Who Dainties love, shall Beggars prove;* and moreover, *Fools make Feasts, and wise Men eat them.*

Here you are all got together at this Vendue of *Fineries* and *Knicknacks.* You call them *Goods;* but if you do not take Care, they will prove *Evils* to some of you. Many a one, for the Sake of Finery on the Back, have gone with a hungry Belly, and half-starved their Families. *Silks and Sattins, Scarlet and Velvets,* as *Poor Richard* says, *put out the Kitchen Fire.*

These are not the *Necessaries* of Life; they can scarcely be called the *Conveniences;* and yet only because they look pretty, how many *want* to *have* them! The *artificial* Wants of Mankind thus become more numerous than the *Natural;* and, as *Poor Dick* says, *for one poor Person, there are an hundred indigent.* By these, and other Extravagancies, the Genteel are reduced to poverty, and forced to borrow of those whom they formerly despised, but who through Industry and Frugality have maintained their Standing; in which Case it appears plainly, that *A Ploughman on his Legs is higher than a Gentleman on his Knees,* as *Poor Richard* says. Perhaps they have had a small Estate left them, which they knew not the Getting of; they think, *'tis Day, and will never be Night;* that a little to be spent out of *so much,* is not worth minding; *a Child and a Fool,* as *Poor Richard* says, *imagine Twenty shillings and Twenty Years can never be spent* but, *always taking out of the Meal-tub, and never putting in, soon comes to the bottom;* as *Poor Dick* says, *When the Well's dry, they know the Worth of Water.* But this they might have known before, if they had taken his Advice; *If you would know the Value of Money, go and try to borrow some; for, he that goes a borrowing goes a sorrowing;* and indeed so does he that lends to such People, when he goes *to get it in again. Poor Dick* farther advises, and says,

> *Fond Pride of Dress is sure a very Curse;*
> *E'er Fancy you consult, consult your Purse.*

And again, *Pride is as loud a Beggar as Want, and a great deal more saucy.* When you have bought one fine Thing, you must buy ten more, that your Appearance may be all of a Piece; but *Poor Dick* says, *'Tis easier to suppress the first Desire, than to satisfy all that follow it*. And 'tis as truly Folly for the Poor to ape the Rich, as for the Frog to swell, in order to equal the ox.

> *Great Estates may venture more,*
> *But little Boats should keep near Shore.*

'Tis, however, a Folly soon punished; for *Pride that dines on Vanity, sups on Contempt,* as *Poor Richard* says. And in another Place, *Pride breakfasted with Plenty, dined with Poverty, and supped with Infamy.*

∞

# Thomas Jefferson to Martha Jefferson, *March 28, 1787*

HERE IS Jefferson to Patsy again. She is now fourteen, the oldest of his children and a student in a convent in Paris when Jefferson, detecting a proclivity to idleness in his otherwise perfect daughter, exhorted her to be industrious. He stressed to Patsy the dangers of idleness, urging her to run from it "as you would from the precipice of a gulph." Jefferson told her that the "American character," as opposed to the European, would be one of self-reliance and independence, of finding "means within" ourselves. Industry was an important and necessary "habit" to inculcate for citizens in a country of such vast opportunities.

. . . *It* is your future happiness which interests me, and nothing can contribute more to it (moral rectitude always excepted) than the contracting a habit of industry and activity. Of all the cankers of human happiness, none corrodes it with so silent, yet so baneful a tooth, as indolence. Body and mind both unemployed, our being becomes a burthen, and every object about us loathsome, even the dearest. Idleness begets ennui, ennui the hypochondria, and that a diseased body. No laborious person was ever yet hysterical. Exercise and application produce order in our affairs, health of body, chearfulness of mind, and these make us precious to our friends. It is while we are young that the habit of industry is formed. If not then, it never is afterwards. The fortune of our lives therefore depends on employing well the short period of youth. If at any moment, my dear, you catch yourself in idleness, start from it as you would from the precipice of a gulph. You are not however to consider yourself as unemployed while taking exercise. That is necessary for your health, and health is the first of all objects.

*Thomas Jefferson*

For this reason if you leave your dancing master for the summer, you must increase your other exercise. I do not like your saying that you are unable to read the antient print of your Livy, but with the aid of your master. We are always equal to what we undertake with resolution. A little degree of this will enable you to decypher your Livy. If you always lean on your master, you will never be able to proceed without him. It is a part of the American character to consider nothing as desperate; to surmount every difficulty by resolution and contrivance. In Europe there are shops for every want. It's inhabitants therefore have no idea that their wants can be furnished otherwise. Remote from all other aid, we are obliged to invent and to execute; to find means within ourselves, and not to lean on others. Consider therefore the conquering your Livy as an exercise in the habit of surmounting difficulties, a habit which will be necessary to you in the country where you are to live, and without which you will be thought a very helpless animal, and less esteemed.

I do not doubt either your affection or dispositions. But great exertions are necessary, and you have little time left to make them. Be industrious then, my dear child. Think nothing unsurmountable by resolution and application, and you will be all that I wish you to be.

∞

## Thomas Jefferson to Martha Jefferson, *May 5 and May 21, 1787*

JEFFERSON WROTE several more letters to his fourteen-year-old daughter telling her that industry is "the true secret, the grand recipe for felicity." By applying ourselves to our studies, our work, our hobbies, etc., we become self-reliant. Jefferson thought that if we equip ourselves with talents and skills, we will enjoy life to the fullest.

Jefferson tells Patsy that she should be "always doing."
Jefferson's preoccupation with rooting out idleness in his
daughter might seem strange to us children of the television age. Watching television—a passive activity—can be
entertaining, but I think most of us would agree that it is
not the most rewarding of activities for either the mind or
body or soul and that much of it today is simply degrading.
Whatever television is or is not, it is not "doing."

## MAY 5, 1787

*Determine* never to be idle. No person will have occasion
to complain of the want of time, who never loses any. It is
wonderful how much may be done, if we are always doing.
And that you may be always doing good, my dear, is the ardent
prayer of yours affectionately.

## MAY 21, 1787

*I* expect to be at Paris about the middle of next month. By
that time we may begin to expect our dear Polly. It will be a
circumstance of inexpressible comfort to me to have you both
with me once more. The object most interesting to me for the
residue of my life, will be to see you both developing daily
those principles of virtue and goodness which will make you
valuable to others and happy in yourselves, and acquiring those
talents and that degree of science which will guard you at all
times against ennui, the most dangerous poison of life. A mind
always employed is always happy. This is the true secret, the
grand recipe for felicity. The idle are the only wretched. In a
world which furnishes so many emploiments which are useful,
and so many which are amusing, it is our own fault if we ever
know what ennui is, or if we are ever driven to the miserable
resource of gaming, which corrupts our dispositions, and
teaches us a habit of hostility against all mankind. We are now
entering the port of Toulouse, where I quit my bark; and of

course must conclude my letter. Be good and be industrious, and you will be what I shall most love in this world. Adieu my dear child. Yours affectionately.

∞

## Benjamin Franklin, "Brave Men at Fires," 1733

BENJAMIN FRANKLIN and his fellow members of the Junto Club established Philadelphia's first voluntary fire company. Franklin also founded the first fire insurance company in America to protect homeowners and business-men against fire losses.

The following selection demonstrates that industry is not just a virtue for purely selfish ends. Rather, as Franklin says in this entry, industry makes us "worthy" members of civil society, for it enables us to be of service to our neighbors.

### TO THE PUBLISHER OF THE GAZETTE.

An experienc'd Writer, has said, there was never a great Man that was not an industrious Man, and I believe that there never was a good Man that was a lazy Man. . . .

The brave Men who at Fires are active and speedy with their best Advice and Example, or the Labour of their Hands, are uppermost in my Thoughts. This kind of Industry seems to me a great Virtue. He that is afraid to leave a warm Bed, and to walk in the Dark, and to dawb or tear his Clothes or his Skin; He that makes no Difference between Virtue and Vice, and takes no Pleasure in Hospitality; and He that cares not who suffers, if he himself gains by it, or suffers not; will not any one of them, be industriously concern'd (if their own Dwellings are out of Danger) in preserving from devouring Flames either private or publick Buildings.

But how pleasing must it be to a thinking Man to observe, that not a Fire happens in this Town, but soon after it is seen and cry'd out, the Place is crowded by active Men of different Ages, Professions and Titles; who, as of one Mind and Rank, apply themselves with all Vigilance and Resolution, according to their Abilities, to the hard Work of conquering the increasing Fire. Some of the chiefest in Authority, and numbers of good Housekeepers, are ever ready, not only to direct but to labour, and are not seen to shun Parts or Places the most hazardous; and Others who having scarce a Coat in the World besides that on their Backs, will venture that, and their Limbs, in saving of Goods surrounded with Fire, and in rending off flaming Shingles. They do it not for Sake of Reward of Money or Fame: There is no Provision of either made for them. But they have a Reward in themselves, and they love one another. . . .

Ye Men of Courage, Industry, and Goodness, continue thus in well doing; and if you grow not ostentatious, it will be thought by every good Man who sees your Performances; here are brave Men, Men of Spirit and Humanity, good Citizens, or Neighbours, capable and worthy of civil Society, and the Enjoyment of a happy Government.

## Samuel Adams to John Scollay, December 30, 1780

SAMUEL ADAMS, second cousin of John Adams, lived by the same austere principles that he preached to others. As a young man, he had been inspired by the sermons of George Whitefield, the leading preacher of America's First Great Awakening, enjoining listeners to lead a life of piety and simplicity. Though Adams's father was a prosperous man who bequeathed to Sam his malt company, Adams displayed little skill or concern for making money. He wore the same old wig and shabby red suit and coat every day. When he was elected as a Massachusetts delegate to the First Continental Congress, his friends worried that he would make a bad impression and not be as influential. Thus the men and women of Boston outfitted Adams with a new suit, a new wig and hat, six pairs of the best silk hose, six pairs of new shoes, and even gave him some spending money. Off he went, looking brand new.

Adams's austerity was not the general rule for most of the Founders, and Adams sometimes carried things a little too far. Still, the sentiments he expresses are not without foundation—in all our affluence, it's not a bad idea to be reminded every now and then that a republican form of government presupposes much more of its citizens than any other form of government. And the "more" it presupposes comes from the inside, not the outside.

*Our* Government, I perceive, is organizd on the Basis of the new Constitution. I am affraid there is more Pomp & Parade than is consistent with those sober Republican Principles, upon which the Framers of it thought they had founded it. Why should this new Œra be introducd with Entertainments expensive & tending to dissipate the Minds of the People? Does it become us to lead the People to such publick Diversions as promote Superfluity of Dress & Ornament, when it is as much as they can bear to support the Expense of cloathing a naked Army? Will Vanity & Levity ever be the Stability of Government, either in States, in Cities, or what, let me hint to you is of the last Importance, in *Families?* Of what Kind are those Manners, by which, as we are truly informed in a late Speech, "not only the freedom but the very Existence of Republicks is greatly affected?" How fruitless is it, to recommend "the adapting the Laws in the most perfect Manner possible, to the Suppression of Idleness Dissipation & Extravagancy," if such Recommendations are counteracted by the Example of Men of Religion, Influence & publick Station? It was asked in the Reign of Charles the 2d of England, How shall we turn the Minds of the People from an Attention to their Liberties? The Answer was, by making them extravagant, luxurious, effeminate.

*Samuel Adams*

## Noah Webster, "Advice to the Young," 1834

THE "love of finery," Webster points out, can be found in all peoples and all countries. Still, Webster believed that

Americans live in a different kind of country, a country that depends on republican simplicity.

*In* your mode of living, be not ambitious of adopting every extravagant fashion. Many fashions are not only inconvenient and expensive, but inconsistent with good taste. The love of finery is of savage origin; the rude inhabitant of the forest delights to deck his person with pieces of shining metal, with painted feathers, and with some appendage dangling from the ears or nose. The same love of finery infects civilized men and women, more or less, in every country, and the body is adorned with brilliant gems and gaudy attire. But true taste demands great simplicity of dress. A well made person is one of the most beautiful of all God's works, and a simple neat dress, displays this person to the best advantage.

∾

## George Washington to Bushrod Washington, January 15, 1783

ONE OF the wealthiest of the Founders, Washington took the time at the closing of the Revolutionary War to urge plain dress and discipline in his favorite nephew, Bushrod. One of Washington's biographers, Washington Irving, wrote that Washington wore a plain, brown "homespun" suit to his first inauguration as president. When Lafayette sent Washington the keys to the Bastille as a present, he sent a pair of simple silver shoe buckles to reciprocate. Certainly republicanism is modest dress. Yet, not all the founders agreed: John Hancock dressed like a peacock in Boston, while John Adams wore a silk suit with a sword dangling from the side to his inauguration.

As Washington says, expensive clothes do not make the man. Some great men dressed up, some down.

*Dear* Bushrod: You will be surprized perhaps at receiving a letter from me; but if the end is answered for which it is written, I shall not think my time miss-spent.

Your Father, who seems to entertain a very favorable opinion of your prudence, and I hope you merit it: in one or two of his letters to me, speaks of the difficulty he is under to make you remittances. Whether this arises from the scantiness of his funds, or the extensiveness of your demands, is matter of conjecture, with me. I hope it is not the latter, because common prudence, and every other consideration which ought to have weight in a reflecting mind is opposed to your requiring more than his conveniency and a regard to his other Children will enable him to pay; and because he holds up no idea in his Letter, which would support me in the conclusion. Yet when I take a view of the inexperience of Youth, the temptations in, and vices of Cities; and the distresses to which our Virginia Gentlemen are driven by an accumulation of Taxes and the want of a market; I am almost inclined to ascribe it, in part to both. Therefore, as a friend, I give you the following advice.

Let the object, which carried you to Philadelphia, be always before your Eyes; remember, that it is not the mere study of the Law, but to become eminent in the Profession of it which is to yield honor and profit; the first was your choice, let the second be your ambition, and that dissipation is incompatible with both. . . .

Do not conceive that fine Clothes make fine Men, any more than fine feathers make fine Birds. A plain genteel dress is more admired and obtains more credit than lace and embroidery in the Eyes of the judicious and sensible.

❧

## *Thomas Jefferson to Martha Jefferson Randolph, January 5, 1808*

JEFFERSON EXHORTED frugal living to his daughters, but for Jefferson himself, this precept did not translate into practice. It is well known that Jefferson died heavily in debt—at his death, his debt would be the equivalent of several million dollars today. Part of his financial woes was due to his indulgences in books, fine wines, and upkeep and remodeling of Monticello. However, some of his financial troubles can be traced to events beyond his control, i.e., the devaluation of the currency during the Revolutionary War; a debt he inherited from his father-in-law; a $20,000 defaulted loan he had co-signed for a friend; and simple bad luck at farming. Jefferson also believed that years of public service, which had taken him away from managing his farm, contributed to his plight.

Whatever the case, these debts "overwhelmed" Jefferson, who viewed them as "a deadly blast of all my peace of mind during my remaining days."

*But* I know nothing more important to inculcate into the minds of young people than the wisdom, the honor, and the blessed comfort of living within their income, to calculate in good time how much less pain will cost them the plainest stile of living which keeps them out of debt, than after a few years of splendor above their income, to have their property taken away for debt when they have a family growing up to maintain and provide for. Lessons enough are before their eyes, among their nearest acquaintances if they will but contemplate and bring the examples home to themselves. Still there is another evil against which we cannot guard, unthrifty marriages; because characters are not known until they are tried. But even here, a wife imbued with principles of prudence, may go far towards arresting or lessening the evils of an improvident management. In your moralising conversations with your children, I have no doubt you endeavor to warn them against the rocks on which they see so many shipwrecked. Altho we cannot expect that none of our posterity are to become the victims of imprudence or misfortune, yet we cannot but be particularly anxious to ward off the evil from those in present being, who having been brought up in our bosoms, cannot suffer without our own suffering equally.

*Benjamin Franklin*

∞

## *Benjamin Franklin,* Autobiography

BENJAMIN FRANKLIN recalls in his *Autobiography* how he made it big. His success depended much on his own initiative and industry but also on his supportive wife. Here, Franklin shares a charming anecdote about his wife's introduction of "luxury" into their family. As we say in today's idiom, "It happens." This in many families is indeed the way of the world.

. . . *We* have an English proverb that says, "He that would thrive, must ask his wife." It was lucky for me that I had one as much disposed to industry and frugality as myself. She assisted me cheerfully in my business, folding and stitching pamphlets, tending shop, purchasing old linen rags for the paper-makers, etc., etc. We kept no idle servants, our table was plain and simple, our furniture of the cheapest. For instance, my breakfast was a long time bread and milk (no tea), and I ate it out of a twopenny earthen porringer, with a pewter spoon. But mark how luxury will enter families, and make a progress in spite of principle: being called one morning to breakfast, I found it in a china bowl, with a spoon of silver! They had been bought for me without my knowledge by my wife, and had cost her the enormous sum of three-and-twenty shillings, for which she had no other excuse or apology to make, but that she thought *her* husband deserved a silver spoon and china bowl as well as any of his neighbors. This was the first appearance of plate and china in our house, which afterward, in a course of years, as our wealth increased, augmented gradually to several hundred pounds in value.

∞

## "To Be Useful Even After My Death," Benjamin Franklin's Philanthropy, 1790–1990

*We* began this chapter with Benjamin Franklin's humble entry into the city of Philadelphia. Franklin, who ran away from his home in Boston and arrived in Philadelphia in 1723 with only a few coins in his pocket, died a very wealthy man. Through industry and frugality, he amassed a large fortune. At his death in 1790, he owned numerous properties in Philadelphia, a home in Boston, pasture lands outside Philadelphia, and land in Georgia, Nova Scotia, and elsewhere. When he died, his estate was worth over $250,000—by today's dollars, that makes him the equivalent of a millionaire, several times over.

Franklin never forgot the "kind loans" two friends gave him as a young man which, he noted, served as "the foundation of my fortune." To give other young people the start of their fortune—"to be useful even after my death if possible" as he put it in a codicil to his will—he bequeathed trust funds of 1,000 pounds each to his hometown of Boston and his adopted town of Philadelphia. Franklin instructed that loans were to be made to married craftsmen, under the age of twenty-five years. He required that these craftsmen must have fulfilled their apprenticeships and obtained the recommendations of respectable citizens vouching for their good moral character. Under Franklin's plan, loans would be made at a 5 percent interest. It was his hope that the trust would "be continually augmented by the interest" and would grow over the next one hundred years, even two hundred years.

Franklin calculated that each fund would be worth 131,000 pounds after one hundred years, at which time, he instructed that 100,000 pounds of the fund be invested in public works projects, such as roads, bridges, and in Philadelphia, making the Schuykill River navigable. The remaining 31,000 pounds would continue to be loaned at interest. At the end of two hundred years, Franklin instructed that the sum was to be divided between the town of Boston and the state of Massachusetts; and similarly, between Philadelphia and the state of Pennsylvania. He didn't leave any more explicit instructions, "not presuming to carry my views farther," he wrote.

In 1990, two hundred years after his death, the two trust funds were worth 6.5 million dollars. And some of this money was designated to be used as grants to help young people learn a trade or craft, young people, who, like Franklin in 1723, are eager to make good in life.

VI

# Justice

❧

*The* pledge of allegiance ends by proclaiming "liberty and justice for all." James Madison once wrote that "justice is the end of government." Justice is one of the most important, if not the most important, virtues for a political community. But what is justice? This is a question that has occupied philosophers and sages since the beginning of time. It is a question that the Founders asked themselves in building the institutions of American democracy.

In an ideal community there would be no need for justice because everybody would get along well and respect each other's person and property. Instead of rules of justice, friendship and mutual cooperation would resolve any disagreements or disputes that may arise. However, we do not live in an ideal world. Without rules, even good friends would find it difficult to avoid disagreements and hurt feelings. So justice is important to a community.

The Founders envisioned a generous principle of justice that would satisfy a large and diverse group of citizens. The Founders' idea of justice was universal, meaning that it applied to all people, no matter their religious or ethnic or racial background. To find the Founders' understanding of justice, it is helpful to begin with the Declaration of Independence. The Declaration states that it is a "self-evident" truth that all humans are created equal and are endowed with certain "unalienable rights" to life, liberty, and the pursuit of happiness. According to the Declaration, these rights are given to us not by a king but from God and the Laws of Nature. Thus these rights are sacred and belong to all human beings of all times and places. In sum, American justice is based on equality and merit—no one is entitled to any special treatment or unfair treatment because of one's birth or background. The Founders wrote the Constitution and the Bill of Rights in order to secure these rights through the establishment of a constitutional government.

The Founders did something new. Most countries were ruled by kings and monarchs and were based on the premise that we are *not* equal. In such countries, the wealthy few or the strong were more equal than others. Power was often arbitrary, meaning that rules varied, depending on the whims of the rulers and those with power. In many of these same countries, religious persecution was widespread. An individual was often punished, even killed, if he did not belong to the right religious sect or if he expressed an opinion criticizing those in power.

Our first immigrants came to America to escape such religious and political persecution. Unfortunately, some came as slaves. Even Thomas Jefferson, who drafted the Declaration of Independence, was a slave holder. But there were also Founders who opposed slavery, such as Alexander Hamilton, Benjamin Franklin, John Jay, Benjamin Rush, and John Adams, to name a few. Readings in this chapter explore the Founders' struggle with the problem of slavery. They knew the institution of slavery was at odds with the principles of justice that they cherished. And in fact, though they did not abolish slavery immediately, they gave us the great charter—the Declaration of Independence and the Constitution—that put slavery on the path of eventual extinction.

James Madison, who drafted the Bill of Rights, wrote that justice will always "be pursued, until it be obtained, or until liberty be lost in the pursuit." The story of America is the pursuit of the highest ideal of justice the world has ever seen.

∞

## "An Expression of the American Mind"
## Thomas Jefferson to Henry Lee,
## May 8, 1825

NEARLY FIFTY years after the fact, Jefferson explained to soldier and statesman Henry "Light-Horse Harry" Lee what he intended when he wrote the Declaration of Independence. Here is, arguably, the most consequential political document in the world described as just good old American common sense.

. . . *This* was the object of the Declaration of Independence. Not to find out new principles, or new arguments, never before thought of, not merely to say things which had never been said before; but to place before mankind the common sense of the subject, in terms so plain and firm as to command their assent, and to justify ourselves in the independent stand we are compelled to take. Neither aiming at originality of principle or sentiment, nor yet copied from any particular and previous writing, it was intended to be an expression of the American mind, and to give to that expression the proper tone and spirit called for by the occasion. All its authority rests then on the harmonizing sentiments of the day, whether expressed in conversation, in letters, printed essays, or in the elementary books of public right, as Aristotle, Cicero, Locke, Sidney, etc. . . .

∞

## "Justice Is the End of Government"
## James Madison, Federalist No. 51

THE FOUNDERS believed that it is not enough that government be democratic; they believed that government must also respect the rights and protect the liberties of the people. That is justice. This is Madison's classic statement of this position.

*Justice* is the end of government. It is the end of civil society. It ever has been, and ever will be pursued, until it be obtained, or until liberty be lost in the pursuit. In a society under the forms of which the stronger faction can readily unite and oppress the weaker, anarchy may as truly be said to reign, as in a state of nature where the weaker individual is not secured against the violence of the stronger: And as in the latter state even the stronger individuals are prompted by the uncertainy of their condition, to submit to a government which may protect the weak as well as themselves: So in the former state, will the more powerful factions or parties be gradually induced by a like motive, to wish for a government which will protect all parties, the weaker as well as the more powerful.

∞

## George Mason,
## Virginia Declaration of Rights,
## January 1776

VIRGINIANS PLAYED a most decisive role in the founding of America—we often think of George Washington, Thomas Jefferson, James Madison, and Patrick Henry as the

most prominent of her sons. But we shouldn't forget
George Mason, a wealthy Virginia planter and self-educated
lawyer, who wrote a Bill of Rights for the Virginia Constitution that served as a model for the Declaration of Independence and the Bill of Rights of the Constitution. Mason's
Declaration of Rights not only stipulates the rights of free
government but also the requirements of free government
—that is, citizens with a "firm adherence to Justice, Moderation, Temperance, Frugality, and Virtue."

*A* declaration of rights made by the Representatives of the
good people of Virginia, assembled in full and free Convention;
which rights do pertain to them and their posterity, as the basis
and foundation of Government.

That all men are by nature equally free and independent, and
have certain inherent rights, of which, when they enter into a
state of society, they cannot, by any compact, deprive or divest
their posterity; namely, the enjoyment of life and liberty, with
the means of acquiring and possessing property, and pursuing
and obtaining happiness and safety.

That all power is vested in, and consequently derived from,
the People; that magistrates are their trustees and servants, and
at all times amenable to them.

That Government is, or ought to be, instituted for the common benefit, protection, and security of the people, nation, or
community;—of all the various modes and forms of Government that is best which is capable of producing the greatest
degree of happiness and safety, and is most effectually secured
against the danger of mal-administration;—and that, whenever
any Government shall be found inadequate or contrary to these
purposes, a majority of the community hath an indubitable,
unalienable, and indefeasible right, to reform, alter, or abolish
it, in such manner as shall be judged most conducive to the
publick weal.

*George Mason*

That no man, or set of men, are entitled to exclusive or separate emoluments and privileges from the community, but in consideration of publick services; which, not being descendible, neither ought the offices of Magistrate, Legislator, or Judge, to be hereditary. . . .

That no free Government, or the blessing of liberty, can be preserved to any people but by a firm adherence to justice, moderation, temperance, frugality, and virtue, and by frequent recurrence to fundamental principles.

That Religion, or the duty which we owe to our *Creator,* and the manner of discharging it, can be directed only by reason and conviction, not by force or violence; and, therefore, all men are equally entitled to the free exercise of religion, according to the dictates of conscience; and that it is the mutual duty of all to practice Christian forbearance, love, and charity, towards each other.

∽

## James Madison, "The Greatest Trust Ever Confided to a Political Society," Address to the States, April 25, 1783

MADISON BELIEVED that the future of free government depends upon America's success. Either the "rights of human nature" will be vindicated on the American stage or lost forever.

*Let* it be remembered finally that it has ever been the pride and boast of America, that the rights for which she contended were the rights of human nature. By the blessing of the Author of these rights on the means exerted for their defence, they have prevailed against all opposition and form the basis of thirteen independant States. No instance has heretofore occurred, nor can any instance be expected hereafter to occur, in which the unadulterated forms of Republican Government can pretend to so fair an opportunity of justifying themselves by their fruits. In this view the Citizens of the U.S. are responsible for the greatest trust ever confided to a Political Society. If justice, good faith, honor, gratitude & all the other Qualities which enoble the character of a nation, and fulfil the ends of Government, be the fruits of our establishments, the cause of liberty will acquire a dignity and lustre, which it has never yet enjoyed; and an example will be set which can not but have the most favorable influence on the rights of mankind. If on the other side, our Governments should be unfortunately blotted with the reverse of these cardinal and essential Virtues, the great cause which we have engaged to vindicate, will be dishonored & betrayed; the last & fairest experiment in favor of the rights of human nature will be turned against them; and their patrons & friends exposed to be insulted & silenced by the votaries of Tyranny and Usurpation.

By order of the United States in Congress assembled.

## *Thomas Paine,* Common Sense

MANY AMERICAN colonists were very hesitant to break free from their mother country. They had a strong sentimental attachment to Great Britain. Moreover, many wondered how they could govern themselves without the king's guidance. Thomas Paine's pamphlet, *Common Sense,* published in January of 1776, made the case for independence in plain language that ordinary people could understand. It circulated widely throughout the colonies and was highly effective in winning the public over to the side of independence. In *Common Sense,* Paine opposed the idea that kings were entitled to rule over others. He argued that Americans could "begin the world over again" by demonstrating that the people could govern themselves.

Many editions of *Common Sense* were reprinted until nearly half a million copies were sold. But Paine did not make any money off the book. He donated all his profits to the Continental Congress in order to support the cause for independence.

### THOUGHTS ON THE PRESENT STATE OF AMERICAN AFFAIRS

*In* the following pages I offer nothing more than simple facts, plain arguments, and common sense; and have no other preliminaries to settle with the reader, than that he will divest himself of prejudice and prepossession, and suffer his reason and his feelings to determine for themselves; that he will put *on,* or rather that he will not put *off,* the true character of a man, and generously enlarge his views beyond the present day.

The sun never shined on a cause of greater worth. 'Tis not the affair of a city, a country, a province, or a kingdom, but of a continent—of at least one eighth part of the habitable globe. 'Tis not the concern of a day, a year, or an age; posterity are virtually involved in the contest, and will be more or less affected, even to the end of time, by the proceedings now. Now is the seed time of continental union, faith and honor. The least fracture now will be like a name engraved with the point of a pin on the tender rind of a young oak; the wound will enlarge with the tree, and posterity read it in full grown characters.

As much hath been said of the advantages of reconciliation, which, like an agreeable dream, hath passed away and left us as we were, it is but right, that we should examine the contrary side of the argument, and inquire into some of the many material injuries which these colonies sustain, and always will sustain, by being connected with, and dependant on Great-Britain. To examine that connexion and dependance, on the principles of nature and common sense, to see what we have to trust to, if separated, and what we are to expect, if dependant.

I have heard it asserted by some, that as America hath flourished under her former connexion with Great-Britain, that the same connexion is necessary towards her future happiness, and will always have the same effect. Nothing can be more fallacious than this kind of argument. We may as well assert that because a child has thrived upon milk, that it is never to have meat, or that the first twenty years of our lives is to become a precedent for the next twenty. But even this is admitting more than is true, for I answer roundly, that America would have flourished as much, and probably much more, had no European power had any thing to do with her.

But Britain is the parent country, say some. Then the more

shame upon her conduct. Even brutes do not devour their young, nor savages make war upon their families; wherefore the assertion, if true, turns to her reproach; but it happens not to be true, or only partly so, and the phrase *parent* or *mother country* hath been jesuitically adopted by the king and his parasites, with a low papistical design of gaining an unfair bias on the credulous weakness of our minds. Europe, and not England, is the parent country of America. This new world hath been the asylum for the persecuted lovers of civil and religious liberty from *every part* of France. Hither have they fled, not from the tender embraces of the mother, but from the cruelty of the monster; and it is so far true of England, that the same tyranny which drove the first emigrants from home, pursues their descendants still.

But where says some is the King of America? I'll tell you Friend, he reigns above, and doth not make havoc of mankind like the Royal Brute of Britain. Yet that we may not appear to be defective even in earthly honors, let a day be solemnly set apart for proclaiming the charter; let it be brought forth placed on the divine law, the word of God; let a crown be placed thereon, by which the world may know, that so far as we approve of monarchy, that in America THE LAW IS KING. For as in absolute governments the King is law, so in free countries the law *ought* to be King; and there ought to be no other. But lest any ill use should afterwards arise, let the crown at the conclusion of the ceremony be demolished, and scattered among the people whose right it is.

O ye that love mankind! Ye that dare oppose, not only the tyranny, but the tyrant, stand forth! Every spot of the old world is overrun with oppression. Freedom hath been hunted round the globe. Asia, and Africa, have long expelled her—Europe regards her like a stranger, and England hath given her warning to depart. O! receive the fugitive, and prepare in time an asylum for mankind.

I shall conclude these remarks, with the following timely and well intended hints. We ought to reflect, that there are three different ways, by which an independancy may hereafter be effected; and that *one* of those *three*, will one day or other, be the fate of America, viz. By the legal voice of the people in Congress; by a military power; or by a mob: It may not always happen that our soldiers are citizens, and the multitude a body of reasonable men; virtue, as I have already remarked, is not hereditary, neither is it perpetual. Should an independancy be brought about by the first of those means, we have every opportunity and every encouragement before us, to form the noblest purest constitution on the face of the earth. We have it in our power to begin the world over again. A situation, similar to the present, hath not happened since the days of Noah until now. The birthday of a new world is at hand, and a race of men, perhaps as numerous as all Europe contains, are to receive their portion of freedom from the event of a few months. The Reflexion is awful—and in this point of view, How trifling, how ridiculous, do the little, paltry cavellings, of a few weak or interested men appear, when weighed against the business of a world.

## "We Are Acting for All Mankind"
### Thomas Jefferson to Dr. Joseph Priestley, June 19, 1802

LIKE MADISON and Paine, Jefferson is well aware that he and others were acting not only for America but for the entire world as well. It is up to Americans to show the world that self-government is a viable alternative to the despotism and tyrannics of the past. If we succeed, the world will follow.

*In* the great work which has been effected in America, no individual has a right to take any great share to himself. Our people in a body are wise, because they are under the unrestrained and unperverted operation of their own understanding. Those whom they have assigned to the direction of their affairs, have stood with a pretty even front. If any one of them was withdrawn, many others entirely equal, have been ready to fill his place with as good abilities. A nation, composed of such materials, and free in all its members from distressing wants, furnishes hopeful implements for the interesting experiment of self-government; and we feel that we are acting under obligations not confined to the limits of our own society. It is impossible not to be sensible that we are acting for all mankind; that circumstances denied to others, but indulged to us, have imposed on us the duty of proving what is the degree of freedom and self-government in which a society may venture to leave its individual members. . . .

✎

## "That Diabolical, Hell-conceived Principle of Persecution"
### James Madison to William Bradford, Jr., January 24, 1774

JAMES MADISON was a member of the Episcopalian Church, which happened to be the established church of Virginia. Yet, having witnessed the persecution and eventual imprisonment of a half-dozen Baptist preachers in Culpeper, Virginia, Madison, just out of Princeton College, wrote this letter to his good friend, William Bradford, Jr., to share his outrage. While this sort of religious persecution might be common in the Old World, Madison was impatient with its presence in the colonies.

From an early age then, Madison dedicated his life to

making America, in his words, an "asylum to the perse-cuted and oppressed of every nation and religion." Madison wrote the First Amendment guaranteeing religious liberty to all Americans.

. . . *I* have indeed as good an atmosphere at home as the climate will allow; but have nothing to brag of as the state and liberty of my country. Poverty and luxury prevail among all sorts; pride, ignorance, and knavery among the priesthood, and vice and wickedness among the laity. This is bad enough, but it is not the worst I have to tell you. That diabolical, hell-conceived principle of persecution rages among some; and to their eternal infamy, the clergy can furnish their quota of imps for such business. This vexes me the worst of anything what-ever. There are at this time in the adjacent country not less than five or six well-meaning men in close jail for publishing their religious sentiments, which in the main are very orthodox. I have neither patience to hear, talk, or think of anything relative to this matter; for I have squabbled and scolded, abused and ridiculed, so long about it to little purpose, that I am without common patience. So I must beg you to pity me, and pray for liberty of conscience to all.

❧

## Thomas Jefferson,
## "A Bill for Establishing Religious Freedom"

IN 1779, Jefferson introduced this bill into the Virginia General Assembly, but it was not enacted until 1786. That year, Jefferson was serving as a diplomat in Paris, so his friend and collaborator, James Madison, led the way for the bill's passage. Upon reflection many years later in 1819, Madison wrote to Jefferson: "It was the universal opinion of the century preceding the last that civil government could not stand without the prop of a religious establishment, and that the Christian religion itself, would perish if not supported by a legal provision for its clergy. The experience of Virginia consciously corroborates the disproof of both opinions."

Jefferson was so proud of this bill that he listed it, along with his authorship of the Declaration of Independence and his establishment of the University of Virginia, on his tombstone.

*Well* aware that the opinions and belief of men depend not on their own will, but follow involuntarily the evidence proposed to their minds; that Almighty God hath created the mind free, *and manifested his supreme will that free it shall remain by making it altogether insusceptible of restraint;* that all attempts to influence it by temporal punishments, or burthens, or by civil incapacitations, tend only to beget habits of hypocrisy and meanness, and are a departure from the plan of the holy author of our religion, who being lord both of body and mind, yet chose not to propagate it by coercions on either, as was in his Almighty power to do, *but to extend it by its influence on reason alone* that the impious presumption of legislators and rulers, civil as well as ecclesiastical, who, being themselves but fallible and uninspired men, have assumed dominion over the faith of others, setting up their own opinions and modes of thinking as the only true and infallible, and as such endeavoring to impose them on others, hath established and maintained false religions over the greatest part of the world and through all time: That to compel a man to furnish contributions of money for the propagation of opinions which he disbelieves *and abhors,* is sinful and tyrannical: that our civil rights have no dependance on our religious opinions, any more than our opinions in physics or geometry; that therefore the proscribing any citizen as unworthy the public confidence by laying upon him an incapacity of being called to offices of trust and emolument, unless he profess or renounce this or that religious opinion, is depriving him injuriously of those privileges and advantages to which, in common with his fellow citizens, he has a natural right; that it tends also to corrupt the principles of that *very* religion it is meant to encourage, by bribing, with a monopoly of worldly honours and emoluments, those who will externally profess and conform to it; *that the opinions of men are not the object of civil government, nor under its jurisdiction;* that it is time enough for the rightful purposes of civil government for its officers to interfere when principles break out into overt acts against peace and good order; and finally, that truth is great and will prevail if left to herself; that she is the

*Thomas Jefferson*

proper and sufficient antagonist to error, and has nothing to fear from the conflict unless by human interposition disarmed of her natural weapons, free argument and debate; errors ceasing to be dangerous when it is permitted freely to contradict them.

*We the General Assembly of Virginia do enact* that no man shall be compelled to frequent or support any religious worship, place, or ministry whatsoever, nor shall be enforced, restrained, molested, or burthened in his body or goods, nor shall otherwise suffer, on account of his religious opinions or belief; but that all men shall be free to profess, and by argument to maintain, their opinions in matters of religion, and that the same shall in no wise diminish, enlarge, or affect their civil capacities.

∞

## George Washington to the Hebrew Congregation of Newport, Rhode Island, September 9, 1790

MEMBERS OF the Newport Hebrew Congregation wrote the president to congratulate George Washington on his presidency and to "reflect on those days . . . of difficulty and danger, when the God of Israel, who delivered David from the peril of the sword, shielded [Washington's] head in the day of battle. . . ."

In his beautiful reply, Washington set forth the American principle of religious liberty: Here no one sect "tolerated" another—here we were all, Jews and Christians, equally Americans, and here "there shall be none to make him afraid." What a promise! How rarely, in the story of inhumanity and misery that is history, has this promise been realized.

*Gentlemen,* While I receive with much satisfaction, your Address replete with expressions of affection and esteem, I rejoice in the opportunity of assuring you, that I shall always retain a grateful remembrance of the cordial welcome I experienced in my visit to Newport, from all classes of citizens.

The reflection on the days of difficulty and danger which are past, is rendered the more sweet, from a consciousness that they are succeeded by days of uncommon prosperity and security. If we have wisdom to make the best use of the advantages with which we are now favored, we cannot fail, under the just administration of a good government, to become a great and a happy people.

The citizens of the United States of America, have a right to applaud themselves for having given to mankind examples of an enlarged and liberal policy—a policy worthy of imitation. ALL possess alike liberty of conscience, and immunities of citizenship. It is now no more that toleration is spoken of, as if it was by the indulgence of one class of people, that another enjoyed the exercise of their inherent natural rights. For happily the government of the United States, which gives to bigotry no sanction—to persecution no assistance, requires only that they who live under its protection should demean themselves as good citizens, in giving it on all occasions their effectual support.

It would be inconsistent with the frankness of my character not to avow, that I am pleased with your favorable opinion of my administration, and fervent wishes for my felicity. May the Children of the Stock of Abraham, who dwell in this land, continue to merit and enjoy the good-will of the other inhabitants; while every one shall sit in safety under his own vine and fig tree, and there shall be none to make him afraid. May the Father of all mercies scatter light and not darkness in our paths, and make us all in our several vocations useful here, and in his own due time and way everlastingly happy.

∞

## George Washington, To the Roman Catholics in the United States of America, March 15, 1790

IT IS fitting that the first president, a Protestant, wrote letters to both Jews and Catholics assuring them of the same blessings in America and so to all of all faiths.

*The* prospect of national prosperity now before us is truly animating, and ought to excite the exertions of all good men to establish and secure the happiness of their country, in the permanent duration of its freedom and independence. America, under the smiles of a Divine Province, the protection of a good government, and the cultivation of manners, morals, and piety, cannot fail of attaining an uncommon degree of eminence, in literature, commerce, agriculture, improvements at home and respectability abroad.

As mankind become more liberal they will be more apt to allow that all those who conduct themselves as worthy members of the community are equally entitled to the protection of civil government. I hope ever to see America among the foremost nations in examples of justice and liberality. And I presume that your fellow-citizens will not forget the patriotic part which you took in the accomplishment of their Revolution, and the establishment of their government; or the important assistance which they received from a nation in which the Roman Catholic faith is professed.

I thank you, gentlemen, for your kind concern for me. While my life and my health shall continue, in whatever situation I may be, it shall be my constant endeavour to justify the favourable sentiments which you are pleased to express of my conduct. And may the members of your society in America, animated alone by the pure spirit of Christianity, and still conducting themselves as the faithful subjects of our free government, enjoying every temporal and spiritual felicity.

## James Madison's Letters to Dr. Jacob de la Motta

JACOB DE la Motta played an active role in building a synagogue in Savannah, Georgia. He gave an address at the dedication of the new synagogue, which he sent to James Madison and Thomas Jefferson. Madison gave classic expression to the American principle of toleration: "Equal laws, protecting equal rights" secure all that is good — the rights of conscience, a loyal citizenry, and goodwill among all.

TO DR DE LA MOTTA
MONTPELLIER, AUGUST 1820

*Sir;*—I have received your letter of the 7th instant, with the Discourse delivered at the Consecration of the Hebrew Synagogue at Savannah, for which you will please to accept my thanks.

The history of the Jews must forever be interesting. The modern part of it is, at the same time, so little generally known, that every ray of light on the subject has its value.

Among the features peculiar to the political system of the United States, is the perfect equality of rights which it secures to every religious sect. And it is particularly pleasing to observe in the good citizenship of such as have been most distrusted and oppressed elsewhere a happy illustration of the safety and success of this experiment of a just and benignant policy. Equal laws, protecting equal rights, are found, as they ought to be presumed, the best guarantee of loyalty and love of country; as well as best calculated to cherish that mutual respect and good will among citizens of every religious denomination which are necessary to social harmony, and most favorable to the advancement of truth. The account you give of the Jews of your congregation brings them fully within the scope of these observations.

∞

## James Madison, "A Property in Our Rights," National Gazette, *March 29, 1792*

**IT IS well known, of course, that every American has a right to life, liberty, and *property*. But property meant more to the founders than a plot of land or a piece of merchandise. "In its larger and juster meaning," Madison explains, it embraces our opinions and especially our religious opinions. Ultimately, it is for the protection of these spiritual goods that humans institute government.**

*This* term [property] in its particular application means "that domination which one man claims and exercises over the external things of the world, in exclusion of every other individual."

In its larger and juster meaning, it embraces every thing to which a man may attach a value and have a right; and *which leaves to every one else the like advantage.*

In the former sense, a man's land, or merchandize, or money is called his property.

In the latter sense, a man has property in his opinions and the free communication of them.

He has a property of peculiar value in his religious opinions, and in the profession and practice dictated by them.

He has property very dear to him in the safety and liberty of his person.

He has an equal property in the free use of his faculties and free choice of the objects on which to employ them.

In a word, as a man is said to have a right to his property, he may be equally said to have a property in his rights.

Where an excess of power prevails, property of no sort is duly respected. No man is safe in his opinions, his person, his faculties or his possessions.

Where there is an excess of liberty, the effect is the same, tho' from an opposite cause.

Government is instituted to protect property of every sort; as well that which lies in the various rights of individuals, as that which the term particularly expresses. This being the end of government, that alone is a *just* government, which *impartially* secures to every man, whatever is his *own.* . . .

Conscience is the most sacred of all property; other property depending in part on positive law, the exercise of that, being a natural and inalienable right. To guard a man's house as his castle, to pay public and enforce private debts with the most exact faith, can give no title to invade a man's conscience which is more sacred than his castle. . . .

If there be a government then which prides itself on maintaining the inviolability of property; which provides that none shall be taken *directly* even for public use without indemnification to the owner, and yet *directly* violates the property which individuals have in their opinions, their religion, their persons, and their faculties; nay more, which *indirectly* violates their property, in their actual possessions, in the labor that acquires their daily subsistence, and in the hallowed remnant of time which ought to relieve their fatigues and soothe their cares, the inference will have been anticipated, that such a government is not a pattern for the United States.

If the United States mean to obtain or deserve the full praise due to wise and just governments, they will equally respect the rights of property, and the property in rights.

⚬

## *James Madison,* Federalist No. 10, *November 22, 1787*

THE ANTI-FEDERALISTS, who opposed the Constitution, thought that the country was too vast, and the population too large, to sustain a republican form of government. The French philosopher Montesquieu had taught that republics thrive in small territories with a basically homogenous population, with citizens holding similar opinions and sentiments. As Brutus, the pen name of one of the leading Anti-Federalists, wrote, "History furnishes no example of a free republic, any thing like the extent of the United States."

In an original and enduring contribution to modern political science, Madison argued in *Federalist 10* that an extended republic was not only possible but desirable. One of the greatest problems that threatened the stability of small republics throughout history had been factions. These factions were made up of a large group of citizens with similar interests who, through sheer numbers and force, would oppress the minority.

But Madison viewed the potential size and diversity of the United States as a strength, not a weakness, in that they solved the problem of factionalism. In a large republic, there would be a diversity of interests, guaranteeing that there would not be a permanent majority capable of oppressing others. In other words, everyone, at some time or another, would be in the "minority" given the wide range of interests possible in such a large and diverse nation. Each faction would cancel the other one out.

*Among* the numerous advantages promised by a well constructed Union, none deserves to be more accurately developed than its tendency to break and control the violence of faction. The friend of popular governments, never finds himself so much alarmed for their character and fate, as when he contemplates their propensity to this dangerous vice. He will not fail therefore to set a due value on any plan which, without violating the principles to which he is attached, provides a proper cure for it. The instability, injustice and confusion introduced into the public councils, have in truth been the mortal diseases under which popular governments have every where perished.

By a faction I understand a number of citizens, whether amounting to a majority or minority of the whole, who are united and actuated by some common impulse of passion, or of interest, adverse to the rights of other citizens, or to the permanent and aggregate interests of the community.

When a majority is included in a faction, the form of popular government on the other hand enables it to sacrifice to its ruling passion or interest, both the public good and the rights of other citizens. To secure the public good, and private rights, against the danger of such a faction, and at the same time to preserve the spirit and the form of popular government, is then the great object to which our enquiries are directed: Let me add that it is the great desideratum, by which alone this form of government can be rescued from the opprobrium under which it has so long labored, and be recommended to the esteem and adoption of mankind. . . .

A Republic, by which I mean a Government in which the scheme of representation takes place, opens a different prospect, and promises the cure for which we are seeking. Let us examine the points in which it varies from pure Democracy, and we shall comprehend both the nature of the cure, and the efficacy which it must derive from the Union.

The . . . point of difference is, the greater number of citizens and extent of territory which may be brought within the compass of Republican, than of Democratic Government; and it is this circumstance principally which renders factious combinations less to be dreaded in the former, than in the latter. The smaller the society, the fewer probably will be the distinct parties and interests composing it; the fewer the distinct parties and interests, the more frequently will a majority be found of the same party; and the smaller the number of individuals composing a majority, and the smaller the compass within which they are placed, the more easily will they concert and execute their plans of oppression. Extend the sphere, and you take in a greater variety of parties and interests; you make it less probable that a majority of the whole will have a common motive to invade the rights of other citizens; or if such a common motive exists, it will be more difficult for all who feel it to discover their own stength, and to act in unison with each other. Besides other impediments, it may be remarked, that where there is a consciousness of unjust or dishonorable purposes, communication is always checked by distrust, in proportion to the number whose concurrence is necessary. . . .

In the extent and proper structure of the Union, therefore, we behold a Republican remedy for the diseases most incident to Republican Government. And according to the degree of pleasure and pride, we feel in being Republicans, ought to be our zeal in cherishing the spirit, and supporting the character of Federalists.

∽

## *"No Title of Nobility"*
## *Constitution, Article 1, Section 9, and*
## *James Madison, Congress, May 11, 1789*

VICE-PRESIDENT John Adams and others had supported giving a title to President George Washington, such as "His Highness the President of the United States and Protector of the Rights of the Same." The thought was that such titles would add dignity to the new and untried form of government. For his suggestion, many in the House of Representatives conferred the title "His Rotundity" to Adams.

James Madison, serving in the First Congress, disagreed with Adams not because titles are dangerous to liberty but because "they are not very reconcilable with the nature of our Government, or the genius of the people." This was the same sentiment that was earlier enshrined in the Constitution in art. 1, sec. 9. America was to be a republic.

## U.S. CONSTITUTION, ART. 1, SEC. 9

*No* Title of Nobility shall be granted by the United States: And no Person holding any Office of Profit or Trust under them, shall, without the Consent of the Congress, accept of any present, Emolument, Office, or Title, of any kind whatever, from any King, Prince, or foreign State.

## IN CONGRESS, MAY 11, 1789

*I* do not conceive titles to be so pregnant with danger as some gentlemen apprehend. I believe a President of the United States, clothed with all the powers given in the Constitution, would not be a dangerous person to the liberties of America, if you were to load him with all the titles of Europe or Asia. We have seen superb and august titles given, without conferring power and influence, or without even obtaining respect. One of the most impotent sovereigns in Europe has assumed a title as high as human invention can devise; for example, what words can imply a greater magnitude of power and strength than that of High Mightiness? This title seems to border almost upon impiety; it is assuming the preeminence and omnipotence of the Deity; yet this title, and many others cast in the same mould, have obtained a long time in Europe, but have they conferred power? Does experience sanction such an opinion? Look at the Republic I have alluded to, and say if their present state warrants the idea?

I am not afraid of titles, because I fear the danger of any power they could confer, but I am against them because they are not very reconcilable with the nature of our Government or the genius of the people. Even if they were proper in themselves, they are not so at this juncture of time. But my strongest objection is founded in principle; instead of increasing, they diminish the true dignity and importance of a Republic, and would in particular, on this occasion, diminish the true dignity of the first magistrate himself. If we give titles, we must either borrow or invent them. If we have recourse to the fertile fields of luxuriant fancy, and deck out an airy being of our own creation, it is a great chance but its fantastic properties would render the empty phantom ridiculous and absurd. If we borrow, the servile imitation will be odious, not to say ridiculous also; we must copy from the pompous sovereigns of the East, or follow the inferior potentates of Europe; in either case, the splendid tinsel or gorgeous robe would disgrace the manly shoulders of our chief. The more truly honourable shall we be, by showing a total neglect and disregard to things of this nature; the more simple, the more Republican we are in our manners, the more rational dignity we shall acquire.

✺

## "I Tremble for My Country"
### The Founders on Slavery, 1773–1826

THERE IS no getting around the fact that many of the Founders held slaves. It is also true that most of the Founders—even those who held slaves—struggled and agonized over the existence of an institution so at odds with the principles of American justice. We often look back at the Founders and accuse them of hypocrisy; it is easy to regard ourselves as morally superior to them. But in pointing out their hypocrisy, we are not discovering anything that the Founders themselves were not aware of. Many, such as the slave holder Patrick Henry, admitted that there was no rationale for defending this institution, save for the "inconvenience of living here without them." Most of the Founders knew, in the words of Madison, that slavery was "evil" and the "blot" on "our Republican character."

The delegates to the Constitutional Convention in 1787 recognized this in their debate over what to do about slavery. In art. 1, sec. 2 of the Constitution, slaves are referred to as "three-fifths" of a person. This was a compromise reached with the slave holders of the South, who wanted to count slaves as full persons in order to have more representation, and ultimately more power, in Congress. The three-fifths clause of the Constitution prevented the slave interest from dominating the legislative process. In addition, art. 1, sec. 9 of the Constitution gave Congress power to end the slave trade in 1808. And finally, an important change was made to art. 4, sec. 2, which contains the fugitive-slave clause. The clause had originally described persons "legally" held in bondage. But members of the Convention objected to the word "legally," as it might give the impression of the Constitution's "favoring the idea that slavery was legal in a moral view."* Instead, "under the Laws thereof" was used. Nowhere can the word "slavery" be found in the Constitution—and this was deliberate. Most of the delegates hoped that the document would put the institution of slavery on the path of eventual extinction, and that there would be a time when former slaves would enjoy full rights under the Constitution. Former slave Frederick Douglass, who had once been a great critic of the Constitution, became one of its strongest defenders, and called it "a glorious liberty document" which he

---

* Farrand, *The Records of the Federal Convention,* vol. 2, p. 628.

"found to contain principles and purposes, entirely hostile to the existence of slavery." *

It is difficult for us living in twentieth-century America to understand why the Founders' love of liberty did not move them to give immediate freedom to the slaves. But as difficult as it is to imagine, we must recall how entrenched the institution of slavery was, how deep prejudice ran, and the hostility and fear between the two races. The prevalent fear was that the two races could not live in harmony with each other. How could former masters begin to treat "property" as full citizens and respect the full rights of freed slaves? And was it possible for former slaves simply to forgive their tormentors for the great evil inflicted upon them and their families? This was the quandary; this was what made Jefferson "tremble" for his country.

Many have observed that the founding did not solve the problem of slavery, but actually created it. That is, the sentiments of the revolution raised America's consciousness and created a great anti-slavery movement—in the 1780s, the abolitionist movement began. It was only after the revolution that the northern states began abolishing slavery, beginning with Pennsylvania in 1780. By the early nineteenth century, slavery had disappeared from all northern states. It would later take a Civil War (and 600,000 lives lost in that war) in the nineteenth century and a civil rights movement in the twentieth century to right the wrongs of this evil. The Founders' struggles with the existence of slavery should be considered in this light. What follows are some of the Founders' thoughts.

* Douglass, "The Meaning of July Fourth for the Negro," July 5, 1852.

THOMAS JEFFERSON, *NOTES ON THE
STATE OF VIRGINIA*, QUERY XVIII, 1787

*And* can the liberties of a nation be thought secure when
we have removed their only firm basis, a conviction in the
minds of the people that these liberties are of the gift of God?
That they are not to be violated but with his wrath? Indeed I
tremble for my country when I reflect that God is just: that his
justice cannot sleep for ever: that considering numbers, nature
and natural means only, a revolution of the wheel of fortune,
an exchange of situation, is among possible events: that it may
become probable by supernatural interference! The Almighty
has no attribute which can take side with us in such a contest.
—But it is impossible to be temperate and to pursue this subject
through the various considerations of policy, of morals, of history natural and civil. We must be contented to hope they will
force their way into every one's mind. I think a change already
perceptible, since the origin of the present revolution. The spirit
of the master is abating, that of the slave rising from the dust,
his condition mollifying, the way I hope preparing, under the
auspices of heaven, for a total emancipation, and that this is
disposed, in the order of events, to be with the consent of the
masters, rather than by their extirpation.

JOHN JAY TO R. LUSHINGTON, NEW YORK,
MARCH 15, 1786

*It* is much to be wished that slavery may be abolished. The
honour of the States, as well as justice and humanity, in my
opinion, loudly call upon them to emancipate these unhappy
people. To contend for our own liberty, and to deny that blessing to others, involves an inconsistency not to be excused.

Whatever may be the issue of the endeavours of restrictions
with which narrow policy opposes the extension of Divine benevolence. It is pleasant, my Lord, to dream of these things, and

I often enjoy that pleasure; but though, like some of our other dreams, we may wish to see them realized, yet the passions and prejudices of mankind forbid us to expect it.

THOMAS PAINE TO BENJAMIN RUSH,
MARCH 16, 1790

*I* wish most anxiously to see my much loved America—it is the Country from whence all reformations must originally spring—I despair of seeing an Abolition of the infernal trafic in Negroes—we must push that matter further on your side the water—I wish that a few well instructed Negroes could be sent among their Brethren in Bondage, for until they are enabled to take their own part nothing will be done—

∞

## Declaration of Independence, Draft, Thomas Jefferson, 1776

IN 1775, the population in America was 2.5 million. About one-fifth of all Americans were black, and nearly all of them were slaves living in the South. In Virginia, slaves were half the population, while in South Carolina, slaves outnumbered white inhabitants, constituting two-thirds of the population.* At the time that Jefferson declared that all men were free and equal, about half a million were not.

Jefferson attempted to protest the wrongs of slavery in our founding document, the Declaration of Independence. John Adams believed that the passages condemning slavery were the best parts of the Declaration. Yet the Southern states strongly opposed Jefferson's position and would not

---

* Statistics cited in Bernard Bailyn, *The Great Republic: A History of the American People,* vol. 1, p. 164.

vote for independence so long as it was included. It was stricken from the final draft.

*He* [George III] has waged cruel war against human nature itself, violating it's most sacred rights of life and liberty in the persons of a distant people who never offended him, captivating & carrying them into slavery in another hemisphere, or to incur miserable death in their transportation thither. This piratical warfare, the opprobrium of INFIDEL powers, is the warfare of the CHRISTIAN king of Great Britain. Determined to keep open a market where MEN should be bought & sold, he has prostituted his negative for suppressing every legislative attempt to prohibit or to restrain this execrable commerce. And that this assemblage of horrors might want no fact of distinguished die, he is now exciting those very people to rise in arms among us, and to purchase that liberty of which he has deprived them, by murdering the people on whom he also obtruded them: thus paying off former crimes committed against the LIBERTIES of one people, with crimes which he urges them to commit against the LIVES of another.

∞

# "I Will Not, I Cannot Justify It"
## Patrick Henry to Robert Pleasants,
## January 18, 1773

SO WHAT was the appeal of slavery? Here's one of the Southerners, a great one. In this strikingly honest self-assessment by Patrick Henry we discover a well-worn excuse of the great and not so great—not actively seeking evil but just "being drawn along," ironically, from the man known forever by his words, "Give me liberty, or give me death."

*Is* it not amazing that at a time when the rights of humanity are defined and understood with precision, in a country, above all others, fond of liberty, that in such an age and in such a country we find men professing a religion the most humane, mild, gentle and generous, adopting a principle as repugnant to humanity as it is inconsistent with the Bible, and destructive to liberty? Every thinking, honest man rejects it in speculation; how few in practice from conscientious motives!

Would anyone believe I am the master of slaves of my own purchase! I am drawn along by the general inconvenience of living here without them. I will not, I cannot justify it. However culpable my conduct, I will so far pay my devoir to virtue as to own the excellence and rectitude of her precepts, and lament my want of conformity to them.

I believe a time will come when an opportunity will be offered to abolish this lamentable evil. Everything we do is to

*Patrick Henry*

improve it, if it happens in our day; if not, let us transmit to our descendants, together with our slaves, a pity for their unhappy lot and an abhorrence of slavery. If we cannot reduce this wished-for reformation to practice, let us treat the unhappy victims with lenity. It is the furthest advance we can make toward justice. It is a debt we owe to the purity of our religion, to show that it is at variance with that law which warrants slavery.

I know not when to stop. I could say many things on the subject, a serious view of which gives a gloomy perspective to future times.

⌘

## Alexander Hamilton to John Jay, March 14, 1779

ALEXANDER HAMILTON wrote the following letter endorsing a plan to enlist the slaves of South Carolina in the Continental Army and, in return, giving them their freedom. The plan was the idea of his best friend, John Laurens, who presented it before Congress, which did not adopt it.

*Col.* Laurens, who will have the honor of delivering you this letter, is on his way to South Carolina, on a project, which I think, in the present situation of affairs there, is a very good one and deserves every kind of support and encouragement. This is to raise two three or four batalions of negroes; with the assistance of the government of that state, by contributions from the owners in proportion to the number they possess. If you should think proper to enter upon the subject with him, he will give you a detail of his plan. He wishes to have it recommended by Congress to the state; and, as an inducement, that they would engage to take those batalions into Continental pay.

I foresee that this project will have to combat much opposition from prejudice and self-interest. The contempt we have been taught to entertain for the blacks, makes us fancy many things that are founded neither in reason nor experience; and an unwillingness to part with property of so valuable a kind will furnish a thousand arguments to show the impracticability or pernicious tendency of a scheme which requires such a sacrifice. But it should be considered, that if we do not make use of them in this way, the enemy probably will; and that the best way to counteract the temptations they will hold out will be to offer them ourselves. An essential part of the plan is to give them their freedom with their muskets. This will secure their fidelity, animate their courage, and I believe will have a good influence upon those who remain, by opening a door to their emancipation. This circumstance, I confess, has no small weight in inducing me to wish the success of the project; for the dictates of humanity and true policy equally interest me in favour of this unfortunate class of men.

∞

## James Madison, Federalist No. 38 and No. 42

AT THE Constitutional Convention of 1787, Southern delegates threatened to withdraw from the plan for union over the issue of slavery. Compromises had to be made—as Madison wrote, "[g]reat as the evil is, a dismemberment of the union would be worse." Madison here defends the Constitution—which allowed banning the slave trade in 1808—as putting the institution of slavery on the path of eventual extermination. The words "slavery" and "slave" were deliberately left out of the Constitution. Madison was correct that the "illicit practice" of slavery would end, although it took Abraham Lincoln and a Civil War to accomplish that end.

*Is* the importation of slaves permitted by the new Constitution for twenty years? By the old, it is permitted for ever.

It were doubtless to be wished that the power of prohibiting the importation of slaves, had not been postponed until the year 1808, or rather that it had been suffered to have immediate operation. But it is not difficult to account either for this restriction on the general government, or for the manner in which the whole clause is expressed. It ought to be considered as a great point gained in favor of humanity, that a period of twenty years may terminate for ever within these States, a traffic which has so long and so loudly upbraided the barbarism of modern policy; that within that period it will receive a considerable discouragement from the fœderal Government, and may be totally abolished by a concurrence of the few States which continue the unnatural traffic, in the prohibitory example which has been given by so great a majority of the Union. Happy would it be for the unfortunate Africans, if an equal prospect lay before them, of being redeemed from the oppressions of their European brethren! Attempts have been made to pervert this clause into an objection against the Constitution, by representing it on one side as a criminal toleration of an illicit practice, and on another, as calculated to prevent voluntary and beneficial emigrations from Europe to America. I mention these misconstructions, not with a view to give them an answer, for they deserve none; but as specimens of the manner and spirit in which some have thought fit to conduct their opposition to the proposed government.

∾

## Northwest Ordinance, July 13, 1787

THE NORTHWEST Ordinance outlawed the spread of slavery in the new territories. It demonstrated that the Founders fundamentally wanted to restrict slavery and that Congress had the power to do it. When they were given the chance to restrict slavery, they did.

## ARTICLE VI (NORTHWEST ORDINANCE)

*"There* shall be neither slavery nor involuntary servitude in the said territory, otherwise than in the punishment of crimes, whereof the party shall have been duly convicted: *Provided always,* That any person escaping into the same, from whom labor or service is lawfully claimed in any one of the original States, such fugitive may be lawfully reclaimed, and conveyed to the person claiming his or her labor or service as aforesaid."

∞

## *". . . Brethren and Members of One Great Family"* *Benjamin Rush,* Commonplace Book, *June 18, 1792, and August 22, 1793*

BENJAMIN RUSH was a strong opponent of slavery and a strong advocate for the brotherhood of man. Here he shares in his Commonplace Book some thoughts about ways of bringing together the races. The first place for desegregation was naturally in God's house, and Rush found that at funerals and at churches the conventional barriers separating black from white disappeared.

*June* 18. This day I attended the funeral of Wm. Gray's wife, a black woman, with about 50 more white persons and two Episcopal Clergymen. The white attendants were chiefly the neighbours of the deceased. The sight was a new one in Philadelphia, for hitherto (a few cases excepted) the negroes alone attended each other's funerals. By this event it is to be hoped the partition wall which divided the Blacks from the Whites will be still further broken down and a way prepared for their union as brethren and members of one great family.

*August 22.* Attended a dinner a mile below the tower in 2nd Street to celebrate the raising of the roof of the African Church. About 100 white persons, chiefly carpenters, dined at one table, who were waited upon by Africans. Afterward about 50 black people sat down at the same table, who were waited upon by white people. Never did I see people more happy. Some of them shed tears of joy. A old black man took Mr. Nicholson by the hand and said to him, "May you live long, and when you die, may you not die eternally." I gave them two toasts, viz: "Peace on earth and good will to man," and, "May African Churches everywhere soon succeed African bondage." The last was received with three cheers.

∞

# George Washington, Last Will and Testament, July 9, 1799

WASHINGTON WAS one of the few prominent Founders who freed his slaves at his death. He not only freed them but also provided for their education and established a trust fund to help them in their freedom. This trust fund continued to support his former slaves and their descendants well into the nineteenth century.

*Item* Upon the decease [of] my wife, it is my Will and desire th[at] all the Slaves which I hold in *[my] own right,* shall receive their free[dom.] To emancipate them during [her] life, would, tho' earnestly wish[ed by] me, be attended with such insu[pera-b]le difficulties on account of thei[r interm]ixture by Marriages

with the [Dow]er Negroes, as to excite the most pa[i]nful sensations, if not disagreeabl[e c]onsequences from the latter, while
[both] descriptions are in the occupancy [of] the same Proprie-
tor; it not being [in] my power, under the tenure by whic[h
t]he Dower Negroes are held, to man[umi]t them. And whereas
among [thos]e who will receive freedom ac[cor]ding to this devise, there may b[e so]me, who from old age or bodily infi[rm]it-
ies, and others who on account of [thei]r infancy, that will be
unable to [su]pport themselves; it is [my] Will a[nd de]sire that
all who [come under the first] and second descrip[tion shall be
comfor]tably cloathed and [fed by my heirs while] they live; and
[3] that such of the latter description as have no parents living,
or if living are unable, or unwilling to provide for them, shall
be bound by the Court until they shall arrive at the age of
twenty five years; and in cases where no record can be produced, whereby their ages can be ascertained, the judgment of
the Court upon its own view of the subject, shall be adequate
and final. The Negroes thus bound, are (by their Masters or
Mistresses) to be taught to read and write; and to be brought
up to some useful occupation, agreeably to the Laws of the
Commonwealth of Virginia, providing for the support of Or-
phan and other poor Children. And I do hereby expressly forbid
the Sale, or transportation out of the said Commonwealth, of
any Slave I may die possessed of, under any pretence whatsoever. And I do moreover most pointedly, and most solemnly
enjoin it upon my Executors hereafter named, or the Survivors
of them, to see that this [cl]ause respecting Slaves, and every
part thereof be religiously fulfilled at the Epoch at which it is
directed to take place; without evasion, neglect or delay, after
the Crops which may then be on the ground are harvested,
particularly as it respects [4] the aged and infirm; Seeing that a
regular and permanent fund be established for their Support so
long as there are subjects requiring it; not trusting to the uncertain provision to be made by individuals.

*George Washington*

## *Jefferson's Last Letter,*
## *Thomas Jefferson to Roger C. Weightman,*
## *June 24, 1826*

THIS WAS Jefferson's last letter, declining an invitation to travel to Washington, D.C., to attend a celebration commemorating the fiftieth anniversary of American independence. Jefferson was too ill to attend, but he found the right words, as usual, to express the significance of the occasion. Fifty years after writing the Declaration of Independence, Jefferson could say: "All eyes are opened, or opening, to the rights of man."

*Respected* Sir,—The kind invitation I receive from you, on the part of the citizens of the city of Washington, to be present with them at their celebration on the fiftieth anniversary of American Independence, as one of the surviving signers of an instrument pregnant with our own, and the fate of the world, is most flattering . . . I should, indeed, with peculiar delight, have met and exchanged there congratulations personally with the small band, the remnant of that host of worthies, who joined with us on that day, in the bold and doubtful election we were to make for our country, between submission or the sword; and to have enjoyed with them the consolatory fact, that our fellow citizens, after half a century of experience and prosperity, continue to approve the choice we made. May it be to the world, what I believe it will be, (to some parts sooner, to others later, but finally to all,) the signal of arousing men to burst the chains under which monkish ignorance and superstition had persuaded them to bind themselves, and to assume the blessings and security of self-government. That form which we have substituted, restores the free right to the unbounded exercise of reason and freedom of opinion. All eyes are opened, or opening, to the rights of man. The general spread of the light of science has already laid open to every view the palpable truth, that the mass of mankind has not been born with saddles on their backs, nor a favored few booted and spurred, ready to ride them legitimately, by the grace of God. These are the grounds of hopes for others. For ourselves, let the annual return of this day forever refresh our recollections of these rights, and an undiminished devotion to them.

# VII

# $\mathcal{P}$IETY

*Religion* has been central to the success of the American experiment. America has been viewed from its very beginnings as a land blessed by Divine Providence. Many early Americans believed that America was a "New Jerusalem" or God's new promised land for the oppressed. John Winthrop, the first governor of the Massachusetts Bay Colony, described America as "a city upon a hill"—a beacon of hope for the rest of the world. George Washington believed that he could trace the hand of God in the events and outcome of the Revolutionary War.

America is a country where religious belief *and* religious freedom flourish. In fact, the two go together. Americans of all faiths are free to worship without fear of persecution. The Founders were united in their view that religious faith could not be directed by outward force. They believed that it was everyone's right to arrive at their religious views freely. This religious freedom, they believed, would make one's faith purer, stronger, and more sincere.

A solid religious faith among the people, the Founders thought, was an indispensable support of the American experiment. Although it was not the business of government to legislate religious beliefs, it was in the government's interest to have a religious citizen body. Why? Because religion provides us with a moral anchor and teaches us to be honest, trustworthy, and responsible. Some people are able to be moral without religion, but most of us need religion to show us the right way. As George Washington wrote: "Of all the dispositions and habits which lead to political prosperity, religion and morality are indispensable supports."

The Founders believed that the success of America's institutions depended on a virtuous and religious citizen body. Free government depends on individuals with solid moral characters because freedom can easily turn into license unless it is guided by a firm sense of right and wrong. John Adams wrote: "Our Constitution was made only for a moral and religious people. It is wholly inadequate to the government of any other." The Founders were men of enlightenment and science, but they were also men who walked humbly before their God. The liberty and the rights that Americans enjoy, they held, were a direct gift of God. The Founders believed America would continue to thrive so long as it was inhabited by a religious and free people.

∞

## Washington's Prayer at Valley Forge, 1777

FRANKLIN DELANO Roosevelt observed that during the Revolutionary War, "every winter was a Valley Forge. Throughout the thirteen states there existed fifth columnists—and selfish men, jealous men, fearful men, who proclaimed that Washington's cause was hopeless, and that he should ask for a negotiated peace." Roosevelt observed that "Washington's conduct in those hard times has provided the model for all Americans ever since—a model of moral stamina." *

Prayer and faith sustained Washington through his many trials. Though some have disputed the accuracy of Washington biographer Mason Weems' depiction of Washington's praying at Valley Forge, many of Washington's fellow officers, such as Alexander Hamilton, reported that they often saw General Washington at prayer. Thus, I thought this was a wonderful account worthy of inclusion.

* Fireside Chat, February 23, 1942.

*In* the winter of '77, while Washington, with the American army lay encamped at Valley Forge, a certain good old FRIEND, of the respectable family and name of Potts, if I mistake not, had occasion to pass through the woods near head-quarters. Treading his way along the venerable grove, suddenly he heard the sound of a human voice, which as he advanced increased on his ear, and at length became like the voice of one speaking much in earnest. As he approached the spot with a cautious step, whom should he behold, in a dark natural bower of ancient oaks, but the commander in chief of the American armies on his knees at prayer! Motionless with surprise, friend Potts continued on the place till the general, having ended his devo-

*George Washington*

tions, arose, and, with a countenance of angel serenity, retired to headquarters: friend Potts then went home, and on entering his parlour called out to his wife, "Sarah, my dear! Sarah! All's well! all's well! George Washington will yet prevail!"

"What's the matter, Isaac?" replied she; "thee seems moved."

"Well, if I seem moved, 'tis no more than what I am. I have this day seen what I never expected. Thee knows that I always thought the sword and the gospel utterly inconsistent; and that no man could be a soldier and a christian at the same time. But George Washington has this day convinced me of my mistake."

He then related what he had seen, and concluded with this prophetical remark—"If George Washington be not a man of God, I am greatly deceived—and still more shall I be deceived if God do not, through him, work out a great salvation for America."

When he was told that the British troops at Lexington, on the memorable 19th of April, 1775, had fired on and killed several of the Americans, he replied, *"I grieve for the death of my countrymen, but rejoice that the British are still so determined to keep God on our side,"* alluding to that noble sentiment which he has since so happily expressed; viz. *"The smiles of Heaven can never be expected on a nation that disregards the eternal rules of order and right, which Heaven itself has ordained."*

—From Mason Weems, *Life of Washington*

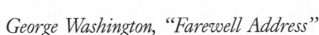

## George Washington, *"Farewell Address"*

AFTER SERVING two presidential terms, George Washington was looking forward to his retirement at Mount Vernon. Yet he worried about the stability of the young nation. Was it going to go the way of all republics before it, that is, toward despotic rule? And could the nation become a government steered by law, not by the force of Washington's or any other great man's reputation? In his Farewell Address he reminds the American people that national strength and stability rest on the pillars of private morality, most especially religion. The word he uses to describe the role of religion and morality in America is not "optional" or "desirable" or "helpful"; it is "indispensable."

. . . *Of* all the dispositions and habits which lead to political prosperity, Religion and morality are indispensable supports. In vain would that man claim the tribute of Patriotism, who should labour to subvert these great Pillars of human happiness, these firmest props of the duties of Men and citizens. The mere Politician, equally with the pious man ought to respect and to cherish them. A volume could not trace all their connections with private and public felicity. Let it simply be asked where is the security for property, for reputation, for life, if the sense of religious obligation desert the oaths, which are the instruments of investigation in Courts of Justice? And let us with caution indulge the supposition, that morality can be maintained without religion. Whatever may be conceded to the influence of refined education on minds of peculiar structure, reason and experience both forbid us to expect that National morality can prevail in exclusion of religious principle.

'Tis substantially true, that virtue or morality is a necessary spring of popular government. The rule indeed extends with more or less force to every species of free Government. Who that is a sincere friend to it, can look with indifference upon attempts to shake the foundation of the fabric.

Promote then as an object of primary importance, Institutions for the general diffusion of knowledge. In proportion as the structure of a government gives force to public opinion, it is essential that public opinion should be enlightened. . . .

Observe good faith and justice towds. all Nations. Cultivate peace and harmony with all. Religion and morality enjoin this conduct; and can it be that good policy does not equally enjoin it? It will be worthy of a free, enlightened, and, at no distant period, a great Nation, to give to mankind the magnanimous and too novel example of a People always guided by an exalted justice and benevolence. Who can doubt that in the course of time and things the fruits of such a plan would richly repay any temporary advantages wch. might be lost by a steady adherence to it? Can it be, that Providence has not connected the permanent felicity of a Nation with its virtue? The experiment, at least, is recommended by every sentiment which ennobles human Nature. Alas! is it rendered impossible by its vices?

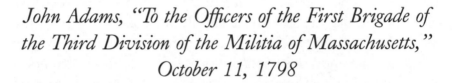

## John Adams, "To the Officers of the First Brigade of the Third Division of the Militia of Massachusetts," October 11, 1798

CAN THERE be any doubt that the American experiment depends on the piety of its citizens? Not according to President John Adams.

*While* our country remains untainted with the principles and manners which are now producing desolation in so many parts of the world; while she continues sincere, and incapable of insidious and impious policy, we shall have the strongest reason to rejoice in the local destination assigned us by Providence. But should the people of America once become capable of that deep simulation towards one another, and towards foreign nations, which assumes the language of justice and moderation while it is practicing iniquity and extravagance, and displays in the most captivating manner the charming pictures of candor, frankness, and sincerity, while it is rioting in rapine

and insolence, this country will be the most miserable habitation in the world; because we have no government armed with
power capable of contending with human passions unbridled
by morality and religion. Avarice, ambition, revenge, or gal-
lantry, would break the strongest cords of our Constitution as a
whale goes through a net. Our Constitution was made only for
a moral and religious people. It is wholly inadequate to the
government of any other.

∽

## Northwest Ordinance; Article 3, July 13, 1787

THE NORTHWEST Ordinance, originally drafted by
Thomas Jefferson, was enacted by the Congress under the
Articles of Confederation. The significance of the Northwest Ordinance was that, unlike Great Britain, which refused to allow a colony to become a full-fledged member
of its commonwealth, the Northwest Ordinance provided
the means by which a territory could eventually apply for
statehood and become part of the United States, not just a
colony of it. In addition, the Northwest Ordinance, as
noted earlier, outlawed slavery in the territories.

The territory stretching to the Mississippi was a wilderness populated by Indians. Eager settlers were ready to go
forth, but it was important that they regulate their conduct
with the Indians and among themselves. Thus the ordinance stipulated trial by jury, freedom of conscience, education and the importance of religion, morality, and justice.
Again note the word used to modify religion's place in the
territories of America—"necessary."

Religion, morality, and knowledge being necessary to good
government and the happiness of mankind, schools and the
means of education shall forever by encouraged. The utmost

good faith shall always be observed towards the Indians; their lands and property shall never be taken from them without their consent; and in their property, rights, and liberty they never shall be invaded or disturbed unless in just and lawful wars authorized by Congress; but laws founded in justice and humanity shall, from time to time, be made, for preventing wrongs being done to them and for preserving peace and friendship with them.

∞

## The Question of Representation: Benjamin Franklin's Invocation for Prayer at the Constitutional Convention, June 28, 1787

FOR TEN weeks delegates to the Constitutional Convention bitterly debated the question of representation. At issue was whether representation was to be based on the population of each state or if each state would be given one vote. Delegates from the small states supported the New Jersey Plan, which proposed one vote per state and a one-house Confederation Congress; delegates from the larger states supported the Virginia Plan, which based representation in both houses on population.

The debate over which plan to adopt became very heated and threatened to dissolve the Convention. Historians have called this period the "critical juncture" in the Convention. Tempers flared, impatience and frustration grew, so much so that on June 28, Franklin, the oldest delegate there at eighty-one, invoked the aid of the Almighty.

The delegates never acted on Franklin's motion for prayer for several reasons: the problem of maintaining the secrecy vital to the proceedings of the convention; the panic this might provoke among the public sensing the desperation of the delegates; and the fact that the convention had no money to pay a clergyman.

But Franklin's motion, at least for a short while, brought calm to the proceedings, and by mid-July a compromise was reached. And while it might have seemed odd for the perhaps least reverent Founder of them all to suggest prayer, historians agree that his motion was sincere, and that in his saying "God governs in the affairs of men," in that company, he was not alone in his belief.

*The small progress* we have made after 4 or five weeks close attendance & continual reasonings with each other—our different sentiments on almost every question, several of the last producing as many noes as ays, is methinks a melancholy proof of the imperfection of the Human Understanding. We indeed seem to *feel* our own want of political wisdom, since we have been running about in search of it. We have gone back to ancient history for models of Government, and examined the different forms of those Republics which having been formed with the seeds of their own dissolution now no longer exist. And we have viewed Modern States all round Europe, but find none of their Constitutions suitable to our circumstances.

In this situation of this Assembly, groping as it were in the dark to find political truth, and scarce able to distinguish it when presented to us, how has it happened, Sir, that we have not hitherto once thought of humbly applying to the Father of lights to illuminate our understandings? In the beginning of the Contest with G. Britain, when we were sensible of danger we had daily prayer in this room for the divine protection.—Our prayers, Sir, were heard, and they were graciously answered. All of us who were engaged in the struggle must have observed frequent instances of a Superintending providence in our favor. To that kind providence we owe this happy opportunity of consulting in peace on the means of establishing our future national felicity. And have we now forgotten that powerful friend? or do we imagine that we no longer need his assistance? I have lived, Sir, a long time, and the longer I live, the more convincing proofs I see of this truth—*that God governs in the affairs of men*. And if a sparrow cannot fall to the ground without his notice, is it probable that an empire can rise without his aid? We have been assured, Sir, in the sacred writings, that "except the Lord build the House they labour in vain that build it." I firmly believe this; and I also believe that without his concurring aid we shall succeed in this political building no better than the Builders of Babel: We shall be divided by our little partial local interests; our projects will be confounded, and we ourselves shall become a reproach and bye word down to future ages. And what is worse, mankind may hereafter from this unfortunate instance, despair of establishing Governments by Human Wisdom and leave it to chance, war and conquest.

I therefore beg leave to move—that henceforth prayers imploring the assistance of Heaven, and its blessings on our deliberations, be held in this Assembly every morning before we proceed to business, and that one or more of the Clergy of this City be requested to officiate in that service.

∞

## George Washington to Samuel Langdon, September 28, 1789

IN THIS letter, Washington succinctly captures the feeling, prevalent in the new nation, that God played a decisive role in the founding of a new people.

. . . *The* man must be bad indeed who can look upon the events of the American Revolution without feeling the warmest gratitude towards the great Author of the Universe whose divine interposition was so frequently manifested in our behalf. And it is my earnest prayer that we may so conduct ourselves as to merit a continuance of those blessings with which we have hitherto been favored. I am etc.

∾

# Benjamin Rush, Commonplace Book, May 27, 1790

IN THIS brief reflection to himself in his *Commonplace Book,* Rush reminds Christians to look for the face of Jesus in all human beings.

## ON SOLITUDE

*The* powers of the human mind appear to be arranged in a certain order like the strata of earth. They are thrown out of their order by the fall of man. The moral powers appear to have occupied the highest and first place. They recover it in solitude, and after sleep, hence the advantage of solitary punishments, and of consulting our morning pillow in cases where there is a doubt of what is right, or duty. The first thoughts in a morning if followed seldom deceive or mislead us. They are generally seasoned by the moral powers.

In Macbeth a lady is restrained from the murder of a king by his resemblance of her father as he slept. Should not all men be restrained from acts of violence and even of unkindness against their fellow men by observing in them something which resembles the Saviour of the World? If nothing else certainly, a human figure?

❦

## "So Help Me God," George Washington, First Inaugural Address, April 30, 1789

ON APRIL 14, 1789, Washington was notified by an old friend that he had been unanimously elected to the presidency. Washington entered the office of the presidency with some doubts as to whether he would be able to meet the expectations of his fellow citizens. He was deeply aware of the enormous task ahead of him and the impact it would have on generations to come. Before the eyes of mankind, Washington would lead the experiment of self-government.

According to Washington Irving, on the day of his inauguration, Washington wore a homespun suit of brown cloth, put his hand on the Bible held by James Otis, and repeated the oath of office. Irving reports that upon concluding the oath, "Mr. Otis would have raised the Bible to [Washington's] lips but he bowed down reverently and kissed it." Washington also added "so help me God" to the official presidential oath of office, and every president since has followed his example.

In the excerpt below, Washington gives thanks to the Almighty for the blessings America had received during the Revolution and Constitution making, and asks for His continued support. Unlike many contemporary speeches where God and Providence are part of a string of mentions, in our first president's first address, the presence of Providence suffuses the entire speech as it suffuses creation.

*Fellow* Citizens of the Senate and the House of Representatives. . . .

Such being the impressions under which I have, in obedience to the public summons, repaired to the present station; it would be peculiarly improper to omit in this first official Act, my fervent supplications to that Almighty Being who rules over the Universe, who presides in the Councils of Nations, and whose providential aids can supply every human defect, that his benediction may consecrate to the liberties and happiness of the People of the United States, a Government instituted by themselves for these essential purposes: and may enable every instrument employed in its administration to execute with success, the functions allotted to his charge. In tendering this homage to the Great Author of every public and private good, I assure myself that it expresses your sentiments not less than my own; nor those of my fellow-citizens at large, less than either. No People can be bound to acknowledge and adore the invisible hand, which conducts the Affairs of men more than the People of the United States. Every step, by which they have advanced to the character of an independent nation, seems to have been distinguished by some token of providential agency. And in the important revolution just accomplished in the system of their United Government, the tranquil deliberations and voluntary consent of so many distinct communities, from which the event has resulted, cannot be compared with the means by which most Governments have been established, without some return of pious gratitude along with an humble anticipation of the future blessings which the past seem to presage. These reflections, arising out of the present crisis, have forced themselves too strongly on my mind to be suppressed. You will join with me I trust in thinking, that there are none under the influence of which, the proceedings of a new and free Government can more auspiciously commence. . . . In these honorable qualifications, I behold the surest pledges . . . that the foundations of our National policy will be laid in the pure and immutable principles of private morality; and the pre-eminence of a free Government, be exemplified by all the attributes which can win the affections of its Citizens, and command the respect of the world.

I dwell on this prospect with every satisfaction which an

ardent love for my Country can inspire: since there is no truth
more thoroughly established, than that there exists in the
economy and course of nature, an indissoluble union between
virtue and happiness, between duty and advantage, between
the genuine maxims of an honest and magnanimous policy,
and the solid rewards of public prosperity and felicity: Since we
ought to be no less persuaded that the propitious smiles of
Heaven, can never be expected on a nation that disregards the
eternal rules of order and right, which Heaven itself has ordained: And since the preservation of the sacred fire of liberty,
and the destiny of the Republican model of Government, are
justly considered as *deeply,* perhaps as *finally* staked, on the
experiment entrusted to the hands of the American people.

Having thus imparted to you my sentiments, as they have
been awakened by the occasion which brings us together, I
shall take my present leave; but not without resorting once
more to the benign parent of the human race, in humble supplication that since he has been pleased to favour the American
people, with opportunities for deliberating in perfect tranquility, and dispositions for deciding with unparellelled unanimity
on a form of Government, for the security of their Union, and
the advancement of their happiness; so his divine blessing may
be equally *conspicuous* in the enlarged views, the temperate
consultations, and the wise measures on which the success of
this Government must depend.

## *Mercy Warren,* History of the Rise, Progress, and Termination of the American Revolution

IN 1805, Mercy Warren published a three-volume history
of the American Revolution. In concluding her history,
Warren reflected on the decline of republican virtue or, as

she put it, "the relaxation of manners" since the Revolution. The excerpt following contains those thoughts and her advice that to sustain the work of the revolutionaries, Americans must sustain their moral and religious character.

*Nothing* seemed to be wanting to the United States but a continuance of their union and virtue. It was their interest to cherish true, genuine republican virtue, in politics; and in religion, a strict adherence to a sublime code of morals, which has never been equalled by the sages of ancient time, nor can ever be abolished by the sophistical reasonings of modern philosophers. Possessed of this palladium, America might bid defiance both to foreign and domestic intrigue, and stand on an eminence that would command their veneration of nations, and the respect of their monarchs; but a defalcation from these principles may leave the sapless vine of liberty to droop, or to be rooted out by the hand that had been stretched out to nourish it.

The world might reasonably have expected, from the circumstances connected with the first settlement of the American colonies, which was in consequence of their attachment to the religion of their fathers, united with a spirit of independence relative to civil government, that there would have been no observable dereliction of those honorable principles, for many ages to come. From the sobriety of their manners, their simple habits, their attention to the education and moral conduct of their children, they had the highest reason to hope, that it might have been long, very long, before the faith of their religion was shaken, or their principles corrupted, either by the manners, opinions, or habits of foreigners, bred in the courts of despotism, or the schools of licentiousness.

This hope shall not yet be relinquished. There has indeed been some relaxation of manners, and the appearance of a change in public opinion not contemplated when revolutionary scenes first shook the western world. But it must be acknowledged, that the religious and moral character of Americans yet stands on a higher grade of excellence and purity, than that of most other nations. It has been observed, that "a violation of manners has destroyed more states than the infraction of laws." It is necessary for every *American,* with becoming energy to endeavour to stop the dissemination of principles evidently destructive of the cause for which they have bled. It must be the combined virtue of the rulers and of the people to do this, and to rescue and save their civil and religious rights from the outstretched arm of tyranny, which may appear under any mode or form of government.

∞

## *Alexander Hamilton to Elizabeth Hamilton, July 1804*

THESE TWO letters were written as Hamilton prepared for a duel against Aaron Burr.

Burr had run for president against Thomas Jefferson, and though Hamilton was a bitter rival of Jefferson, he supported Jefferson rather than Burr. Burr then set his sights on becoming governor of New York and possibly leading a secessionist movement in New York, breaking up the Union and building a strong Northern confederacy. Hamilton attacked Burr and his plan in the press. As a result, Burr was defeated. Enraged, Burr challenged Hamilton to a duel. Though Hamilton did not believe in dueling (he lost his son Philip to a duel), he believed that the code of honor did not give him any out.

In these letters, one gets the sense that Hamilton never intended to shoot at Burr and had a premonition that he was to die.

For most of his life, Hamilton was not what one would

call a traditional Christian. But historians have shown that later in life, he had a conversion of sorts, and these letters extolling his wife to "fly to the bosom of God and be comforted" show that he believed in the promise of a "better world." Indeed, on his deathbed he made several requests that he receive a last Communion, which he eventually did.

### To Mrs. Hamilton, July 10, 1804

This letter, my dear Eliza, will not be delivered to you, unless I shall first have terminated my earthly career, to begin, as I humbly hope, from redeeming grace and divine mercy, a happy immortality. If it had been possible for me to have avoided the interview, my love for you and my precious children would have been alone a decisive motive. But it was not possible, without sacrifices which would have rendered me unworthy of your esteem. I need not tell you of the pangs I feel from the idea of quitting you, and exposing you to the anguish I know you would feel. Nor could I dwell on the topic, lest it should unman me. The consolations of religion, my beloved, can alone support you; and these you have a right to enjoy. Fly to the bosom of your God, and be comforted. With my last idea I shall cherish the sweet hope of meeting you in a better world. Adieu, best of wives—best of women. Embrace all my darling children for me.

### To Mrs. Hamilton, Tuesday evening, ten o'clock

This is my second letter. The scruples of a Christian have determined me to expose my own life to any extent, rather than subject myself to the guilt of taking the life of another. This much increases my hazards, and redoubles my pangs for you. But you had rather I should die innocent than live guilty. Heaven can preserve me, and I humbly hope will; but, in the contrary event, I charge you to remember that you are a Christian. God's will be done! The will of a merciful God must be good. Once more, Adieu, my darling, darling wife.

∞

## George Washington, Thanksgiving Proclamation, New York, October 3, 1789

OUR FIRST Thanksgiving was, of course, held by the Pilgrims in the fall of 1621. Washington's Thanksgiving Proclamation was our first national Thanksgiving. Abraham Lincoln in 1863 made it an annual national holiday to be celebrated on the last Thursday of November. Originally it was a day of thanks and prayer and supplication and request for divine blessing. A few helpings of those would go nicely and wouldn't hurt with the stuffing and gravy of today.

*Whereas* it is the duty of all Nations to acknowledge the providence of Almighty God, to obey his will, to be grateful for his benefits, and humbly to implore his protection and favor, and Whereas both Houses of Congress have by their joint Committee requested me "to recommend to the People of the United States a day of public thanks-giving and prayer to be observed by acknowledging with grateful hearts the many signal favors of Almighty God, especially by affording them an opportunity peaceably to establish a form of government for their safety and happiness."

Now therefore I do recommend and assign Thursday the 26th, day of November next to be devoted by the People of these States to the service of that great and glorious Being, who is the beneficent Author of all the good that was, that is, or that will be. That we may then all unite in rendering unto him our sincere and humble thanks, for his kind care and protection of the People of this country previous to their becoming a Nation, for the signal and manifold mercies, and the favorable interpositions of his providence, which we experienced in the course and conclusion of the late war, for the great degree of tranquillity, union, and plenty, which we have since enjoyed, for the peaceable and rational manner in which we have been enabled to establish constitutions of government for our safety and happiness, and particularly the national One now lately instituted, for the civil and religious liberty with which we are blessed, and the means we have of acquiring and diffusing useful knowledge and in general for all the great and various favors which he hath been pleased to confer upon us.

And also that we may then unite in most humbly offering our prayers and supplications to the great Lord and Ruler of Nations and beseech him to pardon our national and other transgressions, to enable us all, whether in public or private stations, to perform our several and relative duties properly and punctually, to render our national government a blessing to all the People, by constantly being a government of wise, just and constitutional laws, discreetly and faithfully executed and obeyed, to protect and guide all Sovereigns and Nations (especially such as have shown kindness unto us) and to bless them with good government, peace, and concord. To promote the knowledge and practice of true religion and virtue, and the encrease of science among them and Us, and generally to grant unto all Mankind such a degree of temporal prosperity as he alone knows to be best.

∞

## John Adams, Diary, *February 16 and May 28, 1756*

A RECENT graduate of Harvard University, and unsure if he wanted to pursue the study of law or theology, Adams took a job in 1755 as schoolmaster in Worcester, Massachusetts. Of course, the young and ambitious Adams was thinking of bigger things outside of his small classroom. Adams brooded a lot during his three years as schoolmaster and recorded his broodings in his diary. Well aware that vanity was his "cardinal vice and cardinal folly," he freely confessed his weaknesses, in turmoil that his worldly ambitions overwhelmed the Biblical teachings for humility.

Students who read Adams will discover that the Founders were not stodgy, serene, entirely cerebral, and purely spiritual beings. Here is the hard, self-doubting, suffering mind and soul trying to figure out what it's all about. The question of meaning is often fought out with difficulty in men's souls. For some men, like Washington, God's presence is a constant comfort and source of repose—they are God's serene souls. For others God's presence often feels like accusation and judgment. For much of his life that was Adams's predilection and he found himself often "wrestling with angels." Here is God's tortured soul.

*February 16, 1756*

*Oh!* that I could wear out of my mind every mean and base affectation, conquer my natural Pride and Self Conceit, expect no more defference from my fellows than I deserve, acquire that meekness, and humility, which are the sure marks and Characters of a great and generous Soul, and subdue every unworthy Passion and treat all men as I wish to be treated by all. How happy should I then be, in the favour and good will of all honest men, and the sure prospect of a happy immortality!

*May 1756*

Drank Tea at Mr. Putnams.—What is the proper Business of Mankind in this Life? We came into the World naked and destitute of all the Convcniences and necessaries of Life. And if we were not provided for, and nourished by our Parents or others should inevitably perish as soon as born. We increase in strength of Body and mind by slow and insensible Degrees. 1/3 of our Time is consumed in sleep, and 3/4 of the remainder, is spent in procuring a mere animal sustenance. And if we live to the Age of three score and Ten and then set down to make an estimate in our minds of the Happiness we have enjoyed and the Misery we have suffered, We shall find I am apt to think, that the overbalance of Happiness is quite inconsiderable. We shall find that we have been through the greatest Part of our Lives pursuing Shadows, and empty but glittering Phantoms rather than substances. We shall find that we have applied our whole Vigour, all our Faculties, in the Pursuit of Honour, or Wealth, or Learning or some other such delusive Trifle, instead of the real and everlasting Excellences of Piety and Virtue. Habits of Contemplating the Deity and his transcendent Excellences, and correspondent Habits of complacency in and Dependence upon him, Habits of Reverence and Gratitude, to God, and Habits of Love and Compassion to our fellow men and Habits of Temperance, Recollection and self Government will afford us a real and substantial Pleasure. We may then exult in a Consciousness of the Favour of God, and the Prospect of everlasting Felicity.

∞

## Benjamin Rush, "On Slavekeeping," 1773

BENJAMIN RUSH shows that ministers of faith have a first duty to show their congregants the sins of slavery, writing that they should "neglect not the weightier laws of justice and humanity." As Rush says, the Bible—from the Hebrew Bible to the New Testament—makes it plain that God, as Jefferson would later put it, "has no attribute which can take sides with" Americans who support the existence of slavery. Religion is the law of a free people.

*But* chiefly—ye ministers of the gospel, whose dominion over the principles and actions of men is so universally acknowledged and felt,—Ye who estimate the worth of your fellow creatures by their immortality, and therefore must look upon all mankind as equal;—let your zeal keep pace with your opportunities to put a stop to slavery. While you inforce the duties of "tithe and cummin," neglect not the weightier laws of justice and humanity. Slavery is an Hydra sin, and includes in it every violation of the precepts of the Law and the Gospel. In vain will you command your flocks to offer up the incense of faith and charity, while they continue to mingle the sweat and blood of Negro slaves with their sacrifices.—If the blood of Abel cried aloud for vengeance;—If, under the Jewish dispensation, cities of refuge could not screen the deliberate murderer —if even manslaughter required sacrifices to expiate it,—and if a single murder so seldom escapes with impunity in any civilized country, what may you not say against that trade, or those manufactures—or laws, which destroy the lives of so many thousands of our fellow-creatures every year?—If in the Old Testament "God swears by his holiness, and by the excellency of Jacob, that the earth shall tremble, and every one mourn that dwelleth therein for the iniquity of those who oppress the poor and crush the needy," "who buy the poor with silver, and the needy with a pair of shoes," what judgments may you not denounce upon those who continue to perpetrate these crimes, after the more full discovery which God has made of the law of equity in the New Testament. Put them in mind of the rod which was held over them a few years ago in the Stamp and Revenue Acts. Remember that national crimes require national punishments, and without declaring what punishment awaits this evil, you may venture to assure them, that it cannot pass with impunity, unless God shall cease to be just or merciful.

<br>

## Abigail Adams to John Adams, October 9, 1775

AN EPIDEMIC had hit the town of Braintree, Massachusetts, home of Abigail and John Adams—an epidemic that killed John Adams's brother and struck John and Abigail's young son, Tommy. Abigail was exhausted and weak without her husband, who was in Philadelphia serving in the Continental Congress. In August, Abigail had sent to John a "bill of mortality" listing the eight neighbors who had just died that week, along with others. Elizabeth Smith, Abigail's mother, who came to help her daughter, was stricken herself and, after suffering for a couple of weeks, died under Abigail's care. Abigail was almost "ready to faint under this severe and heavy stroke."

As the following letter demonstrates, Abigail Adams was restored by her faith in God and never doubted His divine goodness. America's Founders lived with death in their midst, at their hearth on a regular basis. Such adversity did not provoke them to doubt or to curse God but, rather, to thank Him for the blessings left to them. These people had much reason "to murmur at providence" but did not.

*But* the heavy stroke which most of all distresses me is my dear Mother. I cannot overcome my too selfish sorrow, all her tenderness towards me, her care and anxiety for my welfare at all times, her watchfulness over my infant years, her advice and instruction in maturer age; all, all indear her memory to me, and highten my sorrow for her loss. At the same time I know a patient submission is my duty. I will strive to obtain it! But the lenient hand of time alone can blunt the keen Edg of Sorrow. He who deignd to weep over a departed Friend, will surely forgive a sorrow which at all times desires to be bounded and restrained, by a firm Belief that a Being of infinite wisdom and unbounded Goodness, will carve out my portion in tender mercy towards me! Yea tho he slay me I will trust in him said holy Job. What tho his corrective Hand hath been streatched against me; I will not murmer. Tho earthly comforts are taken away I will not repine, he who gave them has surely a right to limit their duration, and has continued them to me much longer than I deserved. I might have been striped of my children as many others have been. I might o! forbid it Heaven, I might have been left a solitary widow.

Still I have many blessing[s] left, many comforts to be thankfull for, and rejoice in. I am not left to mourn as one without hope.

∾

## *John Adams to Benjamin Rush, July 19, 1812*

JOHN ADAMS and Benjamin Rush carried on a lively correspondence, especially during the years of 1805–1813. Their letters were full of reminiscences of their revolutionary days. They also discussed their views on philosophical, moral, and religious questions of the day.

*In* the month of March last I was called to the house in another part of town which was built by my father, in which he lived and died and from which I buried him; and in the chamber in which I was born I could not forbear to weep over the remains of a beautiful child of my son Thomas that died of the whooping cough. Why was I preserved 3/4 of a century, and that rose cropped in the bud? I, almost dead at top and in all my limbs and wholly useless to myself and the world? Great Teacher, tell me.

What has preserved this race of Adamses in all their ramifications, in such numbers, health, peace, comfort, and mediocrity? I believe it is religion, without which they would have been rakes, fops, sots, gamblers, starved with hunger, frozen with cold, scalped by Indians, &c., &c., &c., been melted away and disappeared. . . .

∽

## John Adams to Thomas Jefferson, December 3, 1813

THE CORRESPONDENCE between Adams and Jefferson is among the most famous exchange of letters in America. In these letters, many historians have noted, we find the thoughts, ideas, and feelings of the founding. Many have argued that these two men were not only addressing each other but also future generations of Americans.

One of the more popular topics that these two men discussed was religion. Here is a tribute to the persuasiveness of George Whitefield, the leading preacher of America's First Great Awakening.

*I* know of no Philosopher, or Theologian, or Moralist ancient or modern more profound; more infallible than Whitefield, if the Anecdote that I have heard be true.

He began; "Father Abraham"! with his hands and Eyes gracefully directed to the Heavens as I have more than once seen him; "Father Abraham," "who have you there with you"? ["]have you Catholicks?" No. "Have you Protestants". No. "Have you Churchmen". No. "Have you Dissenters". No. "Have you Presbyterians"? No. "Quakers?" No. ["]Anabaptists"? No. "Who have you then?" "Are you alone"? No.

"My Brethren,! You have the Answer to all these questions in the Words of My Text, "He who feareth God and worketh Righteousness, shall be accepted of him."

〜〜

## Benjamin Franklin, Appeal for the Hospital, August 15, 1751

BENJAMIN FRANKLIN was involved in founding the first hospital in America and many other charitable projects in Philadelphia that relieved the suffering of the poor and the sick. Franklin notes that it is by exercising the virtue of charity that "most of all recommends us to the Deity" and believed that if we take care of the neediest among us, God will take care of us.

I was sick, and ye visited me.      Matth. xxv.


. . . But tho' every Animal that hath Life is liable to Death, Man, of all other Creatures, has the greatest Number of *Diseases* to his Share; whether they are the Effects of our Intemperance and Vice, or are given us, that we may have a greater Opportunity of exercising towards each other that Virtue, which most of all recommends us to the Deity, I mean CHARITY.

The great Author of our Faith, whose Life should be the constant Object of our Imitation, as far as it is not inimitable, always shew'd the greatest Compassion and regard for the SICK; he disdain'd not to visit and minister Comfort and Health to the meanest of the People; and he frequently inculcated the same Disposition in his Doctrine and Precepts to his Disciples. For this one Thing, (in that beautiful Parable of the Traveller wounded by Thieves) the *Samaritan* (who was esteemed no better than a *Heretick,* or an *Infidel* by the *Orthodox* of those Times) is preferred to the *Priest* and the *Levite;* because he did not, like them, pass by, regardless of the Distress of his Brother Mortal; but when he came to the Place where the half-dead Traveller lay, *he had Compassion on him, and went to him, and bound up his Wounds, pouring in Oil and Wine, and set him on his own Beast, and brought him to an Inn, and took Care of him.*—*Dives*, also, the rich Man, is represented as being excluded from the Happiness of Heaven, because he fared sumptuously every Day, and had Plenty of all Things, and yet neglected to comfort and assist his poor Neighbour, who was helpless and *full of Sores*, and might perhaps have been revived and restored with small Care, *by the Crumbs that fell from his Table, or, as we say, with his loose Corns.*—*I was sick, and ye Visited me*, is one of the Terms of Admission into Bliss, and the Contrary, a Cause of Exclusion: That is, as our Saviour himself explains it, *Ye have visited, or ye have not visited, assisted and comforted those who stood in need of it, even tho' they were the least, or meanest of Mankind.* This Branch of *Charity* seems essential to the true Spirit of Christianity; and should be extended to all in general, whether Deserving or Undeserving, as far as our Power reaches. Of the ten Lepers who were cleansed, *nine* seem to have been much more unworthy than the *tenth*, yet in respect to the Cure of their Disease, they equally shared the Goodness of God. And the great Physician in sending forth his Disciples, always gave them a particular Charge, *that into whatsoever City they entered, they should heal* ALL *the Sick*, without Distinction.

When the good *Samaritan* left his Patient at the Inn, *he gave Money to the Host, and said,* TAKE CARE OF HIM, *and what thou spendest more, I will repay thee.* We are in this World mutual Hosts to each other; the Circumstances and Fortunes of Men and Families are continually changing; in the course of a few Years we have seen the Rich become Poor, and the Poor Rich; the Children of the Wealthy languishing in Want and Misery, and those of their Servants lifted into Estates, and abounding in the good Things of this Life. Since then, our present State, how prosperous soever, hath no Stability, but what depends on the good Providence of God, how careful should we be not to *harden our Hearts* against the Distresses of our Fellow Creatures, lest He who owns and governs all, should punish our Inhumanity, deprived us of a Stewardship in which we have so unworthily behaved, *laugh at our Calamity and mock when our Fear cometh*. Methinks when Objects of Charity, and Opportunities of relieving them, present themselves, we should hear the Voice of this *Samaritan,* as if it were the Voice of God sounding in our Ears, TAKE CARE OF THEM, *and whatever thou spendest, I will repay thee.*

— *The Pennsylvania Gazette,* August 8, 1751

(A continuation of same subject one week later)

. . . It is hoped therefore, that whoever will maturely consider the inestimable Blessings that are connected to a proper Execution of the present Hospital Scheme in this City, can never be so void of Humanity and the essential Duties of Religion as to turn a deaf Ear to the numberless Cries of the Poor and Needy, and refuse for their Assistance, a little of that Superfluity, which a bountiful Providence has so liberally bestowed on them.

*The Pennsylvania Gazette,* August 15, 1751

∞

## Samuel Adams to Hannah Adams
## August 17, 1780

HANNAH ADAMS was the devoted daughter of Samuel Adams. In this affectionate letter, Samuel Adams reminds his daughter that it is her "heavenly Father" that makes all blessings possible.

## LETTER TO HANNAH ADAMS, AUGUST 17, 1780

*Nothing* I assure you, but want of leisure, has prevented my acknowledging the receipt of your very obliging letter of the 12th of July. You cannot imagine with how much pleasure I received it. I have no reason to doubt your sincerity when you express the warmest affection for your mother and me, because I have had the most convincing proof of it in the whole course of your life. Be equally attentive to every relation into which all-wise Providence may lead you, and I will venture to predict for my dear daughter, an unfailing source of happiness in the reflections of her own mind. If you carefully fulfill the various duties of life, from a principle of obedience to your heavenly Father, you shall enjoy that peace which the world cannot give nor take away. In steadily pursuing the path of wisdom and virtue I am sometimes inclined to think you have been influenced with a view of pleasing me. This is indeed endearing, and I owe you the debt of gratitude. But the pleasing an earthly parent, I am persuaded, has not been your principal motive to be religious. If this has any influence on your mind, you know you cannot gratify me so much, as by seeking most earnestly, the favor of Him who made and supports you—who will supply you with whatever his infinite wisdom sees best for you in this world, and above all, who has given up his Son to purchase for us the reward of eternal life—Adieu, and believe that I have all the feelings of a father.

# Thomas Jefferson to Thomas Jefferson Smith, February 21, 1825

A FRIEND asked Jefferson to give some advice to his young son, named after Jefferson, Thomas Jefferson Smith. Jefferson wrote a letter that was to be shown to Smith when he was old enough to appreciate it.

I think the litany of brief exhortations—"few words" is spectacular. In our age, all could be taken to heart with profit, especially "Murmur not at the ways of Providence." We live in a time of complaint from many who have much —perhaps too much.

*This* letter will, to you, be as one from the dead. The writer will be in the grave before you can weigh its counsels. Your affectionate and excellent father has requested that I would address to you something which might possibly have a favorable influence on the course of life you have to run; and I too, as a namesake, feel an interest in that course. Few words will be necessary, with good dispositions on your part. Adore God. Reverence and cherish your parents. Love your neighbor as yourself, and your country more than yourself. Be just. Be true. Murmur not at the ways of Providence. So shall the life into which you have entered, be the portal to one of eternal and ineffable bliss. And if to the dead it is permitted to care for the things of this world, every action of your life will be under my regard. Farewell.

# THE DECLARATION OF INDEPENDENCE

## in Congress, July 4, 1776 *

THE UNANIMOUS DECLARATION OF THE THIRTEEN UNITED STATES OF AMERICA

When in the Course of human events, it becomes necessary for one people to dissolve the political bands which have connected them with another, and to assume among the powers of the earth, the separate and equal station to which the Laws of Nature and of Nature's God entitle them, a decent respect to the opinions of mankind requires that they should declare the causes which impel them to the separation.—We hold these truths to be self-evident, that all men are created equal, that they are endowed by their Creator with certain unalienable Rights, that among these are Life, Liberty and the pursuit of Happiness.—That to secure these rights, Governments are instituted among Men, deriving their just powers from the consent of the governed,—That whenever any Form of Government becomes destructive of these ends, it is the Right of the People to alter or to abolish it, and to institute new Government, laying its foundation on such principles and organizing its powers in such form, as to them shall seem most likely to effect their Safety and Happiness. Prudence, indeed, will dictate that Governments long established should not be changed for light and transient causes; and accordingly all experience hath shown, that mankind are more disposed to suffer, while evils are sufferable, than to right themselves by abolishing the forms to which they are accustomed. But when a long train of abuses and usurpations, pursuing invariably the same Object evinces a design to reduce them under absolute Despotism, it is their right, it is their duty, to throw off such Government, and to provide new Guards for their future security.—Such has been the patient sufferance of these Colonies; and such

* Reprinted from the facsimile of the engrossed copy of the original manuscript in the Library of Congress.

is now the necessity which constrains them to alter their former Systems of Government. The history of the present King of Great Britain is a history of repeated injuries and usurpations, all having in direct object the establishment of an absolute Tyranny over these States. To prove this, let Facts be submitted to a candid world.—He has refused his Assent to Laws, the most wholesome and necessary for the public good.—He has forbidden his Governors to pass Laws of immediate and pressing importance, unless suspended in their operation till his Assent should be obtained; and when so suspended, he has utterly neglected to attend to them.—He has refused to pass other Laws for the accommodation of large districts of people, unless those people would relinquish the right of Representation in the Legislature, a right inestimable to them and formidable to tyrants only.—He has called together legislative bodies at places unusual, uncomfortable, and distant from the depository of their public Records, for the sole purpose of fatiguing them into compliance with his measures.—He has dissolved Representative Houses repeatedly, for opposing with manly firmness his invasions on the rights of the people.—He has refused for a long time, after such dissolutions, to cause others to be elected; whereby the Legislative powers, incapable of Annihilation, have returned to the People at large for their exercise; the State remaining in the mean time exposed to all the dangers of invasion from without, and convulsions within.—He has endeavoured to prevent the population of these States; for that purpose obstructing the Laws of Naturalization of Foreigners; refusing to pass others to encourage their migration hither, and raising the conditions of new Appropriations of Lands.—He has obstructed the Administration of Justice, by refusing his Assent to Laws for establishing Judiciary powers.—He has made Judges dependent on his will alone, for the tenure of their offices, and the amount and payment of their salaries.—He has erected a multitude of New Offices, and sent hither swarms of Officers to harrass our people, and eat out their substance.—He has kept among us, in times of peace, Standing Armies, without the Consent of our legislatures.—He has affected to render the Military independent of and superior to the Civil power.—He has combined with others to subject us to a jurisdiction foreign to our constitution, and unacknowledged by our laws; giving his Assent to their Acts of pretended Legislation:—For quartering large bodies of armed troops among us:—For protecting them, by a mock Trial, from punishment for any Murders which they should commit on the inhabitants of these States:—For cutting off our Trade with all parts of the world:—For imposing Taxes on us without our Consent:—For depriving us in many cases of the benefits of Trial by Jury:—For transporting us beyond Seas to be tried for pretended offences:—For abolishing the free Systems of English Laws in a neighbouring Province, establishing therein an Arbitrary government, and enlarging its Boundaries so as to render it at once an example and fit instrument for introducing the same absolute rule into these Colonies:—For taking away our Charters, abolishing our most valuable Laws, and altering fundamentally the Forms of our Governments:—For suspending our own Legislatures, and declaring themselves invested with power to legislate for us in all cases whatsoever.—He has abdicated Government here, by declaring us out of his Protection and waging War against us. —He plundered our seas, ravaged our Coasts, burnt our towns, and destroyed the lives of our people.—He is at this time transporting large armies of foreign mercenaries to compleat the works of death, desolation and tyranny, already begun with circumstances of Cruelty & perfidy scarcely paralleled in the most barbarous ages, and totally unworthy the Head of a civilized nation.—He has constrained our fellow Citizens taken Captive on the high Seas to bear Arms against their Country, to become the executioners of their friends and Brethren, or to fall themselves by their Hands.—He has excited domestic insurrections amongst us, and has endeavoured to bring on the inhabitants of our frontiers, the merciless Indian Savages, whose known rule of warfare, is an undistinguished destruction of all ages, sexes and conditions. In every stage of these Oppressions We have Petitioned for Redress in the most humble terms: Our repeated Petitions have been answered only by repeated injury. A Prince, whose character is thus marked by every act which may define a Tyrant, is unfit to be the ruler of a free people. Nor have We been wanting in attention to our British brethren. We have warned them from time to time of attempts by their legislature to extend un unwarrantable jurisdiction over us. We have reminded them of the circumstances of our emigration and settlement here. We have appealed to their native justice and magnanimity, and we have conjured them by the ties of our common kindred to disavow these usurpations, which, would inevitably interrupt our connections and correspondence. They too have been deaf to the voice of justice and of consanguinity. We must, therefore, acquiesce in the necessity, which denounces our Separation, and hold them, as we hold the rest of mankind, Enemies in War, in Peace Friends.—

We, Therefore, the Representatives of the United States of America, in General Congress, Assembled, appealing to the Supreme Judge of the world for the rectitude of our intentions, do, in the Name, and by Authority of the good People of these Colonies, solemnly publish and declare, That these United Colonies are, and of Right ought to be Free and Independent States; that they are Absolved from all Allegiance to the British Crown, and that all political connection between them and the State of Great Britain, is and ought to be totally dissolved; and that as Free and Independent States, they have full Power to levy War, conclude Peace, contract Alliances, establish Commerce, and to do all other Acts and Things which independent States may of right do.—And for the support of this Declaration, with a firm reliance on the protection of Divine Providence, we mutually pledge to each other our Lives, our Fortunes, and our sacred Honor.

John Hancock

Samuel Chase
William Paca
Thomas Stone
Charles Carroll of Carrollton

George Wythe
Richard Henry Lee
Thomas Jefferson
Benjamin Harrison
Thomas Nelson, Jr.
Francis Lightfoot Lee
Carter Braxton

Robert Morris
Francis Lewis
Lewis Morris

Richard Stockton
John Witherspoon
Francis Hopkinson
John Hart
Abraham Clark

Josiah Bartlett
William Whipple

Samuel Adams
John Adams
Robert Treat Paine
Elbridge Gerry

Benjamin Rush
Benjamin Franklin

John Morton
George Clymer
James Smith
George Taylor
James Wilson
George Ross

Caesar Rodney
George Read
Thomas M. Kean

William Floyd
Philip Livingston

Arthur Middleton
Button Gwinnett

Stephen Hopkins
William Ellery

Roger Sherman
Samuel Huntington
William Williams
Oliver Wolcott

Matthew Thornton

William Hooper
Joseph Hewes
John Penn

Edward Rutledge
Thomas Heyward, Jr.
Thomas Lynch, Jr.
Lyman Hall
George Walton

# THE CONSTITUTION
# OF THE UNITED STATES

We, the People of the United States, in Order to form a more perfect Union, establish Justice, insure domestic Tranquility, provide for the common defence, promote the general Welfare, and secure the Blessings of Liberty to ourselves and our Posterity, do ordain and establish this Constitution for the United States of America.

## ARTICLE I

SECTION 1. All legislative Powers herein granted shall be vested in a Congress of the United States, which shall consist of a Senate and House of Representatives.

SECTION 2. The House of Representatives shall be composed of Members chosen every second Year by the People of the several States, and the Electors in each State shall have <the> Qualifications requisite for Electors of the most numerous Branch of the State Legislature.

No Person shall be a Representative who shall not have attained to the Age of twenty five Years, and been seven Years a Citizen of the United States, and who shall not, when elected, be an Inhabitant of that State in which he shall be chosen.

Representatives and direct Taxes shall be apportioned among the several States which may be included within this Union, according to their respective Numbers, which shall be determined by adding the whole Number of free Persons, including those bound to Service for a Term of Years, and excluding Indians not taxed, three fifths of all other persons. The actual Enumeration shall be made within three Years after the first Meeting of the Congress of the United States, and within every subsequent Term of ten Years, in such Manner as they shall by Law direct. The Number of Representatives shall not exceed one for every thirty Thousand, but each State shall have at Least one Representative; and until such enumeration shall be made, the State of New Hampshire shall be entitled to chuse three, Massachusetts eight, Rhode-Island and Providence Plantations one, Connecticut five, New-York six, New Jersey four, Pennsylvania eight, Delaware one, Maryland six, Virginia ten, North Carolina five, South Carolina five, and Georgia three.

When vacancies happen in the Representation from any State, the Executive Authority thereof shall issue Writs of Election to fill such Vacancies.

The House of Representatives shall chuse their Speaker and other Officers; and shall have the sole Power of Impeachment.

SECTION 3. The Senate of the United States shall be composed of two Senators from each State, chosen by the Legislature thereof, for six Years; and each Senator shall have one Vote.

Immediately after they shall be assembled in Consequence of the first Election, they shall be divided as equally as may be into three Classes. The Seats of the Senators of the first Class shall be vacated at the Expiration of the second Year, of the second Class at the Expiration of the fourth Year, and of the third Class at the Expiration of the sixth Year, so that one third may be chosen every second Year; and if Vacancies happen by Resignation, or otherwise, during the Recess of the Legislature of any State, the Executive thereof may make temporary Appointments until the next Meeting of the Legislature, which shall then fill such Vacancies.

No Person shall be a Senator who shall not have attained to the Age of thirty Years, and been nine Years a Citizen of the United States, and who shall not, when elected, be an Inhabitant of that State for which he shall be chosen.

The Vice President of the United States shall be President of the Senate, but shall have no Vote, unless they be equally divided.

The Senate shall chuse their other Officers, and also a President pro tempore, in the Absence of the Vice President, or when he shall exercise the Office of the President of the United States.

The Senate shall have the sole Power to try all Impeachments. When sitting for that Purpose, they shall be on Oath or Affirmation. When the President of the United States <is tried> the Chief Justice shall preside: And no Person shall be convicted without the Concurrence of two thirds of the Members present.

Judgment in Cases of Impeachment shall not extend further than to removal from Office, and disqualification to hold and enjoy any Office of honor, Trust, or Profit under the United States: but the Party convicted shall nevertheless be liable and subject to Indictment, Trial, Judgment and Punishment, according to Law.

SECTION 4. The Times, Places and Manner of holding Elections for Senators and Representatives, shall be prescribed in each State by the Legislature thereof; but the Congress may at any time by law make or alter such Regulations, except as to the Places of chusing Senators.

The Congress shall assemble at least once in every Year, and such meeting shall be on the first Monday in December, unless they by Law appoint a different Day.

SECTION 5. Each House shall be the Judge of the Elections, Returns and Qualifications of its own Members, and a Majority of each shall constitute a Quorum to do Business; but a smaller Number may adjourn from day to day, and may be authorized to compel the Attendance of absent Members, in such Manner, and under such Penalties as each House may provide.

Each House may determine the Rules of its Proceedings, punish its Members for disorderly Behaviour, and, with the Concurrence of two thirds, expel a Member.

Each House shall keep a Journal of its Proceedings, and from time to time publish the same, excepting such Parts as may in their Judgment require Secrecy; and the Yeas and Nays of the Members of either House on any question shall, at the Desire of one fifth of those present, be entered on the Journal.

Neither House, during the Session of Congress, shall, without the Consent of the other, adjourn for more than three days, nor to any other Place than that in which the two Houses shall be sitting.

SECTION 6. The Senators and Representatives shall receive a Compensation for their services, to be ascertained by Law, and paid out of the Treasury of the United States. They shall in all Cases, except Treason, Felony and Breach of the Peace, be privileged from Arrest during their Attendance at the Session of their respective Houses, and in going to and returning from the same; and for any Speech or Debate in either House, they shall not be questioned in any other Place.

No Senator or Representative shall, during the Time for which he was elected, be appointed to any civil Office under the Authority of the United States, which shall have been created, or the Emoluments whereof shall have been encreased during such time; and no Person holding any Office under the United States, shall be a Member of either House during his Continuance in Office.

SECTION 7. All Bills for raising Revenue shall originate in the House of Representatives; but the Senate may propose or concur with Amendments as on other Bills.

Every Bill which shall have passed the House of Representatives and the Senate, shall, before it become a Law, be presented to the president of the United States; if he approve, he shall sign it, but if not, he shall return it, with his Objections, to that House in which it shall have originated, who shall enter the Objections at large on their Journal, and proceed to reconsider it. If after such Reconsideration, two thirds of that House shall agree to pass the Bill, it shall be sent, together with the Objections, to the other House, by which it shall likewise be reconsidered, and if approved by two thirds of that House, it shall become a Law. But in all such Cases the Votes of both Houses shall be determined by yeas and Nays, and the Names of the Persons voting for and against the Bill shall be entered on the Journal of each House respectively. If any Bill shall not be returned by the President within ten Days (Sundays excepted) after it shall have been presented to him, the Same shall be a Law, in like Manner as if he had signed it, unless the Congress by their Adjournment prevent its Return, in which Case it shall not be a Law.

Every Order, Resolution, or Vote to which the Concurrence of the Senate and House of Representatives may be necessary (except on a question of Adjournment) shall be presented to the President of the United States; and before the Same shall take Effect, shall be approved by him, or, being disapproved by him, shall be re-passed by two thirds of the Senate and House of Representatives, according to the Rules and Limitations prescribed in the Case of a Bill.

SECTION 8. The Congress shall have Power To lay and collect Taxes, Duties, Imposts and Excises, to pay the Debts and provide for the common Defence and general Welfare of the United States; but all Duties, Imposts and Excises shall be uniform throughout the United States:

To borrow Money on the credit of the United States;

To regulate Commerce with foreign Nations, and among the several States, and with the Indian Tribes;

To establish an uniform Rule of Naturalization, and uniform Laws on the subject of Bankruptcies throughout the United States;

To coin Money, regulate the Value thereof, and of foreign Coin, and fix the Standard of Weights and Measures;

To provide for the Punishment of counterfeiting the Securities and current Coin of the United States;

To establish Post Offices and post Roads;

To promote the Progress of Science and useful Arts, by securing for limited Times to Authors and Inventors the exclusive Right to their respective Writings and Discoveries;

To constitute Tribunals inferior to the supreme Court;

To define and punish Piracies and Felonies committed on the high Seas, and Offences against the Law of Nations;

To declare War, grant Letters of Marque and Reprisal, and make Rules concerning Captures on Land and Water;

To raise and support Armies, but no Appropriation of Money to that Use shall be for a longer Term than two Years;

To provide and maintain a Navy;

To make Rules for the Government and Regulation of the land and naval Forces;

To provide for calling forth the Militia to execute the Laws of the Union, suppress Insurrections and repel Invasions;

To provide for organizing, arming and disciplining the Militia, and for governing such Part of them as may be employed in the Service of the United States, reserving to the States respectively, the Appointment of the Officers, and the Authority of training the Militia according to the discipline prescribed by Congress;

To exercise exclusive Legislation in all Cases whatsoever, over such District (not exceeding ten Miles square) as may, by Cession of Particular States, and the Acceptance of Congress, become the Seat of the Government of the United States, and to exercise like Authority over all Places purchased by the Consent of the Legislature of the State in which the Same shall be, for the Erection of Forts, Magazines, Arsenals, dock-Yards, and other needful Buildings;—And

To make all Laws which shall be necessary and proper for carrying into Execution the foregoing Powers, and all other Powers vested by this Constitution in the Government of the United States, or in any Department or Officer thereof.

SECTION 9. The Migration or Importation of such Persons as any of the States now existing shall think proper to admit, shall not be prohibited by the Congress prior to the Year one thousand eight hundred eight, but a Tax or duty may be imposed on such Importations, not exceeding ten dollars for each Person.

The Privilege of the Writ of Habeas Corpus shall not be suspended, unless when in Cases of Rebellion or Invasion the public Safety may require it.

No Bill of Attainder or ex post facto Law shall be passed.

No Capitation, or other direct Tax shall be laid, unless in Proportion to the Census or Enumeration herein before directed to be taken.

No Tax or Duty shall be laid on Articles exported from any State.

No Preference shall be given by any Regulation of Commerce or Revenue to the Ports of one State over those of another: nor shall Vessels bound to, or from one State, be obliged to enter, clear, or pay Duties in another.

No Money shall be drawn from the Treasury but in Consequence of Appropriations made by Law; and a regular Statement and Account of the Receipts and Expenditures of all public Money shall be published from time to time.

No Title of Nobility shall be granted by the United States: And no Person holding any Office or Profit or Trust under them, shall, without the Consent of the Congress, accept of any present, Emolument, Office, or Title, of any kind whatever, from any King, Prince, or foreign State.


SECTION 10. No State shall enter into any Treaty, Alliance, or Confederation; grant Letters of Marque and Reprisal; coin Money; emit Bills of Credit; make any Thing but gold and silver Coin a Tender in Payment of Debts; pass any Bill of Attainder, ex post facto Law, or Law impairing the Obligation of Contracts, or grant any Title of Nobility.

No State shall, without the Consent of <the> Congress, lay any Imposts or Duties on Imports or Exports, except what may be absolutely necessary for executing its inspection Laws; and the net Produce of all Duties and Imposts, laid by any State on Imports or Exports, shall be for the Use of the Treasury of the United States; and all such Laws shall be subject to the Revision and Control of <the> Congress.

No State shall, without the Consent of Congress, lay any Duty of Tonnage, keep Troops, or Ships of War in time of Peace, enter into any Agreement or Compact with another State, or with a foreign Power, or engage in War, unless actually invaded, or in such imminent Danger as will not admit of delay.


ARTICLE II


SECTION 1. The executive Power shall be vested in a President of the United States of America. He shall hold his Office during the Term of four Years, and together with the Vice President, chosen for the same Term, be elected as follows

Each State shall appoint, in such Manner as the Legislature thereof may direct, a Number of Electors, equal to the whole Number of Senators and Representatives to which the State may be entitled in the Congress: but no

Senator or Representative, or Person holding an Office of Trust or Profit under the United States, shall be appointed an Elector.

The Electors shall meet in their respective States, and vote by Ballot for two Persons, of whom one at least shall not be an Inhabitant of the same State with themselves. And they shall make a List of all the Persons voted for, and of the Number of Votes for each; which List they shall sign and certify, and transmit sealed to the Seat of the Government of the United States, directed to the President of the Senate. The President of the Senate shall, in the Presence of the Senate and House of Representatives, open all the Certificates, and the Votes shall then be counted. The Person having the greatest Number of Votes shall be the President, if such Number be a Majority of the whole Number of Electors appointed; and if there be more than one who have such Majority, and have an equal Number of Votes, then the House of Representatives shall immediately choose by Ballot one of them for President; and if no Person have a Majority, then from the five highest on the List the said House shall in like Manner choose the President. But in choosing the President, the Votes shall be taken by States, the Representation from each State having one Vote; A quorum for this Purpose shall consist of a Member or Members from two-thirds of the States, and a Majority of all the States shall be necessary to a Choice. In every Case, after the Choice of the President, the person having the greatest Number of votes of the Electors shall be the Vice President. But if there should remain two or more who have equal Votes, the Senate shall choose from them by Ballot the Vice President.

The Congress may determine the Time of chusing the Electors, and the Day on which they shall give their Votes; which Day shall be the same throughout the United States.

No Person except a natural born Citizen, or a Citizen of the United States, at the time of the Adoption of this Constitution, shall be eligible to the Office of President; neither shall any person be eligible to that Office who shall not have attained to the Age of thirty-five Years, and been fourteen Years a Resident within the United States.

In Case of the Removal of the President from Office, or of his Death, Resignation, or Inability to discharge the Powers and Duties of the said Office, the Same shall devolve on the Vice President, and the Congress may by Law provide for the Case of Removal, Death, Resignation, or Inability, both of the President and Vice President, declaring what Officer shall then act as President, and such Officer shall act accordingly, until the Disability be removed, or a President shall be elected.

The President shall, at stated Times, receive for his Services, a Compensation, which shall neither be increased nor diminished during the Period for which he shall have been elected, and he shall not receive within that Period any other Emolument from the United States, or any of them.

Before he enter on the Execution of his office, he shall take the following Oath or Affirmation: "I do solemnly swear (or affirm) that I will faithfully execute the Office of the President of the United States, and will to the best of my Ability, preserve, protect and defend the Constitution of the United States."

SECTION 2. The President shall be Commander in Chief of the Army and Navy of the United States, and of the Militia of the several States, when called into the actual Service of the United States; he may require the Opinion, in writing, of the principal Officer in each of the executive Departments, upon any Subject relating to the Duties of their respective Offices, and he shall have Power to grant Reprieves and Pardons for Offenses against against the United States, except in Cases of Impeachment.

He shall have Power, by and with the Advice and Consent of the Senate, to make Treaties, provided two-thirds of the Senators present concur; and he shall nominate, and by and with the Advice and Consent of the Senate, shall appoint Ambassadors, other public Ministers and Consuls, Judges of the Supreme Court, and all other Officers of the United States, whose Appointments are not herein otherwise provided for, and which shall be established by Law: but the Congress may by Law vest the Appointment of such inferior Officers, as they think proper, in the President alone, in the Courts of Law, or in the Heads of Departments.

The President shall have the Power to fill up all Vacancies that may may happen during the Recess of the Senate, by granting Commissions, which shall expire at the End of their next Session.

SECTION 3. He shall from time to time give to the Congress Information of the State of the Union, and recommend to their consideration such Measures as he shall judge necessary and expedient; he may, on extraordinary Occasions, convene both Houses, or either of them, and in Case of Disagreement between them, with Respect to the Time of Adjournment, he may adjourn them to such Time as he shall think proper; he may receive Ambassadors, and other public Ministers; he shall take Care that the Laws be faithfully executed, and shall Commission all the Officers of the United States.

SECTION 4. The President, Vice President, and all civil Officers of the United States, shall be removed from Office on Impeachment for, and Conviction of, Treason, Bribery, or other high Crimes and Misdemeanors.

## ARTICLE III

SECTION 1. The judicial Power of the United States, shall be vested in one supreme Court, and in such inferior Courts as the Congress may, from time to time, ordain and establish. The Judges, both of the supreme and inferior Courts, shall hold their offices during good Behaviour, and shall, at stated Times, receive for their Services a Compensation, which shall not be diminished during their Continuance in Office.

SECTION 2. The judicial Power shall extend to all Cases, in Law and Equity, arising under this Constitution, the Laws of the United States, and Treaties made, or which shall be made under their Authority—to all Cases affecting Ambassadors, other public Ministers and Consuls—to all Cases of admiralty and maritime Jurisdiction—to Controversies to which the United States shall be a Party—to Controversies between two or more States—between a State and Citizens of another State—between Citizens of different States—between Citizens of the same State, claiming Lands under Grants of different States, and between a State, or the Citizens thereof, and foreign States, Citizens or Subjects.

In all Cases affecting Ambassadors, other public Ministers and Consuls, and those in which a State shall be a Party, the supreme Court shall have original Jurisdiction. In all the other Cases before mentioned, the supreme Court shall have appellate Jurisdiction, both as to Law and Fact, with such Exceptions, and under such Regulations as the Congress shall make.

The Trial of all Crimes, except in Cases of Impeachment, shall be by Jury; and such Trial shall be held in the State where the said Crimes shall have been committed; but when not committed within any State, the Trial shall be at such Place or Places as the Congress may by Law have directed.

SECTION 3. Treason against the United States shall consist only in levying War against them, or in adhering to their Enemies, giving them Aid and Comfort. No Person shall be convicted of Treason unless on the Testimony of Two Witnesses to the same overt Act, or on Confession in open Court.

The Congress shall have Power to declare the Punishment of Treason, but no Attainder of Treason shall work Corruption of Blood, or Forfeiture, except during the Life of the Person attainted.

## ARTICLE IV

SECTION 1. Full Faith and Credit shall be given in each State to the public Acts, Records and judicial Proceedings of every other State. And the Congress may by general Laws prescribe the Manner in which such Acts, Records and Proceedings shall be proved, and the Effect thereof.

SECTION 2. The Citizens of each State shall be entitled to all Privileges and Immunities of Citizens in the several States.

A Person charged in any State with Treason, Felony, or other Crime, who shall flee from Justice, and be found in another State, shall, on Demand of the executive Authority of the State from which he fled, be delivered up, to be removed to the State having Jurisdiction of the Crime.

No Person held to Service or Labour in one State, under the Laws thereof, escaping into another, shall, in Consequence of any Law or Regulation therein, be discharged from such Service or Labour, but shall be delivered up on Claim of the Party to whom such Service or Labour may be due.

SECTION 3. New States may be admitted by the Congress into this Union; but no new State shall be formed or erected within the Jurisdiction of any other state, nor any State be formed by the Junction of two or more States, or Parts of States, without the Consent of the Legislatures of the States concerned, as well as of the Congress.

The Congress shall have Power to dispose of and make all needful Rules and Regulations respecting the Territory or other Property belonging to the United States; and nothing in this Constitution shall be so construed as to Prejudice any Claims of the United States, or of any particular State.

SECTION 4. The United States shall guarantee to every State in this Union a Republican Form of Government, and shall protect each of them against Invasion; and on Application of the Legislature, or of the Executive (when the Legislature cannot be convened), against domestic Violence.

## ARTICLE V

The Congress, whenever two-thirds of both Houses shall deem it necessary, shall propose Amendments to this Constitution, or on the Application of the Legislatures of two-thirds of the several States, shall call a Convention for proposing Amendments, which, in either Case, shall be valid to all Intents and Purposes, as part of this Constitution, when ratified by the Legislatures of three-fourths of the several States, or by Conventions in three-fourths thereof, as the one or the other Mode of Ratification may be proposed by the Congress; Provided, that no Amendment which may be made prior to the Year One thousand eight hundred and eight shall in any Manner affect the first and fourth Clauses in the Ninth Section of the first Article; and that no State, without its Consent, shall be deprived of its equal Suffrage in the Senate.

## ARTICLE VI

All Debts contracted and Engagements entered into, before the Adoption of this Constitution, shall be as valid against the United States under this Constitution, as under the Confederation.

This Constitution, and the Laws of the United States which shall be made in Pursuance thereof; and all Treaties made, or which shall be made, under the Authority of the United States shall be the supreme Law of the Land; and the Judges in every State shall be bound thereby, any Thing in the Constitution or Laws of any State to the Contrary notwithstanding.

The Senators and Representatives before mentioned, and the Members of the several State Legislatures, and all executive and judicial Officers, both of the United States and of the several States, shall be bound by Oath or Affirmation, to support this Constitution; but no religious Test shall ever be required as a Qualification to any Office or public Trust under the United States.

## ARTICLE VII

The Ratification of the Conventions of nine States, shall be sufficient for the Establishment of this Constitution between the States so ratifying the Same.

Done in Convention by the Unanimous Consent of the States present the Seventeenth Day of September in the Year of our Lord one thousand seven hundred and Eighty seven and of the Independence of the United States of America the Twelfth In witness whereof We have hereunto subscribed our Names,

Attest William Jackson,                          GO. WASHINGTON—Presidt.
     Secretary.                                   and deputy from Virginia.

New Hamsphire { JOHN LANGDON
NICHOLAS GILMAN

Massachusetts { NATHANIEL GORHAM
RUFUS KING

Connecticut { WM. SAML. JOHNSON
ROGER SHERMAN

New York: . . .    ALEXANDER HAMILTON

New Jersey {
WIL: LIVINGSTON
DAVID BREARLEY.
WM. PATERSON.
JONA: DAYDON

Pennsylvania {
B FRANKLIN
THOMAS MIFFLIN
ROBT MORRIS
GEO. CLYMER
THOS FITZSIMONS
JARED INGERSOLL
JAMES WILSON
GOUV MORRIS

Delaware {
GEO: READ
GUNNING BEDFORD jun
JOHN DICKINSON
RICHARD BASSETT
JACO: BROOM

Maryland {
JAMES MCHENRY
DAN OF ST THOS JENIFER
DANL CARROLL

Virginia {
JOHN BLAIR—
JAMES MADISON Jr.

North Carolina {
WM. BLOUNT
RICHD. DOBBS SPAIGHT.
HU WILLIAMSON

South Carolina {
J. RUTLEDGE
CHARLES COTESWORTH PINCKNEY
CHARLES PINCKNEY
PIERCE BUTLER.

Georgia {
WILLIAM FEW
ABR BALDWIN

In Convention Monday, September 17th. 1787.

Present
The States of
New Hampshire, Massachusetts, Connecticut, Mr. Hamilton from New York, New Jersey, Pennsylvania, Delaware, Maryland, Virginia, North Carolina, South Carolina and Georgia.

Resolved,

That the preceding Constitution be laid before the United States in Congress assembled, and that it is the Opinion of this Convention, that it should afterwards be submitted to a Convention of Delegates, chosen in each State by the People thereof, under the Recommendation of its Legislature, for their Assent and Ratification; and that each Convention assenting to, and ratifying the Same, should give Notice thereof to the United States in Congress assembled.

Resolved, That it is the Opinion of this Convention, that as soon as the Conventions of nine States shall have ratified this Constitution, the United States in Congress assembled should fix a Day on which Electors should be appointed by the States which shall have ratified the same, and a Day on which the Electors should assemble to vote for the President, and the Time and Place for commencing Proceedings under this Constitution. That after such Publication the Electors should be appointed, and the Senators and Representatives elected: That the Electors should meet on the Day fixed for the Election of the President, and should transmit their votes certified signed, sealed and directed, as the Constitution requires, to the Secretary of the United States in Congress assembled, that the Senators and Reprresentatives should convene at the Time and Place assigned; that the Senators should appoint a President of the Senate, for the sole Purpose of receiving, opening and counting the Votes for President; and, that after he shall be chosen, the Congress, together with the President, should, without Delay, proceed to execute this Constitution.

By the Unanimous Order of the Convention.

GO: WASHINGTON Presidt.

W. JACKSON Secretary.

# THE BILL OF RIGHTS

## ARTICLE I

Congress shall make no law respecting an establishment of religion, or prohibiting the free exercise thereof; or abridging the freedom of speech, or of the press; or the right of the people peaceably to assemble, and to petition the Government for a redress of grievances.

## ARTICLE II

A well-regulated Militia, being necessary to the security of a free State, the right of the people to keep and bear Arms, shall not be infringed.

## ARTICLE III

No Soldier shall, in time of peace be quartered in any house, without the consent of the Owner, nor in time of war, but in a manner to be prescribed by law.

## ARTICLE IV

The right of the people to be secure in their persons, houses, papers, and effects, against unreasonable searches and seizures, shall not be violated, and no Warrants shall issue, but upon probable cause, supported by Oath or affirmation, and particularly describing the place to be searched, and the persons or things to be seized.

## ARTICLE V

No person shall be held to answer for a capital, or otherwise infamous crime, unless on a presentment or indictment of a Grand Jury, except in cases arising in the land or naval forces, or in the Militia, when in actual service in time of War or public danger; nor shall any person be subject for the same offence to be twice put in jeopardy of life or limb; nor shall be compelled in any criminal case to be a witness against himself, nor be deprived of life, liberty, or property, without due process of law; nor shall private property be taken for public use, without just compensation.

## ARTICLE VI

In all criminal prosecutions, the accused shall enjoy the right to a speedy and public trial, by an impartial jury of the State and district wherein the crime shall have been committed, which district shall have been previously ascertained by law, and to be informed of the nature and cause of the accusation; to be confronted with the witnesses against him; to have compulsory process for obtaining witnesses in his favor, and to have the Assistance of Counsel for his defence.

## ARTICLE VII

In suits at common law, where the value in controversy shall exceed twenty dollars, the right of trial by jury shall be preserved, and no fact tried by a jury, shall be otherwise reexamined in any Court of the United States, than according to the rules of the common law.

## ARTICLE VIII

Excessive bail shall not be required, nor excessive fines imposed, nor cruel and unusual punishments inflicted.

## ARTICLE IX

The enumeration in the Constitution, of certain rights, shall not be construed to deny or disparage others retained by the people.

## ARTICLE X

The powers not delegated to the United States by the Constitution, nor prohibited by it to the States, are reserved to the States respectively, or to the people.

# BRIEF BIOGRAPHIES

**Abigail Adams** (1744–1818). Abigail Adams, the daughter of a minister, was educated at home. There she learned from books and from the lively conversations she shared with her family and friends. She became a great letter writer. In her letters to family and friends, Adams vividly described the political characters and events shaping the times, and also shared thoughtful reflections on moral and political questions. She was the wife of John Adams, who considered her the source of all his happiness. When public service took John Adams away from his home, Abigail bravely stayed behind, managing a farm and caring for four children during war and epidemics. Her unwavering piety sustained her in those difficult times.

**John Adams** (1735–1826). John Adams was the leading advocate of American independence in the Continental Congress and a signer of the Declaration of Independence. He served his country in a variety of capacities: In 1779, he drafted the Massachusetts state constitution. He was American ambassador to France and Great Britain. In 1783, along with John Jay and Benjamin Franklin, he signed the peace treaty with Great Britain that ended the American Revolutionary War. Adams also secured loans from Holland that helped to finance the American Revolution. He served, under President George Washington, as America's first vice-president, and later as our second president. Adams's administration was rocked by party factions, which led to his temporary falling out with Thomas Jefferson. Jefferson acknowledged Adams's faults but also said of him: "He is as disinterested as the being who made him; he is profound in his views and accurate in his judgment, except where knowledge of the world is necessary to form a judgment. He is so amiable, that I pronounce you will love him if ever you become acquainted with him."

**Samuel Adams** (1722–1803). Samuel Adams was described by Benjamin Rush as "one of the most active instruments of the American Revolution." Adams, a second cousin of John Adams, was the chief agitator for rebellion years before the Revolutionary War actually commenced. He actively campaigned against the presence of British troops in Boston and was a leader in the Stamp Act riots and the Boston Tea Party. He also served in the First and Second Continental Congresses and was a signer of the Declaration of Independence.

**Benjamin Franklin** (1706–1790). Benjamin Franklin was a statesman, scientist, printer, inventor, entrepreneur, and philanthropist. His famous kite-flying experiment proved that lightning is electrical. Among his many useful inventions are the Franklin stove, the lightning rod, and bifocal glasses. In the area of politics, he served his country in many ways: He was a delegate to the Albany Congress of 1754 where he proposed an early plan to form a colonial union. In 1757, he served in London as an agent of the Pennsylvania Assembly to resolve a tax dispute over proprietary estates with the British government. He was later selected by several colonies to represent them in a reconciliation with Great Britain that failed. He returned from Great Britain in 1775 and served as a delegate to the Second Continental Congress, where he signed the Declaration of Independence. In 1779, he was appointed the American minister to France. He signed the Treaty of Paris that officially ended the war in 1783. He also attended the Constitutional Convention of 1787, where his presence did much to promote the spirit of compromise. He published the *Pennsylvania Gazette, Poor Richard's Almanack* and, with great wit and humor, produced many other writings that attempted to inculcate industry, frugality, and morality in the American people. The French statesman Comte Mirabeau praised Franklin as a "mighty genius" who was "able to restrain alike thunderbolts and tyrants" to the benefit of mankind.

**Alexander Hamilton** (1755–1804). Alexander Hamilton was born in the West Indies. He was the illegitimate son of a Scotchman, who abandoned his family. Hamilton was very bright and showed great promise as a young boy. In 1772, he came to the United States to attend college, but was soon caught up in the revolutionary ferments of the day. He wrote several pamphlets defending the American rebels which caught the attention of the American patriots. During the war, George Washington appointed Hamilton as one of his aide-de-camps. Hamilton led several battalions in the Battle of Yorktown. After the war, Hamilton served as a New York delegate to the Constitutional Convention of 1787. He led the ratification fight in New York and wrote and published, along with John Jay and James Madison, *The Federalist* under the pen name Publius. He was our first secretary of the treasury and secured the stability of America's finances. He died in a gun duel with Aaron Burr fought over political differences. A prominent judge of that time said of Hamilton: "I can truly say that hundreds of politicians and statesmen of the day get both the web and woof of their thoughts from Hamilton's brains. He, more than any man, did the thinking of the time."

**Patrick Henry** (1736–1799). Patrick Henry was a great and dazzling orator, whose famous words "Give me liberty, or give me death" helped to define and inspire the patriots' cause. He was active in Virginia politics, serving as governor and also as a representative in the state legislature. During the ratification debates, he was a leading opponent of the Constitution: He believed it would encroach on the liberties and rights of state governments. He eventually accepted the Constitution and was a key figure in the adoption of the Bill of Rights.

**Thomas Jefferson** (1743–1826). Thomas Jefferson, our third president, first became involved in politics by serving in the Virginia House of Burgesses in 1769 until it was dissolved in 1775. He served as a Virginia delegate to the Continental Congress, where he was chosen to draft the Declaration of Independence. He then returned to Virginia, where he became involved in reforming the laws of the state. He was elected governor in June of 1779. In 1784, he joined Benjamin Franklin and John Adams in France where he negotiated commercial treaties. In 1790, George Washington appointed Jefferson to become our first secretary of state. He served as vice president under John Adams, before becoming president in 1801. In addition to his involvement in politics, Jefferson was a scientist, philosopher, educator, letter writer, farmer, and devoted father and grandfather. In his own epitaph, Jefferson wished to be remembered for three achievements: as author of the Declaration of Independence and the Virginia statute for religious freedom and as the founder of the University of Virginia.

**James Madison** (1751–1836). James Madison is forever known as the Father of the Constitution. Born and raised in Virginia, Madison graduated from the College of New Jersey, where he studied under John Witherspoon. When Madison returned to Virginia, he became active in local politics, serving in the Virginia Constitutional Convention of 1776. He was a leading advocate for religious freedom and tolerance. Of his contribution to the Constitutional Convention of 1787, a fellow delegate noted that Madison's "spirit of industry and application" made him the "best informed Man of any point in debate" and that he was a "Gentleman of great modesty,—with a remarkable sweet temper." Madison took copious notes during the four months that the delegates met, and it is his notes that serve as the most accurate and most elaborate account of the secret proceedings. He joined with Alexander Hamilton and John Jay in writing *The Federalist*. He drafted the Bill of Rights and was our fourth president.

**George Mason**. George Mason, a prominent Virginia planter, drafted Virginia's first constitution in May of 1776. He included in that constitution a Declaration of Rights, which served as a model for the Declaration of Independence and many other state constitutions as well. He served as a delegate to the Constitutional Convention of 1787. He refused to sign it because he believed that it gave the national government too much power over the state governments. He became a strong supporter of the Bill of Rights, which was eventually added to the Constitution.

**Thomas Paine** (1737–1809). Thomas Paine, the gifted author and controversial free thinker, was born in England. He came to the United States in 1774. He helped the revolutionary cause by writing and publishing several pamphlets, among them, *Common Sense* and *The Crisis*. These pamphlets strengthened the patriots' belief in the righteousness of the American cause. He donated all profits from these publications to the Continental Congress and died an impoverished man.

**Benjamin Rush** (1746–1813). Benjamin Rush was a physician with a keen interest in politics. He was a delegate to the Continental Congress, where he signed the Declaration of Independence. He also was a leading advocate for the Constitution at the Pennsylvania Ratifying Convention. John Adams appointed Rush to be the treasurer of the United States Mint and later said of him: "I know no Character living or dead, who has done more real good in America."

**Mercy Warren** (1728–1814). Mercy Warren was a great patriot who defied the conventions of her time by establishing herself as both a mother and a prolific writer of letters, polemics, and plays. Her most famous work was her three-volume *History of the Rise, Progress and Termination of the American Revolution*. She also took an active part in the Anti-Federalist opposition to the proposed Constitution, which she viewed as a threat to the state governments.

**George Washington** (1732–1799). George Washington is known as the Father of Our Country. The Virginian statesman Richard Henry Lee put it best when he described Washington as "first in war, first in peace, and first in the hearts of his countrymen." Before the Revolutionary War, Washington saw military action in the French-Indian War and later served in the Virginia House of Burgesses. He was elected to the First and Second Continental Congresses. In 1775, Congress unanimously appointed Washington to be commander-in-chief of the Continental Army, for which Washington declined any salary. Washington and his men suffered many setbacks and defeats over the course of the Revolutionary War. But under Washington's moral and military leadership, the Continental Army went from being a ragtag group of undisciplined men to becoming victors over the most powerful empire in the world. Washington resigned his commission in December of 1783 and retired to Mount Vernon, vowing never to hold public office again. He was called back to public life as a delegate to the Constitutional Convention of 1787. In 1789, he was unanimously elected the first president of the United States. He served two terms, without accepting any salary.

# TIME LINE OF THE
# AMERICAN REVOLUTION

March 22, 1765:      The Stamp Act becomes law and the colonists protest.

March 5, 1770:       The Boston Massacre

December 16, 1773:   The Boston Tea Party

September 5, 1774:   The First Continental Congress meets in Philadelphia.

March 23, 1775:      Patrick Henry gives his famous "Give me liberty or give me death" speech before the Virginia Assembly.

April 18/19, 1775:   Paul Revere's midnight ride

April 19, 1775:      The Battles of Lexington and Concord

May 10, 1775:        The Second Continental Congress convenes in Philadelphia.

June 15, 1775:       The Continental Congress appoints George Washington to be commander-in-chief of the Continental Army.

June 17, 1775:       The Battle of Bunker Hill

March 17, 1776:      George Washington defends Boston; British troops evacuate the city.

June 7, 1776:        Virginia delegate Richard Henry Lee proposes a resolution for independence in Congress.

June 11, 1776:       The Continental Congress appoints Thomas Jefferson, John Adams, Benjamin Franklin, Roger Sherman, and Robert Livingston to a committee to draft the Declaration. Jefferson is chosen to be the draftsman.

July 2, 1776:        Congress adopts Lee's resolution for independence.

July 4, 1776:        Congress approves the Declaration of Independence, as drafted by Jefferson and amended by the Congress.

August 22–27, 1776:  Battle of Long Island. British forces decisively defeat the Continental Army.

September 15, 1776:  British forces occupy New York City.

September 22, 1776:  Nathan Hale is executed by the British.

December 19, 1776:   Thomas Paine's first of *The Crisis* papers is issued.

December 25, 1776:   Washington crosses the Delaware.

December 26, 1776:     Battle of Trenton, New Jersey

January 3, 1777:       Battle of Princeton, New Jersey

September 19, 1777:    The Continental Congress flees Philadelphia and British troops occupy the city one week later.

October 7, 1777:       Battle of Bemis Heights

October 17, 1777:      Battle of Saratoga

November 15, 1777:     The Continental Congress adopts the Articles of Confederation.

December 21, 1777:     George Washington and his troops begin winter camp at Valley Forge, Pennsylvania.

February 6, 1778:      Treaty of alliance and commerce with France is signed by Benjamin Franklin, Silas Deane, and Arthur Lee.

June 28, 1778:         Battle of Monmouth, New Jersey

December 29, 1778:     British forces occupy Savannah, Georgia.

May 12, 1780:          British forces defeat American troops at Charleston, South Carolina.

October 19, 1781:      British General Charles Cornwallis surrenders at the Battle of Yorktown.

September 3, 1783:     Treaty of Paris is signed by John Adams, Benjamin Franklin, and John Jay, and officially ends the war.

May 25, 1787:          The Constitutional Convention convenes in Philadelphia.

September 15, 1787:    The Convention adopts the Constitution.

October 27, 1787:      *Federalist* No. 1 published.

June 21, 1788:         Constitution becomes law.

December 15, 1791:     Bill of Rights is ratified.

# SOURCES

Adams, Charles Francis. *The Letters of Mrs. Adams*. 2 vols. Boston: Charles C. Little and James Brown, 1841.

Adams, Charles Francis. *The Works of John Adams*. 10 vols. Boston: Little, Brown & Co., 1850–1856.

Andrews, James DeWitt, ed. *The Works of James Wilson*. 2 vols. Chicago: Callaghan and Company, 1896.

Baldwin, James. *The Story of Liberty*. American Book Company, 1919.

Bowen, Catherine Drinker. *Miracle at Philadelphia*. Boston: Little, Brown & Company, 1986.

Brandes, Paul, ed. *John Hancock's Life and Speeches: A Personalized Vision of the American Revolution 1763–1793*. Lanham, MD: Scarecrow Press, 1996.

Brookhiser, Richard. *Founding Father: Rediscovering George Washington*. New York: The Free Press, 1996.

Brubaker, Abram. *The Spirit of America*. Garden City, New York: Doubleday, Page & Co., 1920.

Burstein, Andrew. *The Inner Jefferson: Portrait of a Grieving Optimist*. Charles Hesville: University of Virginia Press.

Butterfield, L.H., ed. *Adams Family Correspondence*. 6 vols. Cambridge, Mass.: Belknap Press of Harvard University, 1963.

Butterfield, L.H., ed. *The Book of Abigail and John: Selected Letters of the Adams Family 1762–1784*. Cambridge, Mass.: Harvard University Press, 1975.

Butterfield, L.H., ed. *Diary and Autobiography of John Adams*. 4 vols. Cambridge, Mass.: Belknap Press of Harvard University, 1961.

Butterfield, L.H., ed. *Letters of Benjamin Rush*. 2 vols. Princeton, N.J.: Princeton University Press, 1951.

Butterfield, L.H., ed. *My Dearest Julia: The Love Letters of Dr. Benjamin Rush to Julia Stockton*. New York: N. Watson Academic Publications, 1979.

Cappon, Lester, ed. *The Adams-Jefferson Letters: The Complete Correspon-*

*dence Between Thomas Jefferson and Abigail and John Adams.* Chapel Hill: University of North Carolina Press for The Institute of Early American History and Culture at Williamsburg, Virginia, 1987.

Cushing, Harry Alonzo, ed. *The Writings of Samuel Adams.* 4 vols. New York: G.P. Putnam's Sons, 1904–1908.

Dwight, Nathaniel. *The Lives of the Signers of the Declaration of Independence.* New York: A.S. Barnes & Company, 1876.

Farmer, Lydia Hoyt. *The Life of Lafayette, the Knight of Liberty in Two Worlds and Two Centuries.* New York: T.Y. Crowell & Co., 1888.

Farrand, Max, ed. *The Records of the Federal Convention of 1787.* Rev. ed., 4 vols. New Haven and London: Yale University Press, 1937.

Fitzpatrick, John C. *The Writings of George Washington from the Original Manuscript Sources, 1745–1799.* 39 vols. Washington, D.C.: Government Printing Office, 1931–1944.

Ford, Paul Leceister, ed. *The Works of Thomas Jefferson.* 12 vols. New York and London: G.P. Putnam's Sons, 1904–1905.

Frost, John. *Lives of the Heroes of the American Revolution.* Boston: Phillips & Samson, 1848.

Grant, Ruth W. and Nathan Tarcov, eds. *John Locke: Some Thoughts Concerning Education and of the Conduct of the Understanding.* Indianapolis: Hackett Publishing Company, Inc., 1996.

Hart, Ann Clark, ed. *Abraham Clark: Signer of the Declaration of Independence.* San Francisco: The Pioneer Press, 1923.

Holland, Rupert Sargent. *Lafayette for Young Americans.* George W. Jacobs & Co, 1922.

Hunt, Gaillard, ed. *The Writings of James Madison.* 9 vols. New York: G.P. Putnam's Sons, 1900–1910.

Irving, Washington, *Life of George Washington.* 3 vols. New York: G.P. Putnam & Co., 1855.

Johnston, Henry P. *The Correspondence and Public Papers of John Jay.* 4 vols. New York and London: G.P. Putnam's Sons, 1890–1893.

Koch, Andrienne. *Jefferson and Madison: The Great Collaboration.* New York: Oxford University Press, 1964.

———. *Madison's "Advice to My Country."* Princeton: Princeton University Press, 1966.

Labaree, Leonard W. *The Papers of Benjamin Franklin.* 27 vols. New Haven: Yale University Press, 1959.

Langguth, A.J. *Patriots: The Men Who Started the American Revolution.* New York: Simon & Schuster, 1988.

Lipscomb, Andrew A. and Albert Ellery Bergh. *The Writings of Thomas Jeffer-*

*son*. 20 vols. Washington, D.C.: Thomas Jefferson Memorial Association, 1905.

Lodge, Henry Cabot. *The Works of Alexander Hamilton*. 12 vols. New York, London: G.P. Putnam's Sons, The Knickerbocker Press, 1904.

Mitchell, Stewart. *New Letters of Abigail Adams, 1788–1801*. Boston: Houghton Mifflin, 1947.

Morris, Anne Cary. *Diary and Letters of Gouverneur Morris*. New York: Charles Scribner's Sons, 1898.

Nicolay, Helen. *The Boys Life of Thomas Jefferson*. New York: D. Appleton-Century Co., 1933.

Padover, Saul, ed. *The Complete Madison: His Basic Writings*. Millwood, New York: Kraus Reprint Co., 1973.

Padover, Saul, ed. *The Mind of Alexander Hamilton*. New York: Harper, 1958.

Paine, Thomas *The Complete Political Works of Thomas Paine*. 2 vols. New York: Peter Eckler, Publisher, 1891

Peterson, Merill D. *The Portable Thomas Jefferson*. New York: Viking Press, 1975.

Randall, Henry S. *The Life of Thomas Jefferson*. 3 vols. Freeport, N.Y.: Books for Libraries Press, 1857.

Randolph, Sarah N. *The Domestic Life of Thomas Jefferson*. New York: Harper & Brothers, Publishers, Franlin Square, 1871.

Rives, William C. *History of the Life and Times of James Madison*. 3 vols. Freeport, N.Y.: Books for Libraries Press, 1859–1868, reprinted 1970.

Rowland, Kate Mason. *The Life of George Mason*. New York: G.P. Putnam's Sons, 1892.

Runes, Dagobert D., ed. *The Selected Writings of Benjamin Rush*. New York: Philosophical Library, 1947.

Rutland, Robert A. *James Madison: The Founding Father*. New York: Macmillan Publishing Company, 1987.

Smith, Richard Norton. *Patriarch: George Washington and the New American Nation*. Boston: Houghton Mifflin Company, 1993.

Smyth, Albert Henry, ed. *The Writings of Benjamin Franklin*. 10 vols. New York: Macmillan Co., 1905–1907.

Stevenson, Burton. *Great Americans As Seen By the Poets*. Philadelphia, London: J.B. Lippincott Company, 1933.

Storing, Herbert J., ed. *The Complete Anti-Federalist*. 7 vols. Chicago: University of Chicago Press, 1981.

Tappan, Eva March. *American Hero Stories*. Boston: Houghton, Mifflin & Co., 1906.

Webster, Noah. *A Collection of Essays and Fugitiv Writings on Moral, Historical, Political and Literary Subjects*. Boston, 1790. Reprint, Delmar, N.Y.: Scholars's Facsimiles & Reprints, 1977.

Webster, Noah. *Value of the Bible and Excellence of the Christian Religion: For the Use of Families and Schools*. San Francisco: Foundation for American Christian Education, 1988.

Weems, Mason. *A History of the Life and Death, Virtues and Exploits of General George Washington*. New York: Grosset & Dunlap Publishing, 1927.

Wilson, Woodrow. *George Washington*. New York: Harper & Brothers, 1896.

Wirt, William. *Sketches of the Life and Character of Patrick Henry*. New York, 1859.

# PERMISSIONS

# INDEX